DEADLY QUARRELS

DEADLY QUARRELS

Lewis F. Richardson
and the Statistical
Study of War

David Wilkinson

UNIVERSITY OF CALIFORNIA PRESS
Berkeley / Los Angeles / London

University of California Press
Berkeley and Los Angeles, California

University of California Press, Ltd.
London, England

Library of Congress Cataloging in Publication Data

Wilkinson, David O   1939-
  Deadly quarrels.

  Bibliography: p. 187
  Includes index.
  1. War.   2.   Sociology, Military—Statistical methods.
3.   Richardson, Lewis Fry, 1881–1953.   I.   Title.
U21.7.W54   301.6'334'0182   78.65472
ISBN 9780520303812

To My Parents

Contents

Preface

While I was a student at Columbia University in 1960–61, William T. R. Fox drew my attention to the theoretical writings of Quincy Wright, in whose research project on the causes of war he had worked at the University of Chicago. During 1962-63, Wright himself visited Columbia; I consequently became acquainted with his magisterial *Study of War*, the outcome of the Causes of War Project, and with two posthumous volumes by Lewis F. Richardson which Wright had had a hand in publishing. Wright persuaded me that Richardson's work on the causation of war, *Statistics of Deadly Quarrels*, deserved close scrutiny, and would reward pursuit; but my first reading of *Statistics of Deadly Quarrels* convinced me that it needed first of all an exegesis, for which I was not then equipped.

In 1972, while I was engaged on other research at the Center for Computer-based Behavioral Studies of the University of California, Los Angeles, its director, Gerald H. Shure, accorded me free access to its excellent interactive PDP-10 computer system, which supported the versatile and rational BASIC programming language. To recover Richardson's work and carry it forward suddenly seemed practicable; I undertook to do so. This volume is the result. I wish to acknowledge the encouragement and support of Quincy Wright and Gerald Shure.

Introduction

The violent and deadly quarrels, the wars in Vietnam, Cambodia, Zimbabwe-Rhodesia, Lebanon, Ethiopia, Iran, Northern Ireland, Nicaragua, are but the latest of a long, long series. The players change; the locale changes; the drama does not. Why not? Why is today's system of world politics one in which threats, terrorism, invasions, and wars are no more than ordinary run-of-the-mill daily events? Is this inevitable? Is it necessary? What causes such a system to operate? Is it possible to change it? What can be done? Or must we adjust the best we can?

These are some of the central questions of the academic study of world politics—the field that deals with the politics of the global human society, of the world social system taken as a whole. These questions are often summed up:

What are the *causes of war*?

What are the *conditions of peace*?

The most common way of contributing to the debate over war causation and peace strategy has been to assert some definite theory, to show how it fits current circumstances, and to deduce immediate practical conclusions.

If we follow this public debate, we may expect to be told that war is a consequence, for instance, of wickedness, lawlessness, alienation, aggressive regimes, imperialism, poverty, militarism, anarchy, or weakness. Seldom will any evidence be offered. Instead the writer is likely to present a peace strategy that matches his theory of war causation. We shall therefore learn that we can have:

1. *Peace through morality.* Peace (local and global) can be brought about by a moral appeal, through world public opinion, to leaders

and peoples not to condone or practice violence, aggression, or war, but to shun and to denounce them.

2. *Peace through law.*   Peace can be made by signing international treaties and creating international laws that will regulate conduct and by resorting to international courts to solve disputes.

3. *Peace through negotiation.*   Peace can be maintained by frank discussion of differences, by open diplomacy, by international conferences and assemblies that will air grievances and, through candor and goodwill, arrive at a harmonious consensus.

4. *Peace through political reform.*   Peace can be established by setting up regimes of a nonaggressive type throughout the world: republics rather than monarchies; democratic rather than oligarchic republics; constitutionally limited rather than arbitrary, autocratic regimes.

5. *Peace through national liberation.*   Peace can be instituted only through the worldwide triumph of nationalism. Multinational empires must be dissolved into nation-states; every nation must have its own sovereign, independent government and all its own national territory, but no more.

6. *Peace through prosperity.*   Peace requires the worldwide triumph of an economic order that will produce universal prosperity and thereby remove the incentive to fight. Some consider this order to be one of universal capitalism, or at least of worldwide free trade; others hold it to be some species of socialism, reformist or revolutionary, elitist or democratic.

7. *Peace through disarmament.*   Peace can be established by reducing and eventually eliminating weapons, bases, and armies—by removing the means to make war.

8. *Peace through international organization.*   Peace can be established by creating a world political organization, perhaps even a constitutional world government resembling national governments, to enforce order and promote progress throughout the world.

9. *Peace through power.*   Peace can be maintained by the peaceable accumulation of forces—perhaps overwhelming, perhaps preponderant or balancing or adequate—sufficient to deter, defeat, or punish aggression.

Much current talk on war and peace amounts to no more than high-handed assertions that my chosen theory is right, and all others therefore are evidently wrong; a more or less grudging reference to one or two recent wars that "demonstrate" my theory and "demolish" yours; and a clarion call for you to abandon your foolish conceits and take vigorous action in conformity with my wise ones. The debate is spiced with epithets: your theory is utopian or cynical, rightist or leftist, dovish or hawkish, isolationist or interventionist, moral or amoral, appeasing or militarist, capitalistic or socialistic, naive or corrupt. The participants appear to have spent most of their time in devising new ways of styling each other's views "rubbish."

There exists, however, a very different sort of contribution to the public debate. Some scholars have held that the truths of politics are not self-evident; that social causes and effects are not plain as day, but complex and obscure, to be known not by direct intuition but only by systematic, methodical, and laborious research, applying the methods of the more success-ful natural sciences. Such scholars have thought it their task to construct a true science of society, so that politicians (or "statesmen" or "political activists" or even "citizens") might become the physicians and the engineers of society.

The notable pioneer of this school of thought about the problem of war was Lewis Fry Richardson (1881–1953); his most seminal work was the *Statistics of Deadly Quarrels* (1960*b*, hereinafter cited as SDQ).

Richardson is one of two persons usually cited as founders of the system-atic study of the causes of war (Quincy Wright is the other).[1] Yet Richardson's work on war was not his primary occupation. His bibliography in the *Obituary Notices of Fellows of the Royal Society* (Gold 1954) lists twenty-nine papers on meteorology, twenty-seven on war causation, nine on approximate solutions, eight on scientific instruments, seven on quantitative mental estimates (including one on telephone acoustics still cited after nearly fifty years), six on the "dynamics of intellection," and four on other aspects of psychology. He had a varied and distinguished career as a chemist, physicist, and meteorologist in industry, government, and academic institu-tions. His forte was the application of mathematics; his first classic was *Weather Prediction by Numerical Process* (1922), a scheme of weather predic-tion thirty years in advance of the high-speed computers required to apply it.

Richardson came of a long line of Quakers. From them he derived "a prejudice that the moral evil in war outweighs the moral good, although the latter is conspicuous." His interest in wars, therefore, lay in finding how to prevent their occurrence (SDQ, pp. xxxvii, 1).

Richardson's Quaker schoolmasters taught him the pleasures of Euclid, gave him "glimpses of the marvels of science," and left him with the "prejudice that scientific method is more trustworthy than rhetoric" and "the conviction that science ought to be subordinate to morals" (SDQ, pp. xx, xxxvii). He was educated at King's College, Cambridge. There "it

---

[1] See Appendix 1 for a discussion of Wright's war data.

occurred to me that . . . I would like to spend the first half of my life under the strict discipline of physics, and afterwards to apply that training to researches on living things" (SDQ, p. xxviii). After leaving Cambridge, Richardson worked in physics, peat hydrology, and meteorological and magnetic observation.

The World War that broke out in 1914 changed Richardson's life and work. The condemnation of war by the Society of Friends "pulled me away from the many warlike applications of physics." By 1915 he was thinking about "the conditions of a lasting peace in Europe" (S. Richardson 1957, p. 302). Unable to reconcile war with his understanding of the teachings and spirit of Christ, Richardson was a conscientious objector. In 1916 he joined the Friends' Ambulance Unit and was attached to a motor ambulance convoy (Section Sanitaire Anglaise number 13) lent to the French Army (SDQ, pp. xxix, xxi, xxiii). During the Third Battle of Champagne (April 1917), the Poste of S.S.A. 13 "was continuously bombarded; so was the whole stretch of road down which the cars had to run; so was the village to which they brought the wounded" (Binyon, 1918, p. 105). The effects of the war on Richardson's life were known to those closest to him; to his work it gave direction and intensity.

During this service Richardson wrote his first paper on war causation, "Mathematical Psychology of War." There was no learned society to which he could offer it. Then, as at the end of his life, "There are many anti-war societies, but they are concerned with propaganda, not research. There is a wide public interest in the subject provided it is expressed in bold rhetoric, but not if it is quantitative scientific study involving statistics and mathematics" (SDQ, pp. xxix, xxvi).

After the war Richardson returned to meteorology. In 1926 he was elected a Fellow of the Royal Society. He then made "a deliberate break with meteorology" and took up the study of psychology. From 1929 until his retirement in 1940 he was principal of Paisley Technical College. It was during this period, and afterward, during his retirement, that he published many papers on the mathematics of international relations.

After Richardson's death, two books edited from his papers, previously published and unpublished, were issued under his name. *Arms and Insecurity* reflects the work begun during World War I; it is an attempt to construct mathematical models of arms races. *Statistics of Deadly Quarrels*, the subject of this study, is a collection, begun in 1940, of data about wars and an analysis of theories of war in terms of those data.

Statistics of Deadly Quarrels is a work often cited and often praised in the recent scholarly literature on war and peace.[2] Its imaginative use of statistical

---

[2] For example, by E. Boulding (1972), Flora (1974), Hayes (1973), Parvin (1973), Rummel (1972, pp. 67–68), Singer (1970, pp. 527, 530. 1972), Singer and Small (1972).

techniques to order and inspect war data has been admired, emulated, and refined.[3] And the war data therein collected have been both utilized[4] and criticized and to some degree displaced.[5]

Richardson's statistical examination of war has now been generally accessible for fifteen years. It seems timely to ask whether it has been assimilated fully, or as fully as it deserves, and thereby essentially transformed into an object of study for the history of the science of politics, or whether on the contrary it remains a useful instrument and provocative source of ideas.

Reviewing the succeeding and derivative literature, one finds a certain unevenness. The numerical portions of Richardson's data—the dates of onset and termination of fighting, the number of belligerent actors per war, and the magnitude of war-related casualties—have been utilized frequently by researchers such as Denton (1966), Denton and Phillips (1968), Horvath (1968), Horvath and Foster (1963), Modelski (1972), Moyal (1949), Rapoport (1957), Rummel (1967), Singer and Small (1972), Stefflre (1974), and Weiss (1963). That many follow-up studies conceivably could have exhausted the possible uses of the numerical data; whether they have done so, in fact, bears examination.

On the other hand, the more imaginative portions of *Statistics of Deadly Quarrels*—the coding and counting of background factors and of historians' causal imputations, the attempts to develop data on potential belligerents who did not fight, the model for generating the distribution of wars by complexity—are far less frequently cited and seem, indeed, almost to have been forgotten. It is appropriate to ask whether this neglect is deserved.

It may be useful as a first step to summarize what Richardson intended to do and did in *Statistics of Deadly Quarrels*. We can then consider what he left incomplete, what has been done with his work since, and what, if anything, is to be made of it now.

---

[3] As in its use of the Poisson distribution (SDQ, pp. 128–131) by Midlarsky (1970, p. 64), Singer and Small (1972, pp. 204–206), and Hayes (1973).

[4] Blainey (1973, p. 71), Choucri and North (1972, pp. 107–108; 1975, pp. 41–42), Denton (1966), Horvath (1968), Horvath and Foster (1963), Modelski (1972), Rummel (1967), Stefflre (1974), Terrell (1972, p. 180), Wesley (1962).

[5] Criticized thoroughly, if respectfully: Small and Singer (1970, p. 146), Singer and Small (1972, pp. 8–9, 17–19, 44, 47–50, 78–81). Displaced among several researchers of the 1970s by the data of Singer and Small (1972); e.g., Finsterbusch and Greizman (1975), Midlarsky (1974), Ray (1974), Rosen (1972), Wallace (1972), Siverson and King (1978*a*, 1978*b*). See Appendix 2 for a discussion of the Singer-Small data.

1

Richardson's Assumptions and Intentions

Richardson, a student of the great statistician Karl Pearson, accepted Pearson's contention that "popular beliefs ought to be tested by statistics." He therefore thought it appropriate "to investigate the causes of war by counting how many there have been of various sorts" and to examine "popular beliefs" about the causes of war by searching for persistent quantitative relations in war data (SDQ, pp. ii, v, xxxv, 16).

Among Richardson's assumptions were a few, not complicated, relating to certain questions much debated in metaphysics and the philosophy of history. Richardson presumed or asserted them without debate and drew appropriate conclusions. One assumption was that history forms a continuum rather than, for instance, an assembly of discrete periods or stages. The past, therefore, could serve to guide the future, for "what has happened often is likely to happen again, whether we wish it or not" (SDQ, p. xxxv); "any new proposal for decreasing the frequency of wars should be judged in view of what has usually happened in the past" (SDQ, p. 295); and consequently it would be desirable and useful to know "what has usually happened."

A second assumption, undebated by Richardson, was that human affairs are partly free, partly determined (but to a degree as yet unknown and in ways as yet undetermined). "The less a type of behavior is subject to free choice, the less also is it subject to moral condemnation. We do not, for example, usually condemn passengers for being sick in a storm at sea. So I did not know quite what [about war] to condemn, until I had found out what was mechanical" (SDQ, p. xxxv).

Public discussion of issues of war and peace was then, as now, moralistic and prescriptive. Richardson abstained from such discussion, searching instead for the "mechanical," the "more fated and . . . less freely choosable forms of international behavior" (SDQ, p. xxxv). But his intention was to serve and to improve the public debate by making it easier to discern the likely consequences for peace of various proposed policies, and thus to create peace plans actually more likely to promote peace than to incite war. "The design of a new machine is not entirely free, for it has to conform to the laws of dynamics" (SDQ, p. 295). "This book's relation to publications on how-to-organize the future is like the relation of dynamics to machine design. Engineers customarily learn the science of dynamics as a guide to the art of machine design. Until statesmen have studied international dynamics, how can they expect their plans for peace to succeed?" (SDQ, p. xxxv) Political planning would be substantially improved if it had a reliable foundation in social dynamics—the study of "what has usually happened" (SDQ, p. 295).

Richardson's training and career led him to believe that it would be useful to give "international dynamics" a mathematical expression. By so doing, unspoken assumptions could better be made explicit and summarized, their consequences deduced, absurd implications detected, and disputable statements pinpointed (SDQ, pp. xliii–xliv). He argued that a mathematical treatment does not require that the individual phenomena so treated be fully and rigidly mechanically determined, so long as they are numerous (SDQ, p. xliii). Wars are numerous. The mathematical methods known collectively as statistics allow one to examine many cases or instances of a single phenomenon and to find patterns, associations, and sequences that regularly recur. Accordingly, Richardson sought to establish persistent quantitative relations of war by statistical means. To do so he required data on a great many instances of war. He set about collecting just such data.

2

Approach, Terms, and Methods

Richardson's war list. Richardson's data collection takes the form of a war list, "a summary of brief analyses published by historians in standard works" (SDQ, p. 184). Of course, Richardson's purposes and methods differed radically from those of the historians who were his sources: he sought the abstract, repetitive, and general at the expense of the concrete, unique, and particular; he sought the maximum compression and brevity in his descriptions, rather than the fullest depth and detail; he intended to reduce events to cases of a phenomenon and their features to instances of standardized abstract qualities, expressed in a code rather than in common language. He cut slices out of the history of this nation and that and then compared the slices: it was with no little self-deprecating and disarming irony that he called his war list a "Potted History Book" (SDQ, p. 184).

Richardson himself undertook the search for wars to include in the war list. Since history is mostly arranged by country, he made a list of 163 territories and peoples with the aid of an atlas and inquired after each, at first in the fourteenth edition of the *Encyclopaedia Britannica*. To test the *Britannica's* coverage, he took samples of more detailed histories, compared his list with Wright's in *A Study of War* (1965: 1st ed., 1942), and searched some seventy volumes on the history of Latin America, French colonies, Russia, Turkey, Central Asia, India, and China (SDQ, pp. 29–30).

Richardson's data search led him in quest of the records of "deadly quarrels" in "the whole world since the beginning of A.D. 1820" (SDQ, p. 7). He took the whole world as his field of study in order to reduce the danger of reproducing a single nation's prejudices against its enemies in his analysis; he selected a time interval longer than personal memory for a similar reason.

A.D. 1820 was a compromise starting date: whereas the statistician's desire for many observations dictated a further extension into the past, more recent wars should be more informative for the future. When he began the study in 1940, a hundred-year interval seemed a fair compromise between the "rival claims of abundant data and of modernity" (SDQ, p. 16). To count only complete wars, he first bounded his intervals at dates when there was a lull in fighting worldwide, 1820-1929, but later he gave in to the tendency to come up to date. Thus some analyses come up to 1939 and others to 1945. The war list itself is comprehensive to 1949 but has one extra case for 1952. The wars Richardson counted were those that *terminated* within the interval 1820-1952. This allowed the list to be brought up to date without thereby including unfinished wars for which casualty data were incomplete and narratives likely to be excessively imperfect and partisan (SDQ, p. 16).

"War": the unit of analysis. Richardson studied "wars" as a species of what he called "deadly quarrels." Species and genus both pose problems. To begin with, the concept of a war "as a discrete thing does not quite fit all the facts" (SDQ, p. 35). Declarations of war and peace do not coincide with the outbreak and cessation of hostilities; provocative incidents may precede, and guerrilla warfare follow, the main outbreak, thereby rendering the "duration" of the war ambiguous (SDQ, pp. 255-256). There are whole–part problems: was the Sino-Japanese war that began in 1937 a part of World War II, which "began" in 1939? There are cases of fighting that erupted, died down (with or without an armistice), and erupted again: do these constitute two wars or two episodes of one war? One state is fighting two widely separated unallied enemies simultaneously: two wars or one? A war between A and B is unrelated at first to a war between C and D, but then A and C ally as do B and D: two wars or one?

Richardson replied to all these dilemmas with the principle that "the average should have priority over the differences" (SDQ, p. 125). That is, he did not determine doubtful cases on any consistent, substantive principle, but rather according to a consistent procedural principle of inconsistency, once one way, once the other: "The wars in the Sudan (1881-1900) are split into three parts, whereas the rather similarly long war in Western China (1861-1877) is kept as a whole" (SDQ, p. 125). Thus the count of wars and their circumstances is less wrong than it would be if one direction of determination were consistently adopted and consistently wrong.

Richardson decided to examine civil wars and international wars side by side in a single study. That decision, since questioned (Singer and Small 1972), must have been questioned at the time, for Richardson defended it at some length. Having begun by trying to list civil wars, he found the distinction between civil and international strife "hopelessly inadequate as a classificatory principle" unless account was taken of the length of time the civil belligerents had spent under a common government and of the degree of social unity that the parties shared. Indeed it was the discovery of the inadequacy of the civil-international distinction that led him to develop his scheme for coding social relationships (SDQ, p. 20). Included in this scheme were symbols for encoding the usual elements in definitions of nationality (common versus different language, religion, race, etc.), as well as for encoding the presence and age of common government. But this having been done, there was no longer any need for placing "civil" conflicts (however defined) into a separate series to be treated as if they were a priori unlike "international" conflicts (however defined). Placing the two types of war in a single series allowed study of wars as such; if a comparison of civil with international wars were wanted, the code for "common government" would allow the series to be partitioned into civil and foreign wars (or rather into pairs of civil and pairs of foreign belligerents). By such comparison, the likeness or unlikeness of civil and foreign war could then be determined a posteriori rather than posited a priori.

The participants.   Finding that the attempt to name "the aggressor" in a war usually leads to insoluble problems, Richardson searched for names of "belligerents" instead. In deciding which groups were to be considered participants in each war, Richardson made no juridical distinctions: "Germans," "Cretan Moslems," "Irgun Zvai Leumi"—the name of a nationality, or the group name of an organized body of fighters, is taken as the name of a single "participant" or "belligerent." Those groups whose participation was mainly formal or was confined to supplying arms and money or involved little bloodshed are omitted. Victims of massacres, as well as groups who did notable fighting but joined late or retired early, are listed as participants. Auxiliaries, such as mercenaries, foreign volunteers, and colonial troops, Richardson included as separate participants (though labeling them auxiliaries by printing their names in a different typeface) when he judged that their loyalty to their principal was not automatic and general but available only against certain enemies and not others (SDQ, pp. 12-14, 32, 35, 36).

"Deadly quarrels."   Richardson treated war as a species of "deadly quarrel." "By a deadly quarrel is meant any quarrel which caused death to humans. The term thus includes murders, banditries, mutinies, insurrections, and wars small and large; but it excludes accidents, and calamities such as earthquakes and tornadoes. Deaths by famine and disease are included if they were immediate results of the quarrel, but not otherwise. In puzzling cases the legal criterion of 'malice aforethought' was taken as a guide" (SDQ, p. 6). Richardson's definition could result of course in legally declared or historically recognized "wars" which produced no casualties being excluded from the war list. The exclusion is reasonable if one accepts that it is not the abstract fact of war but its concrete human consequences that arouse the desire to prevent it and, in order to prevent it, to understand it. It was

undoubtedly these "concrete consequences" that concerned Richardson: his convoy had "carried the wounded . . . of the 16-ieme division of infantry" during World War I (SDQ, p. xxiii).

Richardson's editors noted with some reserve that by his criterion a single data series must include hostilities with death tolls ranging from one (murder) to over 10 million, regardless of the juridical status of quarrel or belligerents (SDQ, pp. vii–viii). Considering all deliberate homicide to be a manifestation of the single psychological instinct of aggressiveness, Richardson was impatient with a priori juridical distinctions: he wished to explore the question of "whether there is any statistical connection among these traditionally separate topics" (SDQ, p. 6). In the event he was able to satisfy his curiosity only in part: statistics on very small deadly quarrels proved nearly unavailable, and those on murders different in kind from those available on large-scale violence. Thus his research came to focus on wars: though some links with lesser deadly quarrels were found, the data series actually collected and analyzed is a series of wars with death tolls ranging from over 100 to over 10 million.

Magnitudes. Recognizing that such a range still meant that "unequal" events would be counted together, and that accurate casualty figures were not easy to find, Richardson decided to measure and classify wars by "magnitude." "The magnitude of a quarrel is defined to be the logarithm to the base ten of the number of people who died because of that quarrel" (SDQ, p. 6). This logarithmic scale has technical advantages: it is well adapted to the imperfect state of knowledge; it automatically prevents any pretense of accuracy in casualty estimates; it allows us to utilize the substantial agreement usually present in apparently conflicting estimates; it permits us to treat some cases as "more important" than others according to a rule likely to minimize the effects of national and personal prejudice; and it renders less doubtful the counting of unequal things, since if these are first arranged in orders of magnitude and then counted within those orders the range of inequality in each count is substantially reduced, and differences between small and large wars are not swallowed up by the overall count (SDQ, pp. 3, 6–7). Richardson grouped wars within unit ranges of magnitude, ±0.5, on the ground that persistent disagreements over magnitude usually ranged within ±0.2 units, so that a wider range would "cause many known facts to be wasted" (SDQ, p. 10).

Thus each quarrel collected by Richardson has attached to it some magnitude measurement. One of the greatest claims to precision is contained in the magnitude of 4.83 given for the Russo-Finnish war of 1939–40 (representing some number of deaths between 66,834 and 68,391, probably 67,000); one of the smallest claims for precision, the magnitude of 4? given, for instance to the First Opium war 1839–42. (4? is an assertion that the death toll *may* fall in the range from 3,163 to 31,622 deaths, but could be in the order of magnitude above or below 4). The magnitudes 4?, 4, 4.$_0$, 4.0, 4.0$_0$, and 4.00

in Richardson's list are statements of a progressively increasing degree of confidence in the accuracy with which each magnitude is believed to have been found: from "somewhere about 10,000 dead, but uncertain by a factor of ten" to "very nearly 10,000 dead but uncertain by a factor of .01" (SDQ, pp. 10, 50, 56).

All the quarrels that Richardson examined fall within the magnitudes 0 to 7, that is within a general range of $10^0 = 1$ to $10^7 = 10$ million quarrel dead. The range of each order in logarithms and actual casualty numbers, and the midpoint of each order in actual casualties, are shown in table 1. Richardson's list of particular quarrels, as finally published, contains (by my count) 315 cases, of magnitudes 3 through 7 (table 2).

Causation. Richardson's interest was not confined to such (relatively) uncontroversial features of a war as its dates, duration, participants, and magnitude. His main concern was with causation: "It is proposed to count wars of different kinds in order to examine their causes" (SDQ p. 4). The term *cause,* perplexing as it is to philosophers of science, was treated by Richardson as having an acceptable commonsense meaning, not as a puzzling or technical term in need of lengthy explication. He spoke of "causes" and "causation" repeatedly and without apology (SDQ, pp. xlv, 4, 5, 16, 17, 128, 129, 210). He did examine these terms—in the manner of a researcher rather than a philosopher. He rejected the idea that there is a useful distinction to be made between "occasions" (precipitants) and underlying causes of war (SDQ, p. xlv). He decided that "we can leave out of account any cause ... which is well known, constantly present, and beyond human control" (SDQ, pp. xlv–xlvi). He distinguished between "ostensible" causes (declared intentions of belligerents) and the background of social relations, recording both (SDQ, p. 19).

TABLE 1

THE MIDPOINTS AND RANGES OF THE RICHARDSONIAN
WAR MAGNITUDES

Magnitude	Midpoint (actual)	Logarithmic bounds		Actual bounds	
		Upper	Lower	Upper	Lower
7	10 million	7.5	6.5	31,622,777	3,162,278
6	1 million	6.5	5.5	3,162,277	316,228
5	100 thousand	5.5	4.5	316,227	31,623
4	10 thousand	4.5	3.5	31,622	3,163
3	1 thousand	3.5	2.5	3,162	317
2	100	2.5	1.5	316	32
1	10	1.5	0.5	31	4
0	1	+0.5	−0.5	3	1

TABLE 2
THE NUMBER OF CASES PER ORDER OF MAGNITUDE IN
RICHARDSON'S WAR-LIST

Magnitude	Number of cases
7	2
6	7
5	26
4	71*
3	209
3 to 7	315
2	not recorded by case
1	not recorded by case
0	not recorded by case

*Richardson's editor counts 70 (SDQ, p. 51).

A sample entry. Matrix I is a complete entry from Richardson's war list. At the upper left appears the name of the war, the Second Opium War, and its rough overall duration, 1856 to 1860. The number just below, 4?, is its magnitude: approximately 10^4 or 10,000 war-dead. The names of the contestants are in small capitals: Chinese, British, French; also their ostensible reasons for fighting. The names are set as headings to the rows and columns of a matrix: the cell where a row and a column intersect contains information concerning the relationship of the two participants whose names head the row and the column. In this case there are two cells, one describing the relations of Chinese and British, the other of Chinese and French. The dates in each cell are the dates when the two belligerents fought one another: here the British are said to have fought the Chinese in two rounds, one from October 1856 to June 1858, another from June 1859 to October 1860.

Just above the dates is a set of three compartments (-/-/-). These contain an encoded statement of the background of prewar social relations. The twelve symbols (with modifiers) in the three compartments of the Chinese-British cell tell us what Richardson asserts that he found in the course of his readings on that pair of belligerents. The empty first compartment states that no circumstances were found which tended to pacify the British-Chinese relationship at the time their quarrel broke out. The second compartment (aCDFGIO) states that at the time of the outbreak, Chinese and British traded (a), were of markedly different physical types (C), customarily dressed differently (D), had markedly different marriage customs (F), felt their religions or philosophies of life to be in contrast (G), spoke different languages (I), and had conflicting legal systems (O); but that, though all these

MATRIX I

Second "Opium War" 1856–60

		References
4?	CHINESE against opium and·"western barbarians."	E 5, 537.
		Latourette.
BRITISH[2] against the seizure of a British ship.	— | a C D F G I O | M$_{14}$ A ⟩ H ⟩ K ⟩⟩ X ⟩⟩ 1856.x–58. vi 1859.vi–60.x	Li Ung Bing. MacNair. Camb. Mod.
FRENCH[2] against the murder of a French missionary.	— | a C D F I O | GA ⟩ H ⟩ K ⟩⟩ X ⟩⟩ 1857.xi–58.vi 1859.vi–60.x	Priestley.

[2] For diplomatic recognition, and better openings for trade.

Result. China was opened to British, French, Russians, and U.S. Americans. Opium was permitted.

relations were conspicuously present, and likely to have had some effect, their actual effect was unknown to Richardson, as they were not mentioned as causes of the war in the histories he consulted (SDQ, pp. 22–25).

The symbols in the third compartment of the Chinese-British cell (M$_{14}$ A ⟩ H ⟩ K ⟩⟩ X ⟩⟩) represent those situations which were actually cited as causes of the quarrel. A previous war, ending fourteen years before this one began, had left a residue of bad feeling (M$_{14}$). The Chinese interfered with British trade (A ⟩). The arrow indicates the direction of the relationship: the tail-group (the group nearer the tail of the arrow) put obstacles in the way of the movement of goods to or from the tip-group. The Chinese restricted British immigration (H ⟩). Chinese and British were generally ignorant of one another (K ⟩⟩). Each was "elated by exceptionally strong pride" and behaved toward the other in ways the other considered overbearing (X ⟩⟩).

The coding scheme. Because Richardson's coding scheme presents certain advantages and disadvantages for analysis, it may be as well to describe it in some detail. In order to carry out his intention to research causes of wars, Richardson first arranged "a list of the types of relations that might be important in preventing or causing quarrels" (SDQ, p. 20). Most of the potential causes on this list were taken from works on history and politics where they were mentioned in connection with particular wars; some were derived from treatises of sociology. A few among the social situations thus listed are:

1.   The belligerents had previously fought as allies against a common enemy;
2.   A third party desired that the belligerents should quarrel;
3.   The belligerents were rivals in trading with third parties.

Altogether some fifty-nine alleged causes were mentioned in history or theory often enough for Richardson to record their occurrence in the cases by means of a code of symbols, a classificatory apparatus, the symbols being letters of the alphabet each assigned a particular social situation. (This entire Richardsonian code is reproduced in the first two columns of Appendix IV.)

Richardson's symbolic code is a bit complex, and it is very clearly designed for a data collection handwritten on file cards and intended for human-eye character recognition and for hand count. A symbol has a meaning conveyed by its typeface, another conveyed by its position in a matrix, another by its position in the cell of the matrix, sometimes another conveyed by an appended accent or arrow or footnote. This coding allows the practiced reader to retrieve Richardson's description of a war very rapidly: a glance at one cell in the World War II matrix where the symbol P appears in a certain position, and another glance at the code list, allows one to say, "Richardson gives as one reason for the hostilities between British and Germans in World War II the fact that the Germans had injured or attacked an ally or friend of the British."

Richardson arranges his fifty-nine "social situations" into three groups, by their "expected valency": Eighteen situations expected usually to make for amity are assigned lower case Roman letters; twenty-five situations expected usually to be causes of dislike, contempt, suspicion, or annoyance are assigned Roman capitals; and sixteen situations expected to be ambivalent because their actual effects seem to have been diverse (provoking affection *and* hostility, restraint *and* attack) are assigned Greek cursive letters.

Some of the situations apply to one group, "the government ... was insecure"; some to two groups; some to three groups (one group supported the other's enemy). Symbols are assigned, in Richardson's coding scheme, only to a pair of belligerents: when a pair is assigned a symbol that applies only to one side, a special notation is required to designate the side to which the symbol applies (e.g., *whose* government was insecure). The arrow modifier accomplishes this: "the government of the tail-group was insecure." The arrow modifier in a two-group situation indicates that the relationship is directional, and in which direction it runs, for example, "the tail-group taxed the tip-group."

Accents are used to particularize a situation: T, the tail-group wished to acquire territory from the tip-group; T', the territory was wanted for habitation; T''', for strategic strongholds. Suffixes are used to date a situation: M, the belligerents had fought one another previously; M_{14}, they had fought fourteen years before the outbreak being coded.

Each symbol is thus multidimensional. It always has a definition, an expected valency (typeface), and an actual valency (compartment). Some also have a date (suffix), a specifier (accent), and/or a direction (arrow).

There are actually two units of analysis, the case (or matrix of rows and columns containing all the opposed belligerents in a war) and the pair (one cell of such a matrix, containing statements about the two belligerents at the head of the cell's row and column). Some characteristics of the war (name, starting date, ending date, magnitude) belong to the case; others (the relationship code) to the pairs; others (name, status—i.e., whether principal or auxiliary) to the participants severally.

Some cases contain only one pair. One, World War II, has over eighty pairs of belligerents. Not all the cells in a matrix contain pair information. Matrix II below contains blank cells (information about the pair is lacking) along with symbols indicating that one pair did not actually fight, another was logically absurd, and a third was treated elsewhere in the matrix.

Richardson's coding scheme is, in short, complex, dense, technical, visual. Let us postpone evaluation of it until after inspecting its consequences, Richardson's analyses and findings.[1]

---

[1] The code, summarized in Appendix 4, is evaluated in chapter 2. The problems of converting it for computer processing are discussed in Appendix 3.

MATRIX II

The Mexican Revolution, 1910–20

Not arrangeable as two sides. The large X excludes the notion of "fighting himself." The large O means "did not in fact fight one another." The large S means "see the other row and column for the same pair of belligerents." The phrase "and followers" is to be understood after the name of each leader.

5.4	MADERO for peasants cautiously	ZAPATA for distribution of land	OROZCO for the revolution	VILLA for brigandage	HUERTA for conservative tyranny	CARRANZA for constitutional land-reform
DIAZ for large landowners and private capitalists.	$-\|i\mu m_{34}\|E\rangle\rho\rangle$ 1910.xi–11.v	$-\|i\|E\rangle\rho\rangle$ –11.v	$-\|i\|-$ –11.v	$-\|i\|M'E\rangle V\rangle$ 1910–11.v	O	$-\|i\mu m_{34}\|\rho\rangle$ 1910.xi–11.v
ZAPATA for distribution of land.	$-\|i\|E\rangle$ 1911.xi–13.ii	X	O	$-\|i\lambda_1\|V\rangle$ 1912.iii	$-\|i\|E\rangle$ 1911.xi–14.vii	$-\|i\|-$ 1914.viii–19.vii
OROZCO irked by lack of reward.	$-\|i\|-$ 1912.iii–13.ii	O	X	$-\|i\lambda_1\|V\rangle$ 1912.iii	$-\|i\|-$ 1912.iii–14.vii	
VILLA for brigandage.		S	S	X	S	$-\|i\lambda_3\|V\rangle$ 1914.viii–15.vii
HUERTA for conservative tyranny.	$-\|i\lambda_1\|E\rangle$ 1913.ii	S	S	$-\|i\|V\rangle$ 1910.xi; 1914.v	X	$-\|i\|-$ 1913–16 and 1920.iv–v
U.S.A. for order and private capitalism.	O	O	O	$-\|\sigma\rangle\|V\rangle$ 1916.i–17.ii	$-\|i\|-$ 1913–14.vii	$-\|i\|-$ 1916.vi
OBREGON for socialism.	O	1915.i	1912.iii–13.ii	1914.vii–15.vii	1913–14.viii	1913 and λ_0; 1920.iv–v

Results. Large estates were divided among peasants. The power of the Catholic Church over education and over property was restricted. Minerals, notably petroleum, were nationalized.

References. Kirkpatrick: Teja Zabre: E 15.393–4: E 16.669.

3
Time, Magnitude, and War

Onsets and endings of war per annum. Using fourth-magnitude wars (as both numerous and likely to have been almost exhaustively listed), Richardson counted the number of outbreaks of such wars in each year of the time interval 1820–1929 inclusive. He found that there were sixty-five of these years in which no such war broke out, thirty-five years in which one war began, six years with two outbreaks in each, four years with three outbreaks in each, and no years at all in which four or more wars broke out. Could the series 65–35–6–4–0 . . . be a function of the series 0–1–2–3–4 . . . ? Richardson saw a considerable resemblance between these historical facts and the Poisson distribution of improbable events.

Phenomena that occur rarely, randomly over a time or space, and independently of one another commonly show a certain particular distribution: most units of time (or space) show no such phenomena; where one such phenomenon occurs, it usually does so alone; seldom are two such phenomena concurrent; three together are even rarer, and so on. Stars in space, raisins in a cake, wrong-number calls per day received per telephone, deaths per cavalry regiment per year from horse kicks—all show empirical distributions that appear to fit the theoretical Poisson distribution of rare events. The theoretical distribution is generated by assuming that there are many occasions on which a certain event can occur, a very low probability of its occurrence on each occasion, determination of its occurrence or nonoccurrence on each occasion by random chance, and no alteration of the probability of one occurrence by a nearby occurrence or nonoccurrence. To find that real events are Poisson-distributed allows one to make some intriguing guesses about their causation.

Testing his hunch, Richardson found that the onsets of wars per year do, in fact, show a Poisson distribution.[1] So indeed do the endings of wars. "The usual abstract basis for the Poisson law . . . is that there was the same large number, k, of occasions on which the event, here the outbreak of war, might have occurred in any year, and the same almost zero probability p of its occurrence at each occasion," so that $pk = \lambda$ where λ is the mean number of war-outbreaks per year, here 59/110, or nearly .5364. If $k = 365$ (days per year), then p, the probability of a war breaking out on any given day, is 59/40150, nearly .00147, or a chance of between 1/10 and 2/10 of 1 percent. The corresponding probability of an "outbreak of peace" is 60/40150, somewhat over .00149, and virtually identical (SDQ, pp. 128–130).

The Poisson distribution of onsets and terminations

> follows logically from the hypothesis that there is the same very small probability of an outbreak of war, or of peace, somewhere on the globe on every day. In fact there is a seasonal variation. . . . But when years are counted as wholes, this seasonal effect is averaged out. . . . The Poisson distribution is not predictive; it does not answer such questions as 'when will the present war end?' or 'when will the next war begin?' On the contrary, the Poisson distribution draws attention to a persistent probability of change from peace to war, or from war to peace. . . . A suggestion made by the Poisson law is that . . . discontent with present circumstances underlies . . . peace and war. [Richardson 1950*a*, pp. 243–244]

One might like to find a different interpretation for k, the number of opportunities for war to break out per year: not days per year, but crises per year, for instance. (In that case p would be the probability of any crisis issuing in a war.) This would direct us to the comparative study of actual crises that did and did not end in war. One would ask what distinguished those settled from those that exploded. Now if war-crises per year were few, it would be to the point to concentrate war-prevention efforts on specific named tensions and crises, massively mobilizing conflict-resolution energies and institutions a few times a year to cope with extremely dangerous situations. But Richardson's data suggest that there are many such war-crises per year, each with a very low probability of ending in war. If this is true, it may be more to the point to look for the general causes of war-crises and work on abating such general causes so as to reduce k; or to support institu-

---

[1] Singer and Small found that for their ninety-three international wars the intervals between onsets fit an exponential Poisson distribution, associated with a pure Poisson distribution in the frequency of onsets per unit of time such as Richardson found (1972, pp. 205–206).

tionalized systems of routine crisis-processing intended to handle a great many crises per annum, and to aim at reducing *slightly* in each the already slight probability of resort to war.

There is more reason for seeking some alternative interpretation for the Poisson distribution of the endings of wars. Richardson may not have been satisfied with the persistent discontent interpretation, for it appears in an article (1950*a*) but not in the final book (1960*b*). But he suggested no substitutes. The difficulty with interpreting war onsets and terminations as equally members of the class of "improbable events" is of course that all ongoing wars in Richardson's interval ended; all peace, that is, relationships potentially but not actually violent, did not. The duration of peace between any pair of named nations was on the average very much longer than the duration of war between the same pair (SDQ, pp. 256, 258, 260, 285). War and the onset of war may qualify as "improbable events." Peace and the onset of peace do not. An alternate interpretation of war-ending should be sought. One source for such an interpretation would be some pattern, some regularity, in the duration of war.

The duration of war.   Richardson's finding that war-terminations have the same Poisson distribution as war-onsets led one of Richardson's editors, C. C. Lienau, to raise the question of the distribution of the *durations* of war and of peace (SDQ, pp. 130, xv–xvi). Weiss (1963) and Horvath (1968) have examined this distribution. I have undertaken another examination of war durations for this study.

For purposes of initial inquiry, I defined the duration of a war as year of ending minus year of starting; a duration of zero is permissible and merely indicates that a war ended in the calendar year in which it began. For 106 cases, magnitudes 4–7, 1820–1952, my count is as shown in table 3.

TABLE 3

ACTUAL DISTRIBUTION OF 106 WARS, MAGNITUDES 4–7, BY
THEIR DURATIONS

Duration	0	1	2	3	4	5	6	Over 6 years	Total cases
Number of wars having this duration	23	19	16	13	8	4	4	19	106

The mean duration is 3.65 years. The distribution shows that a plurality of wars end in their first year (zero duration). The table shows thereafter a steady diminution, which continues beyond the table (after the sixth year). For durations from seven to seventeen, the number of cases is 3, 3, 2, 4, 1, 1, 1, 1, 0, 1, 1. There is one outlier with a duration of thirty-five years. The regularity of the data invites an attempt to formulate a hypothesis to explain the slow diminution.

Richardson stated that "the simplest quantitative expression of the notion of 'fading away to zero' is a geometrical progression ... " (a sequence of numerical items in which, the first term being given, each succeeding term may be derived from the term preceding it if that is multiplied by some fixed common ratio, r [SDQ, p. 200]). Accordingly, following a procedure outlined by Richardson, a geometric progression was fitted to the observed collection, and this proposed "theory" tested. In this application, r is a coefficient of continuation: of N wars ongoing in any year, Nr are hypothesized to go on to the next year, Nr^2 to the year following, and so on. The geometric progression having $r = .765$ (table 4) was found to be a credible summary of the observations, in the sense that the calculated discrepancy between hypothesis and observation was small, and that the chi-square test, one-tailed, gives no reason to suspect the theory when $P > 0.10$, while in fact $P > 0.75$.[2]

TABLE 4

THEORETICAL DISTRIBUTION OF 106 WARS, MAGNITUDES 4–7, BY THEIR DURATIONS

Duration	0	1	2	3	4	Over 4 years	Total cases
"Theory"	24.91	19.06	14.58	11.15	8.53	27.77	106
Chi-square = 0.64617		*Df* = 3		*P* > 0.75			

For the data in question, then, it is safe to say that approximately 23.5 percent of wars ended in their first year; the same percentage of the remaining wars ended in their second year, and so on. One might even venture the interpretation that for any ongoing war, there is a probability of approximately 0.235 that it will end within the year.

Had this finding proven stable and credible, it would have supplied a sort of benchmark for measuring the performance of any general peacemaking system applied to a large enough body of ongoing wars, in the same sense that theoretical expectations of "spontaneous" recoveries might be applied in measuring the performance of a therapeutic system. This application would also conceivably allow the testing of a "political malpractice" or "iatrogenic disease" hypothesis: if, for instance, under an alleged system of peacemaking 10 percent of wars ongoing in any year were regularly brought to an end, we might wish to consider bringing the system itself to an end.

But the finding proved unstable. For 209 cases at magnitude 3,

[2] SDQ, pp. 201–202, Fisher (1936, p. 83), Jeffreys (1939, p. 315).

1820–1952, my count is shown in table 5. For durations from 6 to 11, the number of cases is 1, 2, 2, 1, 1, 2; there is one outlier, duration 30 years. The mean duration at this magnitude was 1.5 years. Using the same procedure as before, a geometric progression with $r = .573$ was found to have a tolerable fit to the observed durations. Approximately 42.7 percent of these wars end in their first year; we might therefore say that for any ongoing, very small war there is a probability of approximately 0.427 that it will end within the year.

TABLE 5

ACTUAL AND THEORETICAL DISTRIBUTION OF 209 THIRD-
MAGNITUDE WARS BY THEIR DURATIONS

Duration	0	1	2	3	4	5	Over 5 years	Total cases
Number of wars	92	56	21	18	5	7	10	209
"Theory"	89.24	51.13	29.3	16.79	9.62	5.51	7.40	208.99
Chi-square = 6.523		Df = 4		$0.25 > P > 0.10$				

This coefficient is very much smaller than that for wars at magnitudes 4–7 and leads us to wish to look at the durations for all 315 cases. These are combined in table 6.

For durations of 9 through 17 years the number of cases is 3, 5, 3, 1, 1, 1, 0, 1, 1; there is one outlier at 30 years and one at 35 years. The mean duration for the whole set of 315 cases is 2.23 years. A geometric progression with $r = .708$ was fitted to the data but found not to be a credible summary because the discrepancy between theoretical expectation and actual observation was much too large.

TABLE 6

ACTUAL AND THEORETICAL DISTRIBUTION OF 315 WARS,
MAGNITUDES 3–7, BY THEIR DURATIONS

Duration	0	1	2	3	4	5	6	7	8	Over 8 years	Total cases
Number of wars	115	75	37	31	13	11	5	5	5	18	315
"Theory"	91.9	65.09	46.1	32.65	23.12	16.38	11.60	8.22	5.82	14.13	314.98
Chi-square = 21.58		Df = 7		$P < 0.01$							

The two series, magnitude 3 and magnitudes 4–7, do not merge neatly. An explanation must be sought. It may lie in the incompleteness of the war list at magnitude 3 or in an effect of magnitude on duration (e.g., great sacrifice tending to inspire stubborn resistance) or of duration on magnitude (e.g., longer fighting tending to produce more casualties). All these hypotheses, and others, are superficially plausible. None can be accepted as yet. We are led to consider more complex interpretive procedures, such as those of Weiss (1963) and Horvath (1968).

Weiss's calculation of war-duration is not the same as that given above. Where Richardson gave calendar months for starting and ending of a war, Weiss used these to calculate duration. When calendar years only are recorded, Weiss assigned a duration of 0.5 years to wars ended in the same year as begun and a duration (year of ending minus year of beginning) to other wars. Data are then clustered about durations of 0.5 year, 1.5 years, and so forth. Each war with near integral duration is divided evenly between the two half-year points on either side. The distributions that emerge are given in table 7.

TABLE 7

ACTUAL DISTRIBUTIONS OF 315 WARS, MAGNITUDES 3–7
(ACCORDING TO WEISS [1963])

Duration in years	0–1	1–2	2–3	3–4	4–5	5–6	6–7	7–8	8–9	9–10	10+	Total
Magnitude 4–7	38	16	12	11	6	6	3	2	2	2	8	106
Magnitude 3	127	30	21	11	5	5	2	2	2	1	3	209
All Magnitudes	165	46	33	22	11	11	5	4	4	3	11	315

I attempted to fit geometrical progressions to these distributions by the method of maximum likelihood. Progressions with $r = 0.43$ to $r = 0.59$ were fitted, but the discrepancies (chi-squares) were too large, and no credible summary could be obtained. Wars were too strongly (and perhaps too forcedly) clustered in the first cell of each row.

Weiss used these duration distributions differently. He succeeded in generating distributions of war durations and magnitudes corresponding to those observed by Richardson by using two probabilities—the probability that in a small interval of time an additional death occurred, and the probability that in the same small interval of time the war was terminated. Each probability term was considered to be a function only of the cumulative number of casualties and of the time in which they had been incurred, that is, of the magnitude and duration of the war up to the time in question, with both probabilities apparently varying with the average death rate in the war up to that time. "It is suggestive that $p(x,t)$ [the probability that a war stops in a small time interval after time 't', when (x) deaths have occurred and before $(x+1)$ deaths] increases as the number of deaths incurred in a specified time increases, and decreases as the time in which a specified number of deaths is incurred increases" (1963, pp. 109, 112). One might have expected the opposite effect.

Horvath (1968) provided another statistical model that omitted the magnitudes and dealt only with the distribution of durations of wars (and of strikes). Weiss's tabulation of Richardson's duration data was followed. The observed curve was fitted with considerable accuracy (chi-square = 3.47, Df = 6, probability of deviations of that size due to chance about 0.75) by a Weibull distribution. Horvath interpreted this as meaning that a war ended after many attempts, the success of any of which would have terminated it, with the chance of success for any such attempt fluctuating continually over some probability distribution of impediments to resolution.

The choice among the various models for explaining duration is not clear-cut. Weiss's was conceptually simple and mathematically complex and linked duration and magnitude via the death rate. Horvath's was mathematically simpler than Weiss's but conceptually more complex. The "model" proposed in this book is simpler than either and would be preferable if observation and theory were limited to magnitude 4 and above; but when magnitude 3 is included, it proves unsatisfactory, and some connection between duration and magnitude such as Weiss provides becomes desirable. Let us therefore tentatively accept the disturbing idea that bloodier fighting brings a quicker end.

Trends in the duration of war.   By my calculation, duration being defined as year of ending minus year of starting, the median duration of all 315 wars is 1 year, the mean 2.23 years. For 106 wars at magnitudes 4–7 inclusive, the median duration is 2 years, the mean 3.65 years; for 209 wars at magnitude 3, the median duration is 1 year, the mean 1.5 years. (The discrepancy between mean and median is to be expected given that there are a few very long wars.)

The Richardson data cover thirteen decades beginning with 1820–1829 and ending with 1940–1949; there is one case ending 1952. The 149 wars ending in the first six decades 1820–1879 have a median duration of 1 year and a mean duration of 2.47 years; the 144 wars ending in the last six decades 1890–1949 have the same median duration, 1 year, and a mean duration of 2.12 years. The median durations of the wars ending in each of the thirteen decades are 2, 1, 1.5, 0, 1, 1, 1, 1, 1, 1, 1, 1, 0.5; the mean durations are 2.49, 3.15, 2.57, 1.58, 2.19, 2.86, 1.4, 2.2, 3.38, 1.23, 1.85, 2.25, 1.56. Fitting the latter series to a least squares regression equation gives a line with a small negative slope, - .0675, predicting a mean duration of 2.61 years in the 1820–1829 decade and 1.8 years in 1940–1949.

A similar relationship holds for the wars broken down by magnitude. For the wars at magnitudes 4–7, mean durations in the thirteen decades are 4.7, 3.5, 3.23, 4.4, 4.29, 4.55, 3.2, 2.25, 5.3, 1.44, 2.45, 4.5, 3.67. These fit a line with negative slope, -.074, and a change in predicted duration from 4.09 to 3.20 years. For wars at magnitude 3, mean durations are 1.38, 3.09, 1.7, 0.57, 1.69, 1, 0.8, 2.19, 1.71, 1.12, 1.4, 0.75, 0.5; these fit a line with negative slope, - .0841, and a change in predicted duration from 1.88 to 0.87 years.

Quincy Wright asserted (1942, p. 235) that there had been a "general trend . . . toward a decrease in the length of wars" since the seventeenth century, when he found averages of five to eight years (1942, p. 651). This trend is not inconsistent with the trends in the Richardson data.

Trends in the frequency of war. Are wars becoming more frequent? Richardson found no sufficient indication of any trend toward more, or fewer, wars. His observations do show a slight decrease in the frequency of wars, but this variation might be merely random (SDQ, pp. 136, 139, 141, 163). The increase in world population from 1820 to 1949 was, he averred, certainly not accompanied by a proportionate increase in the frequency of wars.[3] If the collection of wars could be made complete at magnitude 3, or extended back to A.D. 1700, it might be possible to demonstrate that what appears to be a decrease in the frequency of wars per capita is non-random. Until then, said Richardson, there remains "a suggestion, but not a conclusive proof, that mankind has become less warlike since A.D. 1820" (SDQ, pp. 166, 167). I must admit to reservations concerning the use of the term "warlike" in this connection. There might be, as Richardson's next finding indeed suggests, an inverse relationship over time between the frequency of wars and their average magnitude; in that case a reduced frequency of war would not to my mind stand as evidence of diminished "warlikeness."

[3] Singer and Small (1972) found some evidence of a decline in frequency but an increase in nation-months and battle-deaths in their ninety-three international wars 1816–1965, but they concluded finally that the trends were so weak, erratic and fluctuating that "there is no significant trend upward or down over the past 150 years" (1972, pp. 189–190, 195–201). However, Beer (1974, pp. 20–21) noted that in Singer and Small's list of 93 international wars, and in their "comprehensive" list of 367 major and minor wars 1816–1965, the number of wars that occurred in the nineteenth century was about 10 percent more and in the twentieth century about 10 percent less than would have been expected had the incidence of war been unchanged over time. As he also found evidence of a trend toward increasing magnitude of war over the period in question, Beer hypothesized an overall historical trend toward the "concentration" of war. Beer's hypothesis is more consistent with Richardson's findings than is Singer and Small's "no trend" finding, and than Richardson's "less warlike" suggestion.

Fourth-magnitude wars were significantly less frequent in 1920-1949 than in 1820-1919 and fifth-plus-magnitude wars significantly more frequent than a null hypothesis would have led us to expect. Stephen A. Richardson offered the hypothesis that increasing trade and improved communications and transport have made it harder for small wars to remain insulated (SDQ, p. 142). Alternative explanations for this phenomenon would include deadlier weapons, larger belligerent populations, and more effective mobilization for war.

The distribution of wars by magnitude. As Richardson pointed out, " 'the larger, the fewer' is a true description of all the known facts about world totals of fatal quarrels" (1950*a*, p. 247). He fit several log-log linear functions of varying generality, complexity, and utility to his data on deadly quarrels: in all of them the number of quarrels of a given magnitude diminished as the magnitude increased (SDQ, pp. 143-152).

Many interpretations and derivations of this observed distribution are possible. Weiss (1963), for instance, generated it, using the assumption that the probability that a war ends after x deaths have occurred and before death $x+1$ depends only on x and *decreases* as x increases. Richardson preferred a line of interpretation that assumes quarrel-dead to be a function of the size of the quarreling groups, which is in turn a function of the number of groups of a given size that the population of the world makes available for purposes of quarreling.[4] Richardson was unable to derive the empirical formula relating war-magnitude to frequency from geographic opportunity alone; Wesley however did so (1962).

Trends in the magnitude of war. Richardson's editors attributed to him the generalization that "the increase in world population seems not to have been accompanied by a proportionate increase in the frequency of, *and losses of life from*, war . . . " (SDQ, p. ix; emphasis added). I do not find the emphasized conclusion in Richardson at the point cited (SDQ, p. 167), nor can I infer it from the preceding discussion (SDQ, pp. 141, 157-166). Richardson drew no conclusions concerning general trends for all war magnitudes or total war casualties. He did conclude that there is no general trend to more or fewer total quarrels in the ranges of magnitude 3-5 or 4-6, but that there is evidence of a decline in magnitude 4 wars and a rise in the range of magnitude 5-7 since 1920 (SDQ, pp. 141, 142, 163).

My own tabulation of Richardson's war-death rate for the two half-intervals 1820-1884 and 1885-1949 gives a loss of life of 5.1 million for the first period and 42.5 million for the second—scarcely surprising, since the second half-interval includes both world wars! The editors' conclusion there-

---

[4] This interpretation appeared first in the crude form of "aggregation for aggression" (SDQ, pp. 114-119) and was later refined as "geographical opportunities for fighting" (SDQ, pp. 288-313).

fore seems unwarranted. So does Richardson's own statement that "there is a suggestion, but not a conclusive proof, that mankind has become less warlike since A.D. 1820" (SDQ, p. 167), at least if warlikeness involves war magnitude as well as frequency. There is in that case a strong suggestion of increased warlikeness. In any event, there is an increase in "losses of life from war" by a factor of 8.33, which, when compared to a population increase by a factor of close to 1.50 between 1850 and 1920 (Richardson's calculation, SDQ, p. 158), seems more than proportionate. This increase need not reflect a longer-term trend. Richardson began his interval in the lull that followed the Napoleonic Wars. An interval beginning in A.D. 1745 rather than 1820 or earlier might show a periodicity rather than a trend (see below, section on periodicities; and see Moyal, 1949).

Stefflre (1974) has examined Richardson's war-death data and average population estimates and Singer and Small's (1972) battle-death and number-of-nations data for the global system over thirty-year intervals. World Wars I and II give the death series a notably rising trend which Singer and Small conceded,[5] then blurred,[6] and finally rejected.[7]

Stefflre argued that the trend, observable in both Richardson's and Singer and Small's data when thirty-year intervals were used, could not simply be discounted. He contended that both the Richardson and the Singer-Small data were consistent with the hypothesis that "for each interval in which the human population doubles, there occur wars in which ten times as many people are killed, as are killed by wars in the previous such interval" (1974, p. 304). The data may also be consistent with the hypothesis that for each interval in which world population doubles, the *proportion* of that population killed in war increases tenfold. Stefflre objected to Singer and Small's "normalization" of battle-death statistics for population (and number of nations) and argued instead for regressing casualties on these variables, so as to permit using population and number of nations in estimating future war deaths. Following that procedure he arrived at several estimates for "period 6," 1966–1995, assuming a mean population of 5,000 million and 180 countries. His estimates for battle deaths were 50.6 million and upward, for war deaths 65.7 million and upward.

Beer (1974, pp. 24–28) used casualty data collected by Sorokin (1937) to

[5] The "number of . . . battle deaths rises sharply for both the raw and the normalized figures" when the period 1816–1965 is divided into two seventy-five-year periods; there is "a general upward trend" for total battle deaths for all wars when five thirty-year periods are used (1972, pp. 189–190).

[6] Use fifteen periods of ten years, and fluctuations are accentuated while the trend is obscured; correlate annual measures with time, and the correlation is insignificant (1972, pp. 190, 196–197).

[7] There is "no significant trend upward or down over the past 150 years" (1972, p. 201).

argue that, for European countries at least, absolute numbers of war casualties have risen century by century since A.D. 1101 (except for a decline in the nineteenth century). War casualties as a proportion of the population have similarly risen, but for a slight decline in the eighteenth century and a marked decline in the nineteenth. Beer's projections provide some further support for the notion that there is a long-term trend toward increased war magnitude and increased mortality from war. But in suggesting that the nineteenth century was anomalously placid, they also suggest that linear projections begun from that trough and drawn through the high points of the twentieth century may exaggerate the casualties to be expected from wars to come.

Nevertheless, Stefflre's computations confront an issue that Singer and Small interpreted away and Richardson never really considered. They should be taken quite seriously. His conclusions suggest that we ought to be concerned particularly with high-magnitude wars.

Duration, magnitude, and complexity.   The duration of a war, its magnitude, and the number of pairs of belligerents in the case are interrelated. The distributions across magnitudes of cases, pairs per case, and mean durations of wars (for both Weiss's and Wilkinson's definitions of durations) are given in table 8.

TABLE 8

MAGNITUDES, COMPLEXITIES, AND DURATIONS OF 315 WARS

Magnitude	# of cases	# of pairs per case	Mean duration	
			Weiss	Wilkinson
7	2	65	5.1	5
6	7	6	5.4	5.4
5	26	3.5	4.5	4.6
4	71	2.9	2.8	3.1
3	209	1.5	1.7	1.5
All	315	2.5	2.3	2.2

Weiss (1963) plotted mean durations of Richardson's wars as a function of magnitude. With T = duration in years and m = magnitude, he gave an equation $T = .18 \, m^2$. Using a TI SR-51A linear regression routine and Weiss's data, I find the linear equation $T = .18 \, m^2 + .07$ for data for magnitudes 3-5; for magnitudes 3-6 the equation was $T = .14 \, m^2 + .58$. The more bloody wars also last longer.

Via an R-factor analysis for 779 pairs of belligerents on twenty-one variables formed from Richardson's data, Rummel (1967) found a first dimension defined by the number of pairs in a war, the duration of the war in months, and the number killed. The starting date of the pair-quarrel was correlated with this "intensity dimension." Rummel concluded that "there has been some tendency for violent conflicts between groups of all kinds to become more intense," that is, to involve more pairs, more pair-months, and more war-dead (1967, pp. 178, 180, 182). This conclusion adds some weight to Stefflre's assertion of a trend toward increasing magnitude of wars.

The death toll of wars, together and by magnitude. Richardson estimated that approximately 1.6 percent of deaths from all causes 1820–1945 proceeded from quarrels, 0.3 percent arising from murders and 1.3 percent from wars (SDQ, p. 153). Even if Richardson's definition of war-dead had been broadened to include civilian deaths from exposure and infectious disease incidental to war (SDQ, pp. 6, 8–9), it seems unlikely that this percentage would increase drastically. Perhaps the relative importance of war versus other causes of death should be taken into account in the relative financing of peace research versus medical research; perhaps, indeed, it is.

Of all Richardson's estimated war-dead 1820–1945 in wars of magnitudes 4 through 7, nearly 77 percent died in the two world wars (the two seventh-magnitude wars) (see table 9). If one purpose of the study of wars is to reduce the suffering they entail, this pattern would seem to suggest the strong desirability of searching for causal patterns that characterize the largest wars *as a class* and according their prevention as a class a striking priority. From the fact that while the world wars caused 61 percent of all quarrel-dead 1820–1947 on Richardson's estimate, and murders came next with 16.4 percent (followed by the sixth-magnitude wars with 11.3 percent), further priorities for social research might be inferred.

TABLE 9
RELATIVE IMPACT OF THE GREATEST WARS

Magnitude	% of war-dead in cases at this magnitude	No. of cases	% per case
7	76.84%	2	38.42%
6	14.30	5	2.86
5	7.26	24	.30
4	1.60	63	.03
	100%	94	

Modelski has drawn the appropriate conclusion that

the Richardson scale also suggests a scale of priorities for research on conflicts. The critical type of conflict, and of war, is the global war and deserves the highest research priority. . . . The next important type of disorder is murder and related forms of personal and local conflict; for these the remedies are commonly seen to reside in police work and in personal, and local community, development. Finally, all the in-between forms of armed conflict, including national, civil, international and subnational conflicts, while not unimportant appear to assume lesser priority, and deserve possibly only residual attention. [1972, p. 54]

Periodicities. Several different cycles have been noticed when different measures of war are plotted against time.

Moyal (1949) used Quincy Wright's collection of war data for A.D. 1500–1931 to construct a fifty-year moving average of war outbreaks per annum. The means thus derived, when plotted over time, show a cyclical pattern, with highs centered in 1625 (0.91 outbreaks per annum for the fifty years centered on 1625) and 1880 (1.15) and a low at 1745 (0.24 outbreaks per annum). Moyal concluded that this pattern was consistent with a probability of outbreak λ in any small interval of time that varies in a roughly periodic fashion, with a half-period of approximately 100 years (1949, p. 447; SDQ, pp. 140–141). What might account for such a periodicity? The question takes on additional significance in that the maximum probability of outbreak is larger than the minimum by an impressively large factor of five, which suggests that whatever accounts for the historic variation may be worth examining if we wish to minimize λ for the future. Were there fewer war-crises at the bottom of the cycle? Was there a better mechanism of crisis resolution, a more pacific world view, greater general satisfaction with the status quo, a more centralized power structure? Investigation is warranted.

Denton (1966) apportioned Richardson's war data for 1820–1949 among twenty-six five-year intervals. The case data were used to derive world-system data for the twenty-six periods. The derived data were then factor analyzed in a search for synchronous variations. A "size of war cluster" emerged: the factor score per period plotted against time showed peaks, on an average twenty-four years apart, when many nations participated in wars of high magnitude. The peaks in war size coincide rather closely with Rosecrance's (1963) dates for change or dissolution of "international systems."

Using their own data on ninety-three international wars, 1816–1965, Singer and Small found that there exist "one or more periodicities between 20 and 40 years" in the fluctuation in the number of nation-months of war underway per system member per annum (1972, pp. 208–213). This partially supports an earlier study by Denton and Phillips (1968), using Wright's data for 1480–1900.

Denton and Phillips employed an "index of violence" highly correlated with each of four variables (number of wars, number of belligerents, number of belligerent-years, number of belligerents/number of nations) for eighty-four five-year time intervals to measure the level of violence in the system during each interval. There was some evidence of 20- to 30-year peaks possibly tied to a human cycle of generations; and of 60- to 120-year peaks in which civil wars formed a relatively high proportion of all wars. For the longer cycle they proposed a theoretical explanation: dissatisfaction with the form of society is persistent; the experience of disorder and civil violence arising from attempts at reformation checks further attempts until the memory of disorder fades, at which point reforms are again tried, with disorder and civil violence again the result.

Three collections—those of Wright, Richardson, and Singer and Small— thus show periodic fluctuations suggesting a 20- to 40-year cycle when different, but related, measures are plotted against time. This cycle should be treated accordingly as highly probable, and an attempt made to integrate its different indices and to generate a covering theory.

As for long cycles, the only data collection whose interval is long enough to show them, that of Quincy Wright (interval from 1482 to 1940), was alleged by Moyal to show a 200-year cycle but by Denton and Phillips to show a 60- to 120-year cycle. The collection itself is not without problems (see Appendix 1). Long cycles should not be treated as probable, but merely as hypothetical, until Wright's collection has been reworked on Richardsonian lines.

Time and contagion. Siverson and Duncan (1975) and Davis, Duncan and Siverson (1976, 1978) tried to link the random distribution of war onsets (found by Richardson) to the non-random, cyclic distribution of nation-months of war underway (found by Singer and Small) by hypothesizing that war is contagious, so that "one dyad fighting may increase the probability of other dyads entering the war." They therefore studied the distribution not of *war*-onsets but of *pair*-onsets in time. The latter turn out to be heavily clustered. A pattern of irregular and sporadic onsets alternates with an occasional string-of-firecrackers epidemic of pair-onsets. Since war-onsets are randomly distributed, one war does not generate other wars; this being the case, the epidemics of pair-onsets mean that once a war starts the chance of other parties being drawn in must be increased. War-infectiousness may involve ganging up (several actors simultaneously assaulting another) or free-for-alls (A sees a fight between B and C as an incitement to attack C); it seems not to proceed via imitation (a fight between B and C does not inspire A to attack D). Davis, Duncan and Siverson (1978) hypothesized that multilateral wars tend to spread through alliance structures. The actual pattern of contagion remains to be demonstrated.

If nation-months of war underway worldwide per year change cyclically, not only pair-onsets but also pair-terminations ought to be clustered: outbreaks of peace within ongoing complex wars must also be contagious *within those wars*, whether because settlements tend to be general or because one pair's making up tends to diminish the incentive for third parties to fight either. The contagion of peacemaking also deserves investigation.

Summary.   The Poisson distribution of war-onsets points to a specific type of onset process. A similar distribution of war-terminations may point nowhere. Alternative explanations for the distributions of durations and magnitudes of wars are possible; none quite satisfies. No overall trend in war frequency is certain; a slight decline in frequency may exist. Apparent trends toward shorter wars, higher magnitude wars, and larger total war casualties must be taken seriously despite some inconsistencies. The death toll of wars by magnitude argues for most preventive efforts to be aimed at prospective world wars. Several apparent periodicities in war require and may reward further scrutiny. Wars appear to spread, though not to arise, contagiously.

4

Common Government,
Prior Alliance,
and Prior Enmity

Common government.   One of the social relations between two members of
each pair of belligerents into which Richardson inquired was the presence or
absence of a government common to both at the time the fighting began. Of
496 pairs in the wars of magnitudes 4 through 7 and dated 1820-1945, 94, or
18.95 percent, were coded as having had a common government. Civil fighting was comparatively rare (SDQ, pp. 189, 192).

There was, however, a conspicuous tendency toward a greater proportion
of civil quarrels in the smaller magnitudes. Civil pairs were only 9.75 percent
of total pairs at magnitude 7, but 23.24 percent of total pairs at magnitude 4,
and 47.67 percent at magnitude 3. Richardson's first thought was that this
tendency, which he later reexamined in a geographic context, was probably
"connected with the area and population of political states" (SDQ, pp.
192-194).

By my count,[1] in all cases 1820-1952, magnitudes 3-7, there are 780
pairs of opposed belligerents. The symbol m (common government) is assigned to 237 (30.4%) of these pairs,[2] always in the background compart-

---

[1] See Appendix 6.

[2] This is in contrast to Beer's assertion (1974, p. 32) that Richardson "does not
significantly report domestic violence." In support of this contention, Beer cited Eckstein's assertion (1964, p. 3) that well over 1,200 "unequivocal examples" of internal
war were reported in *The New York Times* from 1946 to 1959. This is a rate of 85.7 per
year. On that basis Richardson should have indeed compiled a list of more than eleven
thousand wars, rather than his paltry 315. Eckstein, however, used no criterion of

ment rather than as an irritant. The distribution of m by magnitude is given in table 10. The percentages differ from those given by Richardson (his count was for a smaller population of pairs). The same general tendency appears, however.

The belligerent pairs fighting in high-magnitude wars tend more to be pairs with no prewar experience of common government than those fighting in low-magnitude wars. Furthermore, of the 237 pairs with prewar common government, 138 (58.2%) fought in wars at the third or smallest magnitude; while of 543 belligerent pairs with no prewar common government, 369 (68.0%) fought in wars of magnitude 4 or above. There is some reason to suspect common government of being, or being associated with, a pacifying influence.

The duration of prewar common government. Richardson was strongly interested in the prospects of world government (SDQ, p. 1; 1960*a*, pp. 19, 181–182). This led him to a concern to establish the effects of common government. "A most important question connected with civil war is whether common government tends to prevent fighting; for, if so, a world government might pacify the world" (SDQ, pp. 189–190).

The median length of time under common government for the ninety-four civil pairs at magnitudes 4–7, 1820–1945, was 23.5 years. "The suggestion is that such a time is too short for a new type of loyalty to become habitual." Taking World War I alone, the median length of time under common government was fifty-one years. "The suggestion is that a very large disturbance was required to loosen old-established loyalties" (SDQ, p. 190).

The number of observed pairs of civil belligerents appears to be related to the number of preceding years of common government: there is a rapid diminution of civil fighting with time, to which Richardson fits a geometrical

---

magnitude in compiling his figures. He counted among "internal wars" all incidents of "localized rioting, widely dispersed turmoil, organized and apparently unorganized terrorism, mutinies, and *coups d'etat.*" Eckstein's original tabulation (1962, pp. 141–147) classified "internal wars" by type. Therein he counted only thirty-five "civil wars" or "guerrilla wars" over the fourteen years 1946–1959 inclusive. This gives a rate of 2.5 such wars per year, comparable to Richardson's civil-pair rate of 237/133 or 1.8 civil fights per year.

The overwhelming majority of his so-called internal wars were subclassified by Eckstein as "rioting." The next largest subcategory was "small-scale terrorism" involving undisciplined and discontinuous intimidation and harassment with an occasional assassination or bombing. Riots and "harassment" seldom involve 317 or more deaths; consequently Richardson seldom listed them. He did not, however, simply disregard them: for the 126 years 1820 to 1945, Richardson estimated by formula that there were 5,630 deadly quarrels of magnitude 2 (32 to 316 dead) and 397,000 of magnitude 1 (4 to 31 dead), or about 44.7 per year and 8.6 per day, respectively (SDQ, pp. 152, 192–194). Since the majority of such events would be internal (SDQ, p. 297) Richardson did indeed "significantly report domestic violence" at rates at least comparable to those of Eckstein.

TABLE 10

MAGNITUDES 3–7, 1820-1952, 780 PAIRS, m VS. MAGNITUDE

| Magnitude | Did the belligerents share a common government before the war? | | Total |
	No	Yes	
7	116 (89.2%)	14 (10.8%)	130
6	35 (83.3%)	7 (16.7%)	42
5	68 (74.7%)	23 (25.3%)	91
4	150 (73.2%)	55 (26.8%)	205
3	174 (55.8%)	138 (44.2%)	312
All	543 (69.6%)	237 (30.4%)	780

Chi-square = 58.010 $Df = 4$ $P = .00000*$

Gamma =   −0.4463   (Row– percentages)

*Statistics calculated by the PREP program of the Center for Computer-based Behavioral Studies, UCLA. Low P is the criterion for rejection of the null hypothesis (expected frequencies proportional to the marginal totals).

progression with a "ratio of decrease" per decade of 0.778 (SDQ, pp. 190–191). If Richardson's empirical formula proved completely predictive of the behavior of a world system under a world state, and if in its first decade of establishment such a system suffered one hundred civil wars, it would generate seventy-eight civil wars in its second decade, sixty-one in its third, ten in its tenth, and so on. Richardson made no such claim, but the suggestion remains that propensity to fight may be an exponential function of time under common government, decreasing toward zero as time goes on, so that, once established, the older the government the fewer civil wars it will generate.

Domination and resistance. Whether or not common government in general pacifies, there are circumstances in which it seems liable to have an opposite effect; for example, two groups share a single government that serves as the instrument by which one dominates the other. Richardson used the symbol rho to code for the prewar attempt by one belligerent to dominate the other: "The tail-group habitually ordered the tip-group to obey" (SDQ, p. 23). By my count of 780 pairs, in cases of magnitudes 3-7, 1820-1952, rho appears in 94/780 (11.3%); in eighty-eight of these rho is set as an irritant (and only in 6 pairs as a factor in the background), in strong contrast to m, the symbol for common government, which is never set as an irritant.

In 81 of the 94 pairs, rho appears along with m; these are therefore wars of insurgency, "insurrection, revolt, rebellion or mutiny" in which the "common government" was actually in the hands of one group (SDQ, pp. 187, 189). In these wars it might be proper to consider the common government as an irritant, even though it is never coded as such by Richardson. It might be wise also to explore the 156/780 (20.0%) of all pairs coded m but not rho (civil war but no insurrection), to see whether rho should be added or m set in the irritant compartment. Such caution is rendered more desirable by Richardson's generally positive attitude toward common government (SDQ, pp. 190, 295-296, 307-313) and world government (SDQ, pp. 1, 180-183, 189-190).

Nevertheless, the 81 pairs coded m and rho form an intriguing subset: insurgencies. Of the insurgent pairs, 39/81 (48.1%) had code symbols set that indicated a marked prewar economic difference or rivalry between the belligerents. For all 780 pairs, the fraction coded as having such a difference or rivalry was 153/780 (19.6%). Of insurgent pairs, 30/81 (37.0%) had fought previously, as compared with 219/780 (28.1%) of all pairs. Of insurgent pairs, 26/81 (32.1%) carry a coding that indicates that some ideology, some system of religious or political ideas, helped to inspire and justify the fighting; 158/780 (20.3%) of all pairs carry such a coding. The hypothesis that domination pacifies, though less successfully than common government without domination, must be entertained.

In thirteen of the ninety-four pairs, rho appears without m. In these instances one side attempted to impose or to reimpose its rule on the other, which resisted that attempt. Does this mean in an alleged "age of imperial expansion" there were more revolts against extant domination than wars of imperial expansion? It is tempting to make such a guess and draw conclusion from it, but it would be prudent first to reconsider the whole list of cases so as to exclude the possibility that rho has simply been undercoded.

Examining cases at magnitudes 4-7, 1820-1945, and counting in them ninety-four pairs of opposed belligerents who shared a common government (m) just before the outbreak, Richardson found fifty-nine coded, and thirty-five not coded rho, indicating prewar domination of one by the other (SDQ, p. 189). The median age of the common government was twenty-one years for the first group, thirty-one years for the second. We might surmise that if common government acquires legitimacy with age, it does so more slowly where it is contaminated by domination. This surmise suggests a relatively shaky future for new states whose political structure is oligarchic or whose origins lie in conquest; likewise for regional blocs or a hypothetical world-state whose origins and structure are imperial rather than federal.

Prior alliance versus prior enmity. How many opposing pairs had fought previously, as allies or as enemies? Three differing counts are given in table 11. Those in the first two columns are derived from Richardson's data: the first column is based on Richardson's two estimates for wars at magnitudes 4-7, 1820-1929 (SDQ, pp. 195-196); the second is based on my count of 468 pairs, in wars at the same magnitudes, 1820-1952. The third column comes from Singer and Small's collection of 209 pairs, in ninety-three international wars generally of magnitudes 4 and above, 1816-1965. The discrepancies in the former-enemies row might be partly owing to Singer and Small's not having counted, and Richardson's having counted, enmities in wars that occurred before the collection was begun. Still, the discrepancies are large enough that, until they are satisfactorily accounted for, conclusions on the topics of enmity, and, less surely, of alliance, must remain rather more speculative than one would like.

TABLE 11

PERCENTAGES OF THOSE WHO FOUGHT WHO WERE
EX-ALLIES OR FORMER ENEMIES

	Richardson	*Wilkinson*	*Singer & Small*
Previously allied	26.0–29.0%	18.8%	21.1%
Former enemies	43.0–47.8%	34.4%	18.7%

Prior alliance. Richardson used the Greek letter lambda to indicate that a pair of actors, fighting each other in a particular war, had been allies in a previous war, and that no war between the two had intervened between the alliance and the particular war under consideration. The suffix to lambda indicates the number of years of unbroken peace between the previous alliance and the hostilities under consideration (SDQ, pp. 195-196).

For wars of magnitudes 4-7, 1820-1929, Richardson collected the suffixes to lambda from wars of all magnitudes and reclassified them by decades. Thus there were 20.5 instances in which former allies fought one another after a peaceful interval of zero to ten years, another 20.5 fights after a peaceful interval of ten to twenty years, five after twenty to thirty years of peace, four after thirty to forty years, and four after forty years (SDQ, p. 196). If the net effect of alliance were pacificatory, one would presumably expect a different pattern: of all previous alliances that ended in war, presumably the most recent alliances, still fresh in memory, should have shown the fewest instances of war, and the oldest alliances the most. The actual data would be more compatible with the interpretation that an alliance was an *irritant* whose effects wore off over a long period of time. This seems counterintuitive, and suggests that comparative case study of the transition from alliance to enmity would be of value. Comparison would be suitable not only within the set of allies becoming enemies but between that set and a set of allies who did *not* become enemies.

Singer and Small (1972, p. 343) have listed forty-one pairs of nations twice allied and never opponents in international wars 1816–1965, and eight pairs with three or more war experiences as allies and none as opponents:

France–England	6
Greece–Yugoslavia/Serbia	4
Belgium–England	3
Belgium–France	3
England–Greece	3
England–Holland	3
England–USA	3
France–USA	3

The preponderance of relatively constitutional, liberal, democratic regimes (and pairs of such regimes) on this list is noteworthy.

The comparison might be even more useful if it included a third set of pairs: enemies never allies. Singer and Small (1972, p. 344) list eighteen pairs of nations twice enemies and never allied in their cases, and four pairs with three of more enmities and no alliances:

Russia–Turkey	5
Austria–Hungary–Italy/Sardinia	4
China–Japan	4
France–Germany/Prussia	3

Inspecting World War I and World War II, Richardson found that "after 25 years there still remained a general tendency for allies and enemies to group themselves together as before, although with many exceptions." Richardson interpreted this as suggesting that comradeship in war probably has a pacifying influence (SDQ, p. 197). Still, almost a third of the ally-pairs in the first war were enemy-pairs in the second. Perhaps alliances tend to occur between actors who are also likely to be opponents, for example neighbors or great powers, and the common element uniting alliance and enmity is contact—contiguity of frontiers or of influence.

Starr (1975) examined the hypothesis that war alliances tend to recur, that is, that wartime allies are more likely to become allies again, and less likely to become enemies, than pairs of actors never linked by wartime alliance or than chance would lead us to expect. From thirty-six war coalitions 1821–1967 containing 172 partners, he derived 625 ally-pairs, examined their next mutual war experience (through 1972), compared the behavior of former allies with that of 342 belligerent-pairs and 3,040 nonparticipant pairs, and found that this hypothesis was confirmed. Furthermore, those ex-allies that did fight one another later, Starr found, were more likely to be major powers; contiguous; former enemies as well as ex-allies; and unequal sharers in territory won by their alliance. The first three of these traits are notable irritants, and the fourth might well be one. The idea that, *ceteris paribus*, alliance is more a pacifier than an irritant as between the allies, therefore remains tenable.

Recurrence of war. Richardson inserted the letter M in the war-list whenever a pair of belligerents had fought each other previously; the number of years of peace between the fights was set as a suffix to M. By my count, for 780 pairs who fought 1820–1952 at magnitudes 3 through 7, 219 (28.1%) were marked by M as having fought before. The percentage is large enough to warrant further examination of the irritant effects of past fighting. Richardson examined eighty-nine recurrences in cases from 1820–1929 at magnitudes 4–7.

The number of recurrences (Richardson termed them "retaliations" whether or not the first war was a *motive* for the second) was greatest for the shortest intervals and generally decreased thereafter as the interval of peace grew: of eighty-nine second-round encounters, thirty-two came in the first ten years after the first round; half of the retaliations began after fifteen or fewer years of peace; and the frequency of retaliations decreased on the average in a geometrical progression with a ratio of 0.65 for each decade of peace. "This decreasing frequency of retaliations as the interval of peace increased is what we should expect if a slow process of forgetting and forgiving went on" (SDQ, pp. 197–202).

The ratio of decrease per decade of the frequency of retaliations per decade (0.65) resembles the ratio of decrease per decade of the frequency of civil wars (0.78), the functions in question both being geometric progressions. Half the retaliations began after fifteen years or less of peace; half the civil wars after 23.5 years or less of common government. The two median times, 15 and 23.5 years, are of the same order of size. These figures may indicate a common underlying process of forgetting: the forgetting of old enmities; the forgetting of former separation and independence (SDQ, pp. 200, 202).

The actual decrease of retaliations during the first 30 years "was followed by a slight rise and persistence during the second 30 years, and then by a sudden fall . . . . [A] rather similar phenomenon, namely an increase from the third to the fourth decade, occurs in the frequency of . . . . civil wars when they are classified according to the duration of the preceding common government . . . ." These deviations might be explained as the results of the rise to influence of a new generation, reared on tales of the earlier war or of lost independence; or they might be random (SDQ, pp. 200-202).

Summary.   There is some reason to believe, cautiously, that common government, whatever its origin, may be a pacifier and that its pacifying effects increase with time. But its associates have still to be examined. Having previously fought seems to be an irritant whose effects diminish with time. The net effect of having been allies is obscure; if there is any, it is apparently mildly pacific.

5
Contiguity and War

Contiguous pairs. Of 178 wars containing only one belligerent pair, magnitudes 3–7, end dates 1820–1945, in only 12 instances (6.7%) were the belligerents noncontiguous by Richardson's count (SDQ, p. 302). On the other hand, of all 710 pairs he counted in all the wars in that time span, 173 (24.4%) are noncontiguous; 321 (45.2%) are foreign contiguous; while 216 (30.4%) are civil pairs (SDQ, p. 297). The difference between 6.7 percent and 24.4 percent may indicate that the causes of quarrels between foreign noncontiguous groups were ordinarily too weak to precipitate warfare without there being some third party, the neighbor of one, whose opportunism or inclination or actual belligerency made him a convenient ally for the other. We might read this as meaning that local quarrels precipitate long-distance fights, or vice versa. In any event, most fighting links neighbors, even though every nation and subnational group plainly possesses more nonneighbors than it has neighbor groups. This fact directs our attention to the problem of the relationship among contiguity, other factors, and fighting.

Frontiers and wars. Richardson found a correlation between the number of frontiers a state has and its number of external wars (SDQ, pp. 176–181). He examined states with more than 200,000 population, independent for at least 109 of the 126 years from 1820 to 1945. He counted all of a state's sea frontiers as one frontier and all its land frontiers with any other single state (or empire) as one frontier, and took for each state a time-mean of the number of its frontiers. He counted one external war for each state when in any case of magnitude 4–7 ended 1820–1945 it took part in at least one belligerent pair the other member of which had its headquarters outside the first state's frontiers. From these counts, Richardson derived for each of thirty-three states a number of frontiers (range 1.6–22.5, mean 6.29)[1] and a number of external wars fought (range 0–26, mean 4.85). Taking external wars as the dependent variable y and frontiers as the independent variable x, Richardson derived a linear regression equation which (as he did not state it) I have recomputed as $y = 1.06\,x - 1.85$, or approximately one war per frontier in a 126-year period, with correlation coefficient $r = 0.77$ and $r^2 = 0.59$. The data are not, however, normally distributed but skewed, and the cases are too few to permit much confidence in the results. Still we may hypothesize that "the possession of many frontiers lets us in for the difficulty of living with many neighbors" (SDQ, p. 179).

Rudolph Rummel's DON project found cross-sectional evidence of a much weaker correlation than that located by Richardson, between the number of borders of a nation and the number of wars it fought ($r = 0.20$), and more generally between number of borders and "foreign conflict behavior," defined by a factor analysis of 326 variables for eighty-two nations in 1955–57 (1972, pp. 371–372). Terrell (1977, p. 100), examining seventy-five countries' behavior between 1955 and 1960, likewise found some correlation ($r = 0.33$, $P < 0.01$) between the number of countries contiguous to any country and that country's "war behavior," a composite measure based upon the country's scores on seven variables: presence or absence of military action; number of wars; number of people killed in all forms of foreign conflict behavior; number of mobilizations; number of troop movements; number of accusations; number of threats. Starr and Most (1976, p. 607), using three war-data sets for the years 1946–1965, found correlations ranging from 0.43 to 0.79 (depending on the period, data set, and set of nations analyzed) between the total borders of a nation and its number of new war participations in the period.[2]

[1] Starr and Most (1976) defined and counted six types of borders: contiguous land frontiers; water borders; proximity-zone "almost" borders; and colonial land, water, and proximity-zone borders. Between 1946 and 1965, the total number of borders grew from 406 to 778 (91.6%), almost proportionally to the growth in membership in the international system (from 66 to 125, up 89.4%); total borders per nation showed little change (6.15 to 6.22). Richardson's mean number of frontiers to a political state, 6.29 for thirty-three states, 1815–1929, "almost as if their countries had been hexagons arranged in a honeycomb pattern" (SDQ, pp. 176–179), thus seems stable during a period of marked changes in sovereign jurisdiction.

[2] Starr and Most (1976, p. 609) nonetheless alleged "an almost complete failure to replicate Richardson's . . . findings on data from the post-World War II era" because they chose to "replicate" by correlating noncolonial land and water borders (only) with new war participations. They considered this to constitute "replication" because, they averred, Richardson's border count was not analogous to their "total borders" but rather to their "noncolony land borders" plus their "noncolony water borders." But this cannot be, for Richardson gave a time-mean (1815–1929) of 22.5 borders to the British

Some association between frontiers and wars seems probable; a statement of the association remains to be found. Even if a stable correlation could be found, and even if it reflected a causal relationship, the practical significance of the latter would be obscure, since to decrease the frontiers of the many-frontier states would probably increase the frontiers of others and thereby retain the mean (approximately six) (SDQ, pp. 181-183). If frontiers (which imply geographic contiguity of independent states) are truly irritants as such, however, presumably the total number of frontiers in the world could be reduced by consolidating formerly independent states. The mean of six frontiers per state would be substantially reduced by subcontinental and continental consolidations. And a world state would eliminate frontiers (and, by definition "external wars"). However, frontiers are not yet shown to be irritants, nor credibly shown to be associated with irritants, merely suspect. Proximity may be the culprit; if so, to remove frontiers is pointless. Garnham (1976a) examined thirty interstate, one-pair wars (one state versus one other state) counted by Singer and Small (1972, pp. 60-69) for the period 1816-1965. For each war, Garnham compared the geographic proximity of the combatants (the distance between their national capitals) to the geographic proximities in that year of each pair of states, members of the international system, that did *not* fight one another. Few such pairs were as proximate or more proximate than the fighting pairs; the hypothesis that war is more probable between relatively proximate pairs of nation-states and less probable between relatively distant pairs is confirmed.

War-models with neighbors more likely to fight. In one of his several attempts at theoretical penetration of the fact that wars with many pairs of opposed belligerents are extremely rare, Richardson developed a formal explanation (Theory X) which assumes that prewar disputes are localized rather than general, interesting only eight nations rather than sixty (the average number of nations in the world during his interval). He found Theory X tolerably in agreement with the historical facts (SDQ, pp. 247, 270-273). But geography is not actually introduced into the mathematical expressions of Theory X: the eight concerned nations need not be contiguous or geographically compact; if they were scattered over the surface of the globe it would in no way affect Theory X. Thus no conclusions concerning the effects of contiguity can be drawn from Theory X.

However, Richardson's next attack on the same topic did "attend to the fact that some states had more numerous contacts than others, and therefore more opportunities either for friendship or for quarrelling" (SDQ, p. 273). Those great powers (Britain, France, Russia, the United States, Italy, Japan,

---

Empire, 15 to France, 8.8 to Holland and 8.5 to Portugal; none of these totals could have been attained without counting many "colony" borders. The "replication" failed because it was no replication at all.

Germany, Austria-Hungary) which for all or part of the period 1820–1929 were also great naval powers are treated as long-range many-contact powers "contiguous" to one another and to all local coastal states. Richardson assumed in this model that any fighting pair must be in contact, but that this contact may be overland or oversea: if oversea, short or long range; if overland, direct (across a frontier) or indirect (over the territory of an intervening state). Richardson's Theory XII, the formal explanation of the rarity of complex wars which employs these distinctions, includes a calculation of the theoretical fraction of any long period of time during which: (1) any given world power is at war with any other given world power; (2) any given world power is at war with any given local belligerent with which it is in touch oversea; and (3) any given local belligerent is at war with any overland local neighbor. These theoretical fractions reappear as three probabilities: x, the probability of war between any two long-range powers, calculated by Richardson to be on the order of 0.001; y, the probability of war between a long-range and a short-range power, on the order of 0.01, or ten times as great as x; and z, the probability of war between neighboring powers, varying conspicuously with circumstances, but on the average "decidedly greater than y, and all the more so than x. That is to say *propinquity tended to war*"[3] (Richardson 1950a, p. 254). "It is plain that . . . the worldwide sea-powers have made much *less* pugnacious use of their opportunities for contact than have the local powers" (SDQ, p. 285; emphasis mine). Richardson suggested (SDQ, pp. 280–281) that this difference may be explained either by nations having a limited capacity for fighting (so that the world powers could not take full advantage of their many opportunities) or by overland contact being real, permanent, and involuntary, but oversea contact only potential, temporary, and voluntary (on the part of the world power). The latter interpretation, at least, would seem to implicate contiguity per se: Not only is it necessary to be in touch to fight, but the more firmly in touch two actors are the larger the fraction of any long period of time in which they may be expected to be at war.

Contiguity and magnitude of war. Richardson recorded in Chapter XI of SDQ a preliminary attempt to relate geographic contiguity to common government and to fighting. He contended that the ratio of civil to external fightings could shed further light upon the influence of common government. We have noted that the ratio of civil to total pairs grows rapidly as magnitude of fighting is reduced. "We may reasonably suppose that the ratio of civil to external fightings varies with magnitude in dependence on three causes": geographical opportunities for contact, the size of the populations fighting, and the influence of common government or its associates. To see how much weight the third cause carries, he proposed to examine the degree to which

---

[3] Theory XII and its predecessors are discussed at greater length in Chap. 6 below.

the first two causes satisfactorily explain the variation of the civil-external ratio with magnitude, by formalization, deduction, comparison with history, and an argument using inequalities.

Each magnitude-center and boundary from 2.5 to 7.5 is associated by definition with a certain number of quarrel-dead, from 316 to 31,622,777 (see table 1). Assume that wars have two "sides," that they end with losses on both sides equal, and that they end when the smaller side loses 2 percent of its population. From the magnitude of a hypothetical war and this initial assumption, we can then calculate the population of the hypothetical "smaller side" in that war, e.g., 7,906 for a magnitude of 2.5; 790,569,425 for a magnitude of 7.5.

Assume next that belligerent sides occupy moderately compact geographical areas—"cells." A world population of about 1.5 billion (at the mid-date of Richardson's interval) can be divided into cells each of whose inhabitants are to be regarded as a possibly belligerent group. In general the number of cells whose population is large enough to sustain losses of a given magnitude varies as an inverse exponential function of the magnitude. Thus in Richardson's formalized "world" there are only two cells of the population (790,569,425) required to fight a 7.5 magnitude war, but 189,736 cells with the population (7,906) needed to fight a 2.5 magnitude war. By another formalization, Richardson calculated the number of frontiers, and hence of geographical opportunities for contiguous fighting, in his formalized world: these are given by a direct linear function of the number of cells.

In this formalized world, then, there are at minimum (by Richardson's calculations) 344 times as many geographical-demographic opportunities for fights producing ten thousand casualties as there are for fights producing ten million. But in history Richardson found only thirty-five times as many quarrels with ten thousand as with ten million casualties.

> The contrast between theory and fact is remarkable. It would be explained if some agency, not regarded in the theory, did in fact tend to provoke fatal quarrels among the larger magnitudes, or to prevent those among the smaller magnitudes, or did both. National governments have, so far, not been regarded in the theory. In the meantime *it seems likely that the contrast between the present theory and history can be explained by supposing either that nationalism provokes wars between nations, or that it prevents wars within nations, or that it does both.* (SDQ, pp. 288–294)

Contiguity, the local pacifier, and common government. The comparison, in Chapter XII of SDQ, of an even more complex formal model than that of Chapter XI with a collection of data on observed fighting led Richardson to the further conclusion that "the fraction of the total time during which any particular pair of contiguous cells fought one another was remarkably less

as the cells were drawn smaller. This proves the existence of a local pacifier."
That is, some strong pacifying influence at work on contiguous human groups
has prevented the occurrence of as much small local fighting as would have
been expected from the opportunities existing for such fighting (SDQ, pp.
295–306).

In accord with yet another formalization, this time of geographical opportunities for civil versus foreign fighting, Richardson contended that at the
fourth magnitude it is likely, and at the third magnitude virtually certain, that
some pacifying influence repressed civil fighting relative to foreign fighting
(SDQ, pp. 307–313). "The existence of a pacifier is here proved." It is either
the habit of obedience to a common government, or some social feature with
a strong positive correlation with common government, for example, common language, common religion, intermarriage, or tendency to direct one's
hatred on to foreigners (SDQ, pp. 295–296).

This reasoning could lead to world-state or world-community policy proposals, depending upon one's judgment as to the identity of the pacifier:
Richardson drew no policy conclusions.

There might seem to be some inherent inconsistency between the hypothesis that contiguity between states along frontiers irritates, while contiguity
within a state under a common government pacifies: one might resolve the
apparent paradox either by arguing that the common government functions
to reduce the irritations that physical contiguity creates, or that the state
displaces internal hostilities onto external objects. Or the apparent paradox
might be dissipated by phrasing it: Fighting appears to rise with contiguous
opportunities but not in proportion to them; common government may
account for the disproportion.

Criticisms.   Horvath and Foster (1963) generated Richardson's observed
distribution of wars by complexity, using a model that takes no account of
propinquity. (That model is however suspect on other grounds; see chap. 6
below.)

Rapoport contended (1957, p. 274) that the cell-method used in Chapters
XI and XII of SDQ was inappropriate for deriving estimates of expected civil
fighting, since the opposed belligerents in civil wars are usually not regional
actors. My own study (1975) of civil warfare leaves me, however, in accord
with Richardson's assumption that they usually are.

Wesley (1962) showed that the distribution of wars recorded by Richardson 1820–1945, magnitudes 3–7, which Richardson was unable to generate
by a model based on geographic opportunity defined in terms of numbers of
frontiers, could be generated if the geographical opportunity for fighting were
instead defined as the total *length* of the frontiers between cells of equal
population. The redefinition seems intuitively less satisfying than the original,
especially since other findings by Richardson show national war participation
to be related to the number of national frontiers (SDQ, pp. 176–183). Still it

now becomes desirable to compare this observation to the actual relationship of the frequency of war between contiguous countries to the length of their common frontier (or, as Wesley suggests, the number of roads across it). If Wesley's model proves superior, Richardson's argument that there exists a local pacifier is jeopardized, while his contention that "propinquity tended to war" is reinforced.

Summary. War tends to link neighbors; a pair of groups is more likely to fight if they are contiguous than if they are not. Why, to what degree, and with what exceptions these statements are true remain for researchers to establish. Proximity and contact may be irritants, common government may reduce or countervail their irritation.

6
Complexity of Wars

The number of actors on each side of a war. One of Richardson's most ingenious investigations was prompted by his observation of a pattern that emerged when his list of wars was classified according to the number of belligerents on each side of each war: one versus one (forty-two cases out of a total of ninety-one, magnitudes 4–7, 1820–1939); two versus one (twenty-four cases); three versus one (five cases); four versus one (five cases); two versus two (three cases); three versus two (two cases); five versus one (two cases); and so on (seven other categories with one or, in one instance, two cases) (SDQ, pp. 294).

Richardson found a similar pattern in a collection of 200 noncivil wars from Quincy Wright's list 1480–1941: 117 were one versus one; 28 were two versus one; 12 were three versus one, and the same number were four versus one; 6 were three versus two; 4 were two versus two; 3 were five versus one; 2 were six versus one; and there was one of each of sixteen other types (SDQ, p. 250).

In both collections *the least complex war* (one versus one) *is the most common type,* accounting for 46.15 percent of Richardson's cases and 58.5 percent of Wright's.

In Richardson's collection there are forty-two wars with two participants, twenty-four with three, eight with four, seven with five, three with six, three with seven, and four with more than seven. In Wright's the corresponding figures are 117, 28, 16, 18, 4, 4, 13. In general, *wars with more participants are less frequent than wars with fewer.*

Two-sided wars with two participants are necessarily one on one, and those with three participants two on one. Those with four could be two on two or three on one; those with five could be three on two or four on one; those with six three on three, four on two or five on one; those with seven four on three, five on two, or six on one; and so on. Is each of these arrangements equally likely or is there a tendency to equalize the number of participants on each side, or conversely to gang up? If each arrangement were equally likely, one-half of the wars with four or five participants would be three on one or four on one, respectively; one-third of the wars with six or seven participants would also be gang-ups of five on one or six on one, respectively. The actual fractions of wars in each category which are many against one are given in table 12.

TABLE 12
WHAT FRACTION OF WARS WITH N + 1 PARTICIPANTS
ARE N AGAINST ONE?

| | *No. of participants* | | | |
	4	5	6	7
Richardson's data	5/8	5/7	2/3	1/3
Wright's data	3/4	2/3	3/4	1/2

In seven of eight data sets, the participants arranged themselves many against one more frequently than would be expected if there were no tendency to do so.

If we label the number of actors on one side r and the number on the other side s, we may take their sum $(r + s)$ as the number of participants in the war and their product rs as the number of pairs of opposed belligerents in the war. (These are approximate rather than exact since some actors fought on both sides and since the rule that every actor on one side fights every actor on the other does not fit every case.)

We can now observe that where, say, $r + s = 4$, its more common subtype (3 against 1) involves a lower rs (fewer belligerent pairs: $3 \times 1 = 3$) than the less common subtype (2 against 2, with an rs of $2 \times 2 = 4$). The same is true where $r + s = 5, 6,$ or 7: The many against one subtypes $(4 - 1; 5 - 1; 6 - 1)$ for each of these types involve, respectively 4, 5, and 6 belligerent pairs, while the less common subtypes $(3 - 2; 4 - 2, 3 - 3; 5 - 2, 4 - 3)$ involve, respectively, 6, 8 or 9, and 10 or 12 belligerent pairs. More generally, as shown in table 13, *wars with more belligerent pairs are less frequent than wars with fewer.*

Such patterns call for inquiry and explanation. After some effort, Richard- found a formula that credibly described all these facts: one-on-one wars most common; fewer many-participant wars; fewer many-pair wars. The proportion

TABLE 13
MANY-PAIR WARS ARE LESS FREQUENT

	Number of belligerent pairs, rs				
	1	*2*	*3-6*	*7 or more*	*Total*
Richardson's data (rounded percentages)	46%	26	20	8	100
Wright's data (rounded percentages)	59%	14	20	8	101

of all observed wars in which *r* belligerents fight *s* belligerents is tolerably close to

$$\frac{5}{9}(rs)^{-2.5}$$

which is a fraction of a reciprocal of a power of *rs*. More explicitly: in this empirical formula as in fact, wars became rapidly rarer as the number, *rs*, of pairs of opposed belligerents slowly increased (SDQ, pp. 247, 252–255).

But this formula is merely descriptive and raises at once the question: *Why* does this relationship exist? To Richardson this meant: Could a hypothetical explanation be found which would provide a quantitative agreement with the historical facts? Explanations that relied on a tendency to join the winning side, or a tendency to mob the aggressor, might explain why three-on-one wars were commoner than two-on-two, or four-on-one than three-on-two, but failed to show why one-on-one wars were commonest of all (SDQ, pp. 262–264). Some theory that would explain the frequency of simple wars and the infrequency of complex wars was needed.

It struck Richardson that there already existed a model whose characteristic property was that complicated events are rarer than simple events. This model was that of chaos; and it had previously been applied in explaining the observed phenomenon that in a gas the collision of two molecules was much more frequent than that of three. The interpretive idea of a chaos relates the number of complicated events to the number of simple events by assuming that the more complicated ones are made up of simpler ones, and that the latter are statistically independent. Two or more events are statistically independent if the occurrence of any one of the events has no effect on the occurrence or nonoccurrence of the other. The probability that *both* of two independent events will happen is the product of their separate probabilities of occurrence. Thus in a chaos theory the probability of two simple events happening together (and thus forming a complex event) is the *product* of their separate probabilities of happening at all. Since probabilities range between zero and one, the product of two probabilities is never larger and is usually smaller than either of its factors. A chaos model will therefore more or less automatically produce fewer complex events than simple events. Richardson consequently began to search for a chaos model that might be applicable to wars (SDQ, pp. 258-260).

Richardson began his serious search for a chaos model to explain the observed war-pattern with what he called Theory VI: "The behavior of any pair of states is statistically independent of the behavior of every other pair of states." It is assumed that whether any one pair of states is at war is entirely unrelated to whether any other pair of states is at war. This assumption would automatically explain why complicated wars are fewer than simple wars, since the only thing that could link one pair of enemies A versus B with another pair A versus C in a simultaneous collision would be the random chance of both pairs being at war at the same time, which would be the product of the probability of AB being at war at any time, with the probability of AC being at war at any time, and as a product normally smaller than either of its elements. It also explains why three-on-one wars are more frequent than two-on-two: the probability of three overlapping pairs simultaneously fighting is the product of their three separate probabilities, which will be larger than the probability of four such pairs (2 x 2) fighting simultaneously, simply because the latter is the product of four rather than three separate probabilities (SDQ, pp. 265-266).

Theory VI, however, is at odds with historical evidence, especially concerning alliances, which links war in one pair with consequent war in another. Such alliances did not generally persist for intervals longer than a century; the stipulation that the theory will be applied only to such lengths of time is therefore added to Theory VI. Richardson next tried out a further specification (called Theory VIII), which hypothesizes that there are about sixty political actors in the world, and that over a long historical time interval the total *duration* of all wars of all types, and of each type, and the ratios of the duration of one type to that of another will be explained by assuming that the probability of war between any two actors was the same at all times, the same for all pairs of actors, independent of any other pairs being at war or not. Richardson devised an appropriate formula and used historical frequencies to calculate what that numerical probability must be. He found that the various historical data cannot be explained by the same numerical probability: Theory VIII crashes (SDQ, pp. 266-269).

Richardson sought an explanation for this failure and a suggestion for a new direction. He found both in the fact that most actual wars have been localized. This suggested to him a model in which each war is the result of a dispute which interests only a few actors, so that only they are likely to join in. The final form (Theory X) of this revised theory hypothesizes that disputes occur at random over the globe; each interests eight and only eight actors; the probability that any pair taken from those eight will be at war is 0.35, the same for every pair, the same for every dispute, and the same in every year. Comparing theory and fact, Richardson found "a tolerable agreement" between them. "With the exception of a small minority of very complicated wars, Theory X succeeds in explaining, not particular wars nor the behavior of named states, but the average behavior of the world over an interval of 120 years or more" (SDQ, pp. 247, 270–273).

Richardson next attempted to contrive a theory that would explain those rare wars in which $r + s$ was greater than 8. Some actors were world powers who had large navies and the opportunity to be in touch with many more than seven nations; others were local powers, coastal or landlocked, with more limited opportunities for quarreling. Theory XI, "chaos restricted by a formalized geography," seeks to take account of this fact by modeling the behavior of world powers and of local powers separately, and by postulating that the probability of wars in a pair will be zero if the members of the pair are not in geographic contact, and will be different depending on whether the members of the pair are (1) both world powers, (2) a world power and a local power, or (3) both local powers. Introducing pairs of actors who could not be at war with one another (unless put in touch by world-power allies or intervening local belligerents) does the same job that had to be done by Theory X—that of reducing the number of potentially belligerent pairs to take account of the actual propensity of actors to fight their neighbors—though it does that job in a different way. And by admitting the possibilities of many-contact world powers, and of the conduction of war by land through the territories of belligerents, Theory XI allows the worldwide wars which history has demonstrated but Theory X could not accommodate. Unfortunately Theory XI fails to fit the data; but its failure is so narrow and so orderly that the failure itself suggests the next (and final) improvement. The probability of war between neighbors seems to vary directly with the complexity of the war; this would be explained if nearby fighting were infectious.

The ultimate Theory XII is one of chaos, contact, and contagion: chaos restricted by geographic opportunities to fight and by the local infectiousness of fighting once begun. Fighting between any pair of actors is, with specified restrictions, statistically independent of the behavior of every other pair of states when the facts are collected from an interval of at least a century. The probability of war between any two actors (the fraction of time during which they are at war) is the same between any two world powers (and on the order of 0.001); the same between any world power and any local power with which it was in contact via a seacoast or a local belligerent (on the order of 0.01); the same as between any two local powers, increasing with the number of pairs of opposed belligerents (as low as 0.008 for one pair, as high as 0.119 for four-pair wars); and the same as between any two actors not in contact (zero). In a general way this theory explains the rare occurrence of very complicated wars, and it satisfactorily describes wars from 1-1 to 2-2 and 3-1 complexities (SDQ, pp. 278-286).

Interpretations. In order to fit the data, this model had to be so constructed that "the worldwide sea-powers . . . made much less pugnacious use of their opportunities for contact than . . . the local powers" (SDQ, p. 285); and so that two states not in contact with each other by a frontier, by sea power, or by alliance of one to an intermediary belligerent could not be at war (SDQ, pp. 276-277). The need to give special recognition to contiguity and contact as necessary conditions and perhaps actual irritants is striking. It led Richardson to disquieting suggestions concerning a possible future effect of aviation: if the limiting effect of geography is removed and the infectiousness of fighting retained, "all-in wars" become possible, the expectation of simple wars rises, and the expectation of complex wars rises even more (SDQ, pp. 248, 264, 277, 286-287). Today aviation is less interesting as a potential nullifier of distance than is missile technology. Should the concern now expressed for instance over the proliferation of "nuclear weapons," perhaps be directed more particularly at proliferation of long-distance delivery systems that bring many potential enemies within the effective range of the possessor?

The fact that the pattern that corresponds best to the observed frequency of complex wars is that of a chaos, "restricted by geography and further modified by the infectiousness of fighting" (SDQ, p. 248), does not of course demonstrate that the real-world probability of fighting between actors in geographic contact is particularly high (as compared with the probability of fighting between states not in touch). But that explanation does mesh with hypotheses about the effect of contiguity derived from other features of the Richardson data than the complexity of wars (see above, chap. 5).

The fit of the explanation likewise does not demonstrate that the probability of adjacent groups' fighting is uniform over all pairs of groups when taken over a time period of about a century, nor that it rises strikingly during periods when there is warfare in the vicinity of a given pair. The second of these elements of Theory XII does seem consistent with common sense; the first does not, but deserves to be compared with data patterns. Perhaps the invariance over time of a mean probability of neighbor-fights, representing a range of empirical probabilities normally or otherwise regularly distributed when calculated against the duration of war within each neighbor-pair ever at war during the Richardson interval, is a hypothesis consistent with Theory XII and also with common sense. One could then seek special explanations of unusual war-proneness and unusual placidity in such relationships without sacrificing the general model. After all, the chaos theories of Richardson, including the surviving Theory XII so far as it remains a chaos theory, purport to examine "the average behavior of [actors] in general during centuries," not "the peculiarities of named [actors] at particular times" (SDQ, pp. 248, 262). They therefore supplement rather than contradict those other Richardsonian theories that derive from the participation of named actors, the abstract qualities of types of actors, and the abstract relations of pairs of actors.

It is at times assumed that there is a built-in tendency for local wars to escalate by other parties (especially world powers) being drawn in, so that peace is truly indivisible, and every war everywhere is implicitly a threat to the peace of the whole world. Richardson's investigation into the complexity of wars tends to support opposite assumptions: peace is divisible; most wars do not become wider; widening of a war is more likely to involve a neighboring actor than a distant world power. There is an apparent contradiction between the hypotheses that fighting is localized and that it is infectious; but the two can be reconciled mathematically (and are) by localizing the infectiousness—by assigning localized fighting a higher probability, the more local fighting is already present.

One is naturally curious as to whether there are any implications for peace strategy in Theory XII. The geographic restriction on chaos suggests that, if the frequency or duration of warfare concerns us, it is the relationships of neighbors that most need third-party pacification or appeasement. The chaos postulate itself suggests that the "expectation" of warfare (the total theoretical duration divided by the time-interval in question) is a function of the number of autonomous groups with war-making capacity at a given time and implies political unification, rather than "national liberation" or "independence," as an appropriate policy objective. (Theory XII does not imply that such an objective is feasible, nor that it is desirable on any other grounds.)

The infectiousness hypothesis suggests that our worries about the contagion of existing conflict should be directed at neighbors rather than at superpowers—but only if it is the *frequency* of such contagion that we seek to limit. The *magnitude* of the war is liable to be particularly affected by the participation of certain named nations.[1] Still, since the number of pairs fighting in a war is related to the magnitude of the war,[2] Richardson's examination of the genesis of complex wars is by inference an examination of the genesis of high-magnitude wars as well. To the degree that such wars are partly attributable to the "infectiousness of fighting" some direction for war-control policy is indicated. The actual incidence of "infectiousness" therefore merits examination.

Actual contagion in the Richardson data.   I count 57/315 cases (18.1%) in which more than one pair of belligerents were opposed; and in which at

[1] See chap. 7 below.

[2] An average of 65 pairs fought in each case at magnitude 7; 6 pairs at magnitude 6; 3.5 pairs at 5; 2.9 pairs at 4; and 1.5 pairs at 3. Cf. Denton's size of war dimension (1966) and Rummel's intensity of war dimension (1967).

least one belligerent pair started its fighting on a later date than at least one other pair; and in which, in my judgment, the later fighting occurred at least in part because the earlier fighting was going on.

This count, strictly preliminary in that it involves no systematic coding but only a scan of Richardson's case list, was made for several reasons. (1) Richardson dealt at a theoretical level with the "infectiousness" of war, theses concerning which are essential to the final version of his chaos theory. But he made no empirical examination of the phenomenon of infectiousness. (2) Three symbols in Richardson's coding scheme touch on the phenomenon of "infectiousness" or contagion, but unsatisfactorily. The symbols are: P (the two groups fought because of the action of one on a third group); eta (the tail-group sympathized with those under the tip-group's control); and gamma (a third party desired that the two should fight). When war spreads, P or eta or gamma will usually appear, but not always; for example, none of the three symbols will do for coding the predatory attack of a third party upon a war-weakened state or its former clients. And neither P nor eta nor gamma always indicates contagion, since the coded relationship that incites the fight in question need not itself have been a deadly quarrel.

The phenomenon of contagion appears on first inspection to have been a frequent one, and a significant one as well: 17 of the 35 cases at magnitudes 5, 6, and 7 involved contagion (by my preliminary count), but only 11 of the 209 cases at magnitude 3. A causal relationship, probably bidirectional, may well be suspected.

Inspection of the fifty-seven cases thought to involve contagion leads one to conclude that the types of contagion are exceedingly diverse. When two groups fight:

1. A third may take the side of its friend, ally, client, or patron;
2. One may go on to attack its foe's supporters;
3. A third may be inspired to attack a fourth who is allied or akin to one of the fighters to whose opponent the third is allied or friendly;
4. A third may take advantage of the preoccupation of the belligerents to loot, dispossess, or conquer one or both, or their now helpless protégés;
5. One may inspire, persuade, pay, or compel a neutral to join in;
6. A third may see a chance, while its dominator is preoccupied, to rebel;
7. A third may be exasperated by war taxes and levies laid upon it by one belligerent, and rebel;
8. A third may join the stronger or nearer or the likely victor, to insure profit or safety;

9.   A third may be located between the belligerents, be invaded by one or both quite incidentally, but resist;

10. A third may use force against one or both to restrain, limit, or end the war;

11. A third, fearing the increment of power that a victor might receive, may attack to prevent the victory—or the increment;

12. A third, fearing that a fourth will intervene for any of these reasons, may intervene to forestall it.

The diversity of these causes and motives is rather like the diversity of grounds for war itself in the traditional literature. To order this diversity by counting various types of contagion and relating them to other characteristics of war would therefore be useful. A review of Richardson's coding scheme and case list to improve our information on the phenomenon of contagion evidently belongs on the research agenda.

General, local, and alliance contagion.   Siverson and Duncan (1975) studied the number of pairs of nations going to war in each year 1816–1965; Davis, Duncan, and Siverson (1976, 1978) examined the time elapsed between the onsets of such pair-belligerencies; both studies confirmed the existence of contagion, such that one pair-belligerency increased the probability of another within the same war. Starr and Most (1976, pp. 615–617) have examined the actual local infectiousness of fighting and find that, during the years 1946–1965, nations at peace but bordering nations already at war were from three to five times more likely themselves to go to war within the next five years than nations at peace and having no warring border nations. These findings are quite consistent with Richardson's Theory XII.

Siverson and King (1978a) found that nations allied before some war with a belligerent in that war were some five times more likely to participate in the war than nations not having such alliances, and that nations at war who had had a prewar alliance were more likely to fight as members of a war coalition than those nations at war which had lacked any prewar allies. The very largest war coalitions appears to have been produced by some factor of contagion additional to alliance. Siverson and King concluded that prewar alliances serve not to increase the probability of onset of a war but to increase the probability that once begun it will spread; i.e. to increase the chance of contagion of fighting, and to increase the probability that a war, once begun, will be complex. They further found (1978b) that the infectious effect of a prewar alliance is greatest for nations in large alliances, with many allies already at war and with a small-power ally already at war.

We may reasonably conclude that fighting once begun has *some* tendency to spread to include nearby actors, prewar allies of belligerents and, perhaps, major powers. More data are needed on the latter tendency; the effect of alliances needs to be integrated into Richardson's model; and there may be other forms of contagion.

A challenge.   Horvath and Foster (1963) were able to generate Richardson's observed distribution of wars of different complexities by postulating a different and computationally somewhat less complex process of random interaction between "nations," on several assumptions. Belligerents enter wars at a constant rate (so many new participations per unit of time); they leave at a constant rate; and the two rates are the same. When they start to fight, they have a certain constant probability of either doing so alone or joining some existing belligerents. Those who ally join with single belligerents, or with two-member alliances, or with N-member alliances, in proportion to the fraction of all current participants already in fighting groups of the given size. Belligerency for all members of an alliance ends simultaneously. Alliances break up (and cease fighting) at a constant rate, the same for alliances of all sizes. Coalitions of a given size (including size one) tend to fight other coalitions of a given size strictly in the ratio that such other coalitions bear to the total number of coalitions existing. On these assumptions, the total number of coalitions and of participations recorded by Richardson for magnitudes 4–7, 1820–1939, were used to generate the expected frequencies of coalitions of various complexities (e.g., 1 vs. 1, 2 vs. 1, etc.), and a good fit was obtained.

Horvath and Foster's assumption of constant and equal rates of entry and exit seems at variance with Richardson's observation of a Poisson distribution in the onset and termination of wars (SDQ, pp. 128–130) and Singer and Small's observation of violent fluctuations in annual amounts of nation months of international war begun and underway (1972, pp. 205–212). Other assumptions, for example, that alliances are joined in proportion to the membership of *all* alliances of that size, or that alliances dissolve completely rather than by solitary departure, are also subject to empirical test, and seem suspect.

Summary.   The very small number of very complex wars requires some explanation. Duration, magnitude, and complexity being interrelated, what explains one may explain the others; as the interrelation is opaque, separate explanations of each phenomenon may be sought first. Richardson develops a model that generates the essential portions of the distribution of wars by complexity: the model is that of "a chaos, restricted by geography, and further modified by the infectiousness of fighting" (SDQ, p. 248). The model has many monitory and prescriptive implications as regards long-range missiles, contiguity, escalation, and unification. A close study of actual contagion of war, as well as of contiguity and war, would be required before these implications could be accepted; all the more because a very different model, though one in its way even more in need of empirical substantiation, can generate the same distribution of complexities.

Richardson's model is probably to be preferred at this point, but not wholeheartedly embraced. It needs modifying to take account of, rather than to set aside, contagion via alliances. For the time being, we may fairly say that fighting has some tendency to spread to entangle the neighbors and the allies of the belligerents.

7

Participation by Named Nations

A chief aggressor? At various times there has been advanced the thesis of a "chief aggressor": Richardson refers in particular to "Lord Vansittart's thesis that Germany has always been the chief aggressor" (SDQ, p. 256), but other nations have also been accused. There has also been implicit in certain proposals for international reconstruction—including the Charter of the United Nations—the idea that certain specific states are warlike and therefore in need of constraint or reorganization, and others peace-loving and therefore deserving of imitation, power, or applause.[1]

The number of deadly quarrels in which a nation was the aggressor cannot have exceeded the number in which that nation was a participant. Richardson found that no single state participated as a belligerent in more than 30 percent of the wars of magnitudes 4–7, 1820–1945, so that no single belligerent could have been the aggressor in more than that percentage of cases. Richardson rejected Lord Vansittart's thesis with regard to Germany and, indeed, any single chief aggressor: "belligerency, and therefore its sub-class aggression, have been widespread," and "so widespread that any scheme to prevent war by restraining any one named nation is not in accordance with the history of the interval A.D. 1820 to 1945" (SDQ, pp. 176, 174). That

---

[1] The United Nations organization (1945–) is the successor to the United Nations alliance (1942–1945), victorious in World War II. The most powerful of the victorious Allies—the United States, the Soviet Union, the United Kingdom, China, and France—were explicitly accorded special powers and privileges by Articles 23 and 106 of the United Nations Charter. The defeated Axis states—Germany, Italy, Japan, Rumania, Bulgaria, Hungary, and Finland—are treated in Articles 107 and 53 as likely to commit "further aggression," and hence needing special supervision and control.

belligerency is widespread actually does not necessarily imply that aggression is also widespread; but the difficulty of defining aggression for any scientific purpose (SDQ, pp. 17-19, 120, 174-175) renders the question moot in any case.

New belligerents.   Richardson recorded the fact that some 20 to 40 percent of all belligerents in each twenty-one-year period from 1841 to 1945 were new, that is, had not appeared on the list of participants before. The rate of appearance of new belligerents seems to tend toward 30 percent. Thus "the problem of keeping the peace is not merely to prevent future aggression by Germany and Japan, nor only to prevent aggression by any of the states at present established, nor even aggression by other dissatisfied groups with names at present well-known, because there is likely to arise a steady supply of new dissatisfactions, and of new groups organizing those unrests" (SDQ, p. 171). This conclusion reinforces one's conviction, derived from such non-quantitative analysis as that of Kenneth Waltz (1954), that political analysis and action are required at the global-system levels as well as at the actor-level: how else can one deal with the prospect of a predictable horde of future belligerents, presently nameless because nonexistent? System-level analysis in this connection would be directed to the questions: Why does the steady supply of new belligerents actually arise? How might it be diminished or choked off?

Infrequent participants.   Richardson took note of the exceptional behavior during 1820-1939 of Switzerland (one participation below magnitude 3) and Sweden (no participation) but drew no conclusions. Two instances permit no conclusions. Still, one might note that these states could be considered to have shared relative prosperity, neutrality (or isolationism, or a policy of no alliances), absence of territorial claims, lack of colonies and overseas colonization, faint ideological commitment, markedly restrained sympathy with foreign subject classes or peoples, reasonably good defensive geographic situations, strong defensive war preparations, strong international trade ties, constitutional government, and less than major power status.

Frequent participants.   Richardson's table of participation (SDQ, p. 173) in ninety-four wars magnitudes 4-7, 1820-1945, lists the number of wars in which each of thirteen named belligerents took part (see table 14).

Taking the first ten nations on this list, Richardson found that of ninety-one wars, magnitudes 4-7, 1820-1939, thirteen involved none of the ten, and the total number of belligerents' names (counting no name twice) was 108, far in excess of ten (SDQ, p. 269). There is therefore no bellicose minority facing a peaceable majority of nations: belligerency was widespread in one sense, though concentrated in another.

Richardson in consequence advanced Ranyard West's thesis that "a changing majority of momentarily good nations may hope to control a changing minority of momentarily bad nations" (SDQ, p. 176). Taken in context, this

TABLE 14

PARTICIPATIONS OF NAMED NATIONS (AFTER RICHARDSON)

Actor	Participations
Britain	28
France	21
Russia	18
Turkey or Ottoman Empire	15
China	14
Spain	11
Germany or Prussia	10
Italy or Piedmont	10
U.S.A.	9
Japan	9
Austria, in various combinations	9
Egypt	7
Greece	6

thesis seems implicitly to accept the identification of participation with aggression which Richardson had thereto rejected. It rests in addition upon examinable but unexamined assumptions.

Does membership in the group of high-participant nations actually fluctuate over time? Richardson's data could be brought to bear on the question; but rather than inquire, Richardson seemed to accept Quincy Wright's assertion that modern states have varied greatly, swiftly, and somewhat mysteriously in their warlikeness. Assuming a high degree and speed of variation, this might still follow from determinable causes.

Is the "temporarily" bellicose minority of states controllable because a minority? Surely controllability is more a function of power than of numbers. It seems worth noting that the first eleven of the thirteen high-participant nations in Richardson's participation table would commonly be spoken of as including three former great powers, slowly decaying during 1820–1945 (Spain, Turkey, China); one state that had great-power status at the start of the interval but later declined (Austria); four states which rose to great-power status during the period (Germany, Italy, U.S.A., Japan); and three states that were great powers more or less throughout (Britain, France, Russia). This observation would suggest an evident and plausible link between power status and war participation. Such a link in turn throws grave doubt on the practicality of the low-participators constraining the high-participators, as this would amount to the weak constraining the strong. The link does serve to mark out a type of actor perhaps peculiarly needing to be pacified, but without suggesting practical means of pacification.

The great-power record.   Table 15 below shows Singer and Small's rankings (1972, pp. 282–284) for Richardson's eleven major participants. With the three circled exceptions, the group accounts for the top eleven places in frequency, magnitude, *and* duration of participation: a remarkable accomplishment!

Furthermore, of 29,189.69 thousand battle deaths and 4532.8 nation months attributed to the Singer and Small wars (1972, pp. 275–280), 26,332.50 thousand (90.2%) of the battle deaths, and 2694.9 (59.5%) of the nation-months, were accounted for by these eleven participants (1972, p. 282). Singer and Small therefore are justified in concluding that "most of the war in the system has been accounted for by a small fraction of the nations, most of which would be found near the top of any hierarchy based on diplomatic status, military-industrial capability, or related indicators" (1972, p. 287).[2]

I have carried Richardson's analysis of the participation of named actors somewhat farther. For all 315 cases, magnitudes 3–7, 1820–1952, participation from the eleven nations at the top of Richardson's list is as follows:[3]

British participated in	74 cases	or 23.5%
French	54 cases	17.1%
Chinese	34 cases	10.8%
Russians	29 cases	9.2%
Turks or Ottomans	28 cases	8.8%
Italians or Piedmontese	18 cases	5.7%
Spanish	16 cases	5.1%
Germans or Prussians	15 cases	4.8%
Americans	14 cases	4.4%
Austrians or Austro-Hungarians	13 cases	4.1%
Japanese	12 cases	3.8%

[2] These powers appear to share another interesting and perhaps significant characteristic. Starr and Most (1976, pp. 605–607) found that sixty-eight members of the international system bordered Britain (or its colonies) at some time during 1946–1955, thirty-eight bordered France, twenty-two the United States, twenty-two Portugal, twenty-one the Soviet Union, nineteen China, and so on. Starr and Most concluded th· major powers (all the above except Portugal) averaged three to seven times as many total borders as the ordinary system member. Given the already examined relations between contiguity and war, it may be worth noting that major powers have not only been virtually contiguous to many states by reason of their ability to dispose of forces (historically, naval forces in particular) at great distances but also *actually* contiguous to more states than the average power.

[3] An earlier version of this study gave slightly different totals, based on different assignments of nationality. For this count, "Chinese" excludes Nien, Kokandians,

TABLE 15

PARTICIPATIONS OF NAMED NATIONS (AFTER SINGER AND SMALL)

	Rank in no. of wars	Rank in no. of battle deaths	Rank in war months
Britain	1-2	6	2
France	1-2	4	1
Russia	4	1	5
Turkey	3	9	3
China	8-9	3	6
Spain	6	⑮	4
Germany/Prussia	⑫	2	11
Italy/Sardinia	5	8	10
United States	7	11	8
Japan	10-11	5	7
Austria-Hungary	8-9	7	⑳

Ninety-two cases (29.2%) involved none of the eleven. Bringing the analysis down to magnitude 3 substantially increases this last figure, as the breakdown by magnitude in table 16 demonstrates.

Table 16 suggests an association between 11-nation participation and war magnitude. The 2 × 2 table 17 shows that association. The number of casualties in a war is positively related to the participation of those frequent participants—great powers, rising and falling powers, former and future impe-

TABLE 16

ABSTENTION FROM WAR BY THE 11 MAIN PARTICIPANTS

Magnitude	Total no. of cases at that magnitude	No. of cases in which none of the 11 participated	Percentage
7	2	0	0.0
6	7	1	14.3
5	26	4	15.4
4	71	8	11.7
3	209	79	37.8
All	315	92	29.2

Kashgarians, Tibetans, Mongols, Turkis, but includes Taiping, Yunnanese, Szechwanese, Kueichowese, Tungans, Manchus, Formosans. "Spanish" excludes Latin Americans and Basques. "Italians" excludes non-Piedmontese before 1859, Garibaldians, and Papal troops in 1859 but includes Volunteers in 1859 and Papal forces in 1860 and 1867. "Austrians" includes anti-Carbonarist Piedmontese 1820 and anti-Carbonarist Neapolitans 1820–21; includes Hungarians in 1848–49 but not after 1919. "Germans" excludes non-Prussian states until 1871. "Americans" includes Texans before annexation but excludes Filibusters. "French" and "British" include volunteers in the Spanish civil war.

TABLE 17
GREAT-POWER PARTICIPATION VERSUS WAR MAGNITUDE

Magnitude	Cases with one or more of the 11	Cases with none of the 11	Total Cases
4-7	93	13	106
3	130	79	209
All	223	92	315

Yule's Q=0.63

rial states, however one wishes to label them, since no label seems entirely satisfactory. This association could be interpreted as meaning that adding a "great power" tends to raise the casualties in a war; or that it is difficult to inflict many casualties without a great power assisting; or that intense conflicts are those that tend to draw in great powers; or all the above.

Table 18 shows association between the *number* of "great power" participants in a conflict and the magnitude of the conflict. The same interpretations as before, appropriately modified, seem possible.

Great-power pairs. It is natural to ask next whether there are any patterns in the interrelationships of the 11 high-participation nations. In the 315 cases, I count 780 pairs of opposed belligerents.

The 780 pairs were taken part in by 11-nation belligerents thus:

British participated in 105 pairs or 13.5%
French   82 or 10.5%
Chinese   59 or 7.6%
Russians   59 or 7.6%
Turks   56 or 7.2%
Germans   56 or 7.2%
Italians   44 or 5.6%
Spanish   38 or 4.9%
Austrians   34 or 4.4%
Japanese   25 or 3.2%
Americans   22 or 2.8%

In 57 of the 780 pairs, both belligerents came from one of the 11 high-participating nations (were "11-nation civil pairs"). In 94/780, one belligerent came from one of the eleven nations, the other from another ("11-nation foreign pairs"). Thus 151/780, or 19.36%, were "11-nation pairs." 294/780, or 37.7%, lacked any 11-nation participant; 335/780, or 42.9%, pitted one of the eleven against an outsider.

TABLE 18
NUMBER OF GREAT-POWER PARTICIPANTS VERSUS
WAR MAGNITUDE

Magnitude	Cases with 2 or more of the 11	Cases with only 1 of the 11	Cases with none	Total
5–7	14 (35%)	16 (8.7%)	5 (5.4%)	35 (11.1%)
4	20 (50%)	43 (23.5%)	8 (8.7%)	71 (22.5%)
3	6 (15%)	124 (67.8%)	79 (85.9%)	209 (66.4%)
All	40 (100%)	183 (100%)	92 (100%)	315 (100%)

The 780 pairs had 780 $\times$ 2 = 1560 participants. These came from the eleven nations as follows:

British	105 or 6.7%
French	87 or 5.6%
Chinese	84 or 5.4%
Russians	63 or 4.0%
Turks	59 or 3.8%
Germans	58 or 3.7%
Italians	48 or 3.1%
Spanish	45 or 2.9%
Austrians	38 or 2.4%
Japanese	27 or 1.7%
Americans	23 or 1.5%

Together the eleven nations contributed 637/1560, or 40.8%, of all belligerent participants.

Table 19 shows the relationship of eleven-nation participation to magnitude. The strongest apparent association is shown in column (G): the low-magnitude pairs show more abstention by the 11. Next strongest is the rise in 11-nation foreign pairs as the magnitude of the war rises, at least to magnitude 6; see column (D).

This relationship emerges in another form in table 20: few 11-nation foreign pairs participate in small wars, many in large. If we interpret this as reflecting the special ability of great powers to inflict and to absorb casualties, we arrive at the not unprecedented policy conclusion that to avert

TABLE 19
PERCENTAGES OF BELLIGERENT PAIRS AT EACH MAGNITUDE INVOLVING GREAT-POWER PARTICIPATION OF VARIOUS TYPES

Magnitude	A	B	C	D	E	F	G
7	2	130	2 (1.5%)	33 (25.4%)	35 (26.9%)	77 (59.2%)	18 (13.9%)
6	7	42	5 (11.9%)	15 (35.7%)	20 (47.6%)	10 (23.8%)	12 (28.6%)
5	26	91	13 (14.3%)	15 (16.5%)	28 (30.1%)	34 (37.4%)	29 (31.9%)
4	71	205	15 (7.3%)	26 (12.7%)	41 (20%)	92 (44.9%)	72 (35.1%)
3	209	312	22 (7.1%)	5 (1.6%)	27 (8.7%)	119 (38.1%)	166 (53.2%)
All	315	780	57 (7.3%)	94 (12.1%)	151 (19.4%)	332 (42.6%)	297 (38.1%)

Column (A) shows the total number of cases of a given magnitude. Column (B) shows the total number of pairs of belligerents in those cases. Column (C) shows the number of 11-nation civil pairs in those cases, and the percentage 11-nation-civil/all pairs at that magnitude. Column (D) shows similar figures for 11-nation foreign pairs, column (E) for all 11-nation pairs, column (F) for pairs linking one of the 11 to an outsider, and column (G) for non-11-nation pairs.

TABLE 20
FIGHTING BETWEEN GREAT POWERS VERSUS WAR MAGNITUDE

| | Magnitude | | | | |
	3	4	5	6	7
No. of cases at that Magnitude	209	71	26	7	2
No. of 11-nation foreign pairs in all cases at that magnitude	5	26	15	15	33
No. of such pairs per case	0.02	0.37	0.58	2.14	16.5

catastrophic death from wars it is particularly urgent to avert fighting between great powers.

The distribution of 11-nation pair-belligerencies among 11-nation pairs is quite uneven. The fifty-seven civil pair-belligerencies are distributed as follows:

Chinese	25
Spanish	7
French	5
Italian	4
Russian	4
Austrian	4
Turkish	3
German	2
Japanese	2
U. S. A.	1
British	0
	57

The frequency of Chinese and the absence of British pairs is noteworthy. Here one must point out that rebellions of ethnic minorities (Turkish vs. Chinese, Irish vs. British, etc.) are not counted as "11-nation civil pairs" in this tally, which counts ethnic-group names rather than occurrences of m (common government). Nor are the twelve or so wars of independence in Spanish America counted against Spain.

The 94 foreign pairs give 94 X 2 = 188 participations. The 188 participations are distributed among the 11 nations as follows:

Russia	27
France	25
Italy	21

Britain	18
Germany	18
China	18
Japan	16
Austria	14
Turkey	13
Spain	9
U. S. A.	9
	188

There are specific historical explanations that could be called on to account for these differences. In part these are generalizable. No doubt a nation's number of frontiers with other great powers, the average distance of its capital from those of all other great powers, and the portion of a long historic interval during which it had great power status would be plausible independent variables.

The 11 nations form (11 × 10/2) = 55 separate pairs among whom 94 pair-belligerencies are distributed, with a mean of 1.71 belligerencies per great power pair (see table 21).

The frequencies in the cells of the 11-nation foreign pair cross-tabulation by nations are all 1, 2, or 3 (within one standard deviation, 1.42, of the mean) with the following exceptions:

Italians-Austrians	6
Russians-Turks	5
Chinese-Japanese	5
French-Germans	4
French-Italians	4
Russians-Germans	4
British-Americans	0
Chinese-Turks	0
Chinese-Spanish	0
Turks-Spanish	0
Turks-Americans	0
Turks-Germans	0
Turks-Austrians	0
Italians-Japanese	0
Spanish-Japanese	0
Spanish-Austrians	0

There are specific historical explanations once more available for the recurring fights. Theoretically one would perhaps draw on propinquity or contiguity, alienness, and retaliation itself; perhaps also to the decline in power of one neighbor simultaneously with the rise of the other. The pairs

TABLE 21
11-NATION FOREIGN PAIRS

Russians and	French	3		Japanese	2
	Italians	3		Austrians	1
	British	2		Turks	2
	Germans	4		Spanish	2
	Chinese	3		Americans	0
	Japanese	3			
	Austrians	1	Germans and	Chinese	1
	Turks	5		Japanese	1
	Spanish	2		Austrians	1
	Americans	1		Turks	0
				Spanish	1
French and	Italians	4		Americans	2
	British	1			
	Germans	4	Chinese and	Japanese	5
	Chinese	3		Austrians	1
	Japanese	2		Turks	0
	Austrians	2		Spanish	0
	Turks	3		Americans	1
	Spanish	2			
	Americans	1	Japanese and	Austrians	1
				Turks	1
Italians and	British	2		Spanish	0
	Germans	1		Americans	1
	Chinese	1			
	Japanese	0	Austrian and	Turks	0
	Austrians	6		Spanish	0
	Turks	2		Americans	1
	Spanish	1			
	Americans	1	Turks and	Spanish	0
				Americans	0
British and	Germans	3			
	Chinese	3	Spanish and	Americans	1
					94

that failed to fight are more diverse: great distances often separated their capitals or territories; they usually had no land frontier; there were limitations (in time or in spatial sphere of influence) on the members' great-power status; deliberate policy probably influenced the Turkish-Austrian pair, policy and coethnicity the British-American pair. Jencks (1973, p. 22) singles out having a language or a liberal-democratic regime in common, and lacking a land frontier, as pacifiers for great-power pairs. The paucity of colingual and/or democratic great powers, and the volatility of frontiers and regimes over Richardson's interval, make this theory hard to test. Still, those pairs that shared either a language or democracy or both for most of the period (Germany-Austria, Britain-France, France-America, Britain-America) fought once at most; and the six pairs that fought most often were indeed usually contiguous, alien and not both democracies.

Implications.   If the several hypotheses offered in explaining variations in the war participation of named nations seem persuasive, implications for peace strategy follow at once. None is novel; some are implied in certain peace plans. Pacification efforts should be directed particularly but not exclusively toward the great powers of any moment because their wars are both frequent and intense. It would be prudent to include in that ambiguous category of great power, for the purposes of pacification, both weakened former great powers with extended territories and aspirant, candidate, or challenger powers. Fighting between members of the great-power group is particularly worth avoiding. Great-power pairs that are adjacent and alien with a record of recent fighting, and in which one is weakening while the other grows stronger, may be particularly in need of pacification. Additional conclusions of use to policy might emerge from a study of the low-participant nations, or from a study of the origins of new belligerent groups.

Modelski, using data from Singer and Small and from his own collection to prove the point, carries the reasoning much farther.

> War can no longer be regarded as a form of activity normally distrib-
> uted over the entire population of states members of the international
> system. Rather it is a form of behavior peculiarly appropriate only to
> those states occupying the position of Great Powers. ... On closer
> analysis the control of war may require no more than dispensing with
> Great Power status in world politics. ... Constructive thinking about
> the control of war thus involves conceiving of the world as capable of
> being organized without Great Power dominance. (1972, p. 47).

The character of a no-great-power order is not made clear. A world state would presumably qualify. So might Auguste Comte's proposal to pacify the globe by dissolving all great powers and dividing the world into 500 equal republics of 3 million people each (1877, pp. 268–269; something over 1,300 would now be needed). These and alternate forms are worth exploring: their character, feasibility, durability, and desirability on grounds other than that of pacificity need to be established.

Summary.   There is no "chief aggressor." Research on the problems of the flow of new belligerents and of low war-participant nations is in order. No "bellicose minority" of nations wholly accounts for warfare in the global system. But some actors, nations, are very high participants, and a group of eleven such are linked to/account for/suffer most of the wars, war-months, and war-deaths. Many questions about the members of this group remain, but in a broad sense they are/have been/will be "great powers." Their participation, especially in opposition to one another, is associated with high casualties. This finding points to a realist/conservative peace strategy of pacifying, or to a utopian/radical strategy of liquidating, the great powers.

8
Economic Causes

The debate over whether some wars, or all, have economic causes or are principally or entirely to be explained by economic causes ebbs and flows and is never quite stilled. "While diligently recording the special causes of each war, writers may perhaps have neglected to mention the general cause of all wars" (SDQ, p. 26): such a collection as Richardson's cannot therefore be used either to refute or to confirm such a general cause, whether that is "human nature," "aggressiveness," a "security dilemma," or "economics" in a general sense. But writers do mention specific economic causes, and these may be tallied.

Richardson did not define an exhaustive logical set of economic-cause symbols with the intention of testing any preconceived economic hypothesis. Rather, as he read histories of particular quarrels, he defined symbols and set them against particular wars according to the historians' indications. Richardsonian symbols that bear on economic relations which historians have asserted to hold between belligerents include the following:

a   The tail-group sent goods to the tip-group as trade

e   Common level of wealth or poverty

theta   The tail-group owed money to the tip-group

sigma   The tail-group organized commercial enterprises on the tip-group's territory

A   The tail-group put obstacles in the way of the movement of goods, A′ to, or A″ from, the tip-group

E   The individuals of the tail-group were evidently richer than those of those of the tip-group

H   The tail-group restricted immigration from the tip-group

P′   The tip-group supported the tail-group's enemy or rival by favors, money, supplies, or fighting

Q   The belligerents were rivals for concessions on the territories of third parties

R   The belligerents were rivals in trading with third parties

T   The tail-group wished to acquire territory from the tip-group, T′ for habitation, T″ for minerals or other portable goods, T‴ for strategic strongholds

U   The tail-group taxed the tip-group

V   The tail-group wished to take loot

Y   The tail-group complained about the insufficiency of their land for their population

Z   The tail-group fought for pay

Now is the time to recall that the lower and upper case Roman letters symbolize relations expected to make for amity and enmity, respectively, and that the Greek cursives denote relations expected to be ambivalent.

The symbols e and Y appeared so infrequently as to be useless for analysis, the latter being absorbed doubtless by T′, while the former may have indicated a relationship either of little interest to the historians of wars or very hard to document. The symbol a appeared often, but never as a cause of war. Z and V occurred more frequently but were not treated as economic causes by Richardson in his analysis.

The only economic cause specifically cited in his sources that Richardson excluded from his symbol list—because there was no satisfactory evidence except for the Nye Committee investigation in the United States in 1934—was the effect of the private manufacture and trade in armaments (SDQ, p. 207). State trading in armaments as a cause of war is presumably covered by P′

or by the noneconomic symbol gamma, "a third party . . . desired that [the belligerents] should quarrel" (SDQ, pp. 207, 23).

The only credible theoretical economic cause that Richardson found to have been omitted from his list—after reviewing an indication of probable economic causes of quarrel composed by J. E. Meade—was the "fall from comfort to poverty," which in the form of the economic crisis of the inter-war years was of substantial importance in bringing on World War II. He chose to exclude this cause nonetheless from his list because of the long delay in its effect, which seemed likely to lead historians to undercite it, so that nonstatistical procedures would be more appropriate for dealing with it (SEQ, pp. 208-209).

The list of symbols provides no particularization of such causes as a desire for territory for the establishment of trading posts, for capital investment, or for slaving, all of them plausible and alleged motives at one time or another during Richardson's interval. Instead the list groups these under the unanaly-zed symbol T, the desire for territory, along with such motives for terri-torial acquisition as nationalism, religious-ideological proselytization, and "pride and glory." This is inconvenient but does not prevent some use being made of the unanalyzed T, simply by reclassifying all its occurrences in the manner most favorable to a hypothesis that is rejected and in the manner most adverse to a conclusion that is accepted (SDQ, pp. 208-209). In the next paragraph, *all* occurrences of T, otherwise unanalyzed, are counted as economic.

In eighty-three wars, magnitudes 4-7, 1820-1929, and counting irritants (symbols in the third compartment of -/-/-) only, Richardson found thirty-three (39.7%) in which one or more of the symbols T, T', and T" appeared as a direct cause; thirteen (15.7%) in which U appeared in third compartment; seven (8.4%) with E; and no more than four occurrences each of A (or A' or A"), sigma (or theta), Q, H, R, and P' (SDQ, pp. 205-206, 209). Of 244 symbols that appeared in the third compartment of (-/-/-) for these eighty-three wars, 71 (29.1%) of all symbols were "economic," that is, included in the list A, A', A", E, sigma, theta, Q, H, T', T", T, R, U, P'. In the whole group of eighty-three quarrels, "There were 25 for which no economic direct cause has been noted in the list" (SDQ, p. 210). By implication 58/83 (70%) had some economic direct cause.

Richardson's investigation of economic causes is probably the least devel-oped portion of his work. By internal evidence it would seem to have been completed in the first year of his investigation (1940), revised between 1945 and 1947 to include one more case, and then left untouched to be reproduced in the edited volume (SDQ, pp. 7, 206, 207). One cannot readily tell which of the cases in the present list were tallied for Richardson's analysis. It seemed desirable to bring the count up to date.

In my recount I dropped from the "economic" group the symbols H (restriction on immigration) and P′ (aid to an enemy) as seldom used and marginally "economic"; I added to that group the symbol V (taking loot) as arguably "economic" and fairly often used, and the symbol Y (desire for land for population) as nearly equivalent to T′ even though seldom used.

For all 315 cases (780 belligerent pairs) 1820–1952, magnitudes 3–7:

1. One or more of thirteen economic symbols (A, A′, A″, E, sigma, theta, Q, R, T′, T″, U, V, Y) was set as an irritant in 153/780 (19.6%) of pairs and in 89/315 (28.3%) of cases;

2. The possibly economic symbol T was set as an irritant in 173/780 (22.2%) of pairs and in 111/315 (35.2%) of cases;

3. When T was treated as a fourteenth economic symbol, the number of pairs having an economic irritant was raised very substantially to 285/780 (36.6%) and the number of cases to 163/315 (51.7%);

4. But upon retrieving the list of 74 cases with T and no other economic symbol, I was able to justify treating only 18 of them as plainly having an "economic" component (usually a desire to settle in territory occupied by others). This reduced the number of "economic" pairs once again, to 184/780 (23.6%) and the number of "economic" cases to 107/315 (34.0%).

There remains a substantial residue of uncertainty. The difference between Richardson's maximum percentage of cases with an economic cause (70%) and mine (51.7%) is due to fewer economic causes being cited at magnitude 3, which I count and Richardson does not. The ambiguous symbol T dominates both counts.

Despite these difficulties, there remain conclusions that may be drawn. Economic direct causes of war have been frequent but not omnipresent. They do not appear to be necessary for war.

Richardson's investigation thus failed to confirm the propositions that all causes or most causes of war are economic, insofar as those propositions are confirmable by counting. The investigation supported the less ambitious thesis that the causes labeled "economic" together form an important set of causes of war, none of which is dominant. This set of causes is not shown to have (or to lack) any unity beyond being economic; that is, the set of economic causes does not appear to be reducible to inequality, commercial rivalry, population pressure, trade barriers, or expansive "economic imperialism." Not only is no single-cause theory of war supported but no theory that one kind of economic cause dominates is supported. Proposals for economic redistribution, control of competition, restraints on population growth or migration, free trade, and defense against economic penetration, all receive some support from these findings. But as they contradict one another, and as their past implementation is frequently implicated in these findings as a cause of war rather than of peace, that support is heavily qualified. It may still be possible to find unity in the set of economic causes, to argue consequently that economics is *a* most important cause, and perhaps in some sense the principal cause of war, and to prescribe accordingly. Richardson's findings clearly do not rule such an argument out. They do, however, raise serious obstacles in its path. Some economic theories rely on rather vague definitions of their terms to buttress the plausibility of their conclusions. Richardson admitted that "the social background always had an economic aspect," that "the boundaries of the class 'economic' are not sharply defined," and that it could be argued that "every human affair is economic." Should one wish to extend the meaning of *cause* to encompass the background, or the meaning of *economic* to encompass every activity dependent on material objects, or the set of symbols labeled "economic" (or the assignment of those symbols to specific cases) to the limits of definition of *economics*, the prominence of economic causes of war could be made larger or even total. Richardson contended that such extension would render useless the terms so extended in meaning (SDQ, p. 210), so that the assertion that economics causes war would become true but trivial, impractical and futile.

In a more general sense, one might contend that under conditions of universal prosperity there would be no particular need to acquire the territory (T,Y) or goods (V) of others, no special ground to resent their wealth (E), enterprise (sigma), or competitive success (Q,R), no reason to block their trade (A), and no incentive to revolt against debt (theta) or taxes (U). Thus if any theme underlies the economic causes, it is the common theme of economics: the world is one of scarcity rather than abundance.

The significance of this judgment is open to interpretation in the light of conflicting views of human nature. Hsün Tzu tells us that man, by nature selfish, seeks gain and profit, and his greedy desires cannot be satisfied: men's desires are many, goods are few; so strife is inevitable (1928, pp. 65, 152, 295, 301, 302). His pupil Han Fei Tzu however declares that our feelings and behavior are not the same in abundance as in scarcity: when men are few and things are many they are peaceable, not because men are then benevolent but because goods are abundant; when men quarrel and pillage it is not because they have become wicked but because goods have become scarce (1959, pp. 276-278). Those inclined to Han Fei's side will find Dwight Eisenhower's old slogan "Peace, Prosperity, and Progress" to the point. Those who agree with Hsün Tzu will seek other avenues to peace.

Affluence, development, and peace. Certain social-evolutionist theorists have argued that as a poor agricultural society is slowly replaced worldwide by a prosperous industrialized society, the world will also become more peaceful. Various arguments for this position have been advanced.

Henri de Saint-Simon believed that successful industrialization would completely satisfy reasonable men of every class and every nation: the vast majority would have an interest in maintaining an established order of prosperity; hence there would be no motive for insurrection or for aggression against one's neighbors, no fear of rebellion or invasion, no need for large armies and police forces; antagonism, exploitation, violence, and war would decline and cease (1825*a*, 1825*b*; Bazard 1830).

Auguste Comte held that affluence could and would produce a higher, peaceful human morality. Material progress is the basis of all moral improvement: the accumulation of capital will steadily liberate human existence from physical labor, material want, and all anxieties about material needs; concordantly, altruism and unselfishness will spontaneously replace egoism and selfishness, and war will be spontaneously extinguished. By the twenty-first or twenty-second century, the nations will come to form one vast family, and human activities will resolve themselves into art, games, and festivals (1875, pp. 116, 122, 140, 147 *et passim*).

More recently, Modelski has speculated (1961, p. 142) that an industrialized international system could be "relatively or largely war-free" because

> functions efficiently filled by war in the agrarian system could now be implemented by industrial structures: the solidarity function of imposing penal sanctions on the offenders against the international order, and the leadership function of helping to enforce international decisions. The place which war has held as a test of international achievement, as a measuring rod of international status, can in Industria be replaced by productive technological or scientific competition or by space exploration. Such a world might discard the military contest for simple 'status-seeking,' which is equally serious, taxing, and time-consuming, and can be carried on for high stakes, but which might nevertheless be pursued without the assumption of violence. Although war as the ultimate contingency may not disappear, its share in accomplishing international purposes may greatly diminish.

It seems that this theory must be mistaken. Richardson's data show that from 1820, when Saint-Simon was publishing his ideas, to 1949, a period in which the world underwent entirely unprecedented economic growth, wars did not become much less frequent; they did become more bloody; and the total number of war-dead rose.

Yet the theory that relates material abundance to peace cannot simply be dismissed. Matthew Melko, having reviewed the history of fifty-two societies that at some time between 2650 B.C. and A.D. 1973 experienced a century of internal peace (i.e., had no civil war over approximately the fourth magnitude), concluded that these societies were on the whole uncommonly prosperous, with their prosperity fairly well distributed, fostered by, and fostering peace (1973, pp. 113–115). Russett counted deaths from domestic group violence in seventy-four countries from 1950 to 1962 (1964, pp. 97–100) and correlated these with numerous national social indicators: some twenty-five variables that appear to reflect a society's level of economic development correlate to violence, with correlation coefficients from twenty-six to fifty-six, in a direction that suggests an association between poverty and violence, or between affluence and peace (1964, p. 272).

Using the tables in Taylor and Hudson's *World Handbook of Political and Social Indicators* for population (1972, pp. 295–298), for total deaths per country from domestic violence 1948–1967 (1972, pp. 110–115), and for gross national product per capita (1972, pp. 314–321), one finds that the richest thirty countries,[1] with GNP per capita over $800, having together about 25 percent of the world population, produced only about 4 percent of the world's deaths from domestic violence.

To examine this fact in another way, I have used *World Handbook* aggregate data and the PREP data manipulation program at UCLA's Center for Computer-Based Behavioral Studies to cross-tabulate per capita GNP against annual death rates from domestic violence. A strong relationship between affluence and peace emerges (table 22).

What are we to make of this? Saint-Simon, Comte, and Modelski tell us that a prosperous industrial society ought to be peaceful. We know that the world has grown more industrialized and more prosperous. Richardson's work shows that it did not grow any more peaceful. Melko asserted that

TABLE 22
DEATHS FROM DOMESTIC VIOLENCE

	Deaths per year per hundred million population		
	Under 103	*Over 103*	*Total*
GNP per capita over $800	27	3	30
GNP per capita under $800	40	65	105
Total	67	68	135

Gamma = –0.8720
Chi-square = 25.146 *Df* = 1
P < 0.00001

[1] Sixteen West and North European countries, five East European countries, the United States, Canada, Puerto Rico, Australia, New Zealand, Japan, Kuwait, Venezuela, and Israel.

societies that have been peaceful have also been relatively prosperous; recent political data indicate that prosperous societies have been relatively peaceful.

One of Quincy Wright's theories (1965, p. 1155) offers us a way of reconciling the theories and the data that seem so puzzling.

> Historic periods of transition from one economy to another have been warlike. Agricultural classes accustomed to a dominant position have usually resisted violently the rise to dominance of commercial or industrial classes. . . .
>
> Commercial classes were superseding the agricultural nobility during the civil wars of the late Roman Republic and the Renaissance in Western Europe. Industrial classes were superseding commercial and agricultural classes during the civil wars of Napoleonic Western Europe, of mid-nineteenth-century United States, Germany, and Japan, and of twentieth-century Italy, Russia, and China. . . .
>
> Geographic frontiers marking the transition from one economy to another have also often been the scene of war. An industrial state in close contact with an agricultural state tends to expand its commerce and industry into, and to draw its food and raw materials from, the latter. Regarding this process as subversive of its culture and dangerous to its independence, the agricultural state is likely to resist by arms.

Cyril E. Black, a comparative historian whose subject is modernization, has contended even more forcefully than Quincy Wright that while a uniformly prosperous society may be tranquil, the transition fron traditional to modern society is likely to be very violent. Having examined some 170 societies over the past few centuries, Black was compelled to conclude (1966, pp. 90–94, 150) that during the modernizing process of industrialization, urbanization, and social reorganization, there is actually an increase in violence—in wars and revolutions—over the pre-modern period; and that only after such a violent transition do societies enter the relatively safe haven of domestic stability which about fourteen First World countries[2] have apparently reached. The "transition from traditional to modern leadership has generally been violent" as the societies in transition to modernity confront the challenge of modern ideas, transfer power from traditional to modernizing leaders during a bitter struggle that lasts several generations, actually transform themselves from rural agrarian to urban industrial societies, and finally reorganize and reintegrate their whole social structures in the new way (1966, pp. 68–69). The peaks of the crises of challenge, transfer, transformation, and integration "are also the periods when domestic or international violence is most likely to occur." Up till now, by and large, the

---

[2] Britain, France, Belgium, Netherlands, Luxembourg, Switzerland, West Germany, Denmark, Norway, Sweden, the United States, Canada, Australia, and New Zealand (1966, pp. 90–91).

modernization process has actually led to an increase in violence (1966, p. 33). "In the great majority of cases political, economic, and social development have been accompanied by wars of liberation and unification ... major revolutions and civil wars ... [and] innumerable minor wars, revolts and disturbances" (1966, p. 164). Thus, for most of the world in the generations ahead the struggle between forces of tradition and modernity, and between rival programs of development, assures prolonged instability—ten to fifteen revolutions a year (1966, pp. 165-166). It will be well into the twenty-first century before a majority of world societies will have completed the main tasks of economic and social transformation and entered the relatively safe haven of social integration (1966, pp. 150-151).

Again crosstabulating *World Handbook* aggregate data via UCLA-CCBS PREP, it appears that death rates from domestic group violence are indeed highest at middle-income levels but noticeably lower in high-income than in low-income countries. (See table 23.)

A closer examination of domestic violence data already cited led Russett to conclude that (1) although the most striking feature of the general pattern is "the low level of violence associated with high economic development (GNP equal to more than $800 per capita)," (2) since "violent deaths seem less frequent at extremely low GNP levels" than in middle-income countries, (3) "underdeveloped nations should probably expect an increase, not a decrease, in domestic violence over the next few decades" (1964, pp. 306-307). At first, aspirations awakened by early development outrun the society's ability to satisfy or control them, but at length development catches up to desire (Russett, 1965, pp. 136-137).

TABLE 23

DEATHS FROM DOMESTIC VIOLENCE

		Deaths per year per hundred million population		
		Under 103	*Over 103*	
	Over $800	27 (90%)	3 (10%)	30 (100%)
GNP per capita	$80-$800	32 (37.2%)	54 (62.8%)	86 (100%)
	Under $80	8 (42.1%)	11 (57.9%)	19 (100%)
		67	68	135 cases

Eckstein (1962, pp. 121–122) distinguished two groups of countries with fewer than five reports of "unequivocal internal war" (civil war, guerrilla war, turmoil, rioting, terrorism, mutiny, coup) in the *New York Times Index* 1946–1959. Examining Russett (1964, pp. 155–157), one finds that the 9 countries in the first group show a median 1957 per capita GNP of $1,056, that of Denmark, one among the richest 10 percent of countries. Using Russett, and Taylor and Hudson (1972, pp. 314–320), one finds that the 15 countries in the second group for which data are available cannot have had a median 1957 per capita GNP exceeding $90. The 1957 median per capita GNP for 122 countries was $191.50. The most peaceful countries were unusually rich—or uncommonly poor.

On the whole, available data seem most consistent with the idea that a high level of material affluence fosters peace rather than war, but that periods and locales of transition from a subsistence economy to one of abundance are likely to experience a sharp increase in violence before any diminution can be expected. Policies of accelerating modernization and development thus buy a good chance of peace and security in the long run at the very probable cost of war and intense suffering in the immediate and foreseeable future. This bargain reverses Faust's, for the price is borne today that posterity may benefit. Even so, if modernization had not been begun throughout the globe, we might not wish to begin it. As it is everywhere begun, we must hope that it can be completed, and quickly; for any delay or setback will exact a cruel payment.

Summary. Economic direct causes of war have been frequent but not omnipresent nor present to the exclusion of other causes. No single-factor economic-cause theory of war is supported. Even within the set of economic causes no one type of economic cause is preponderant. These findings are not fatal to economic theories of war but do pose serious difficulties for them and for economically based peace schemes as well. If there were any economic panacea, it would be prosperity, to be achieved via development and modernization. But the price of peace through prosperity seems to be modernization punctuated by violence.

9

Ethnocultural Heterogeneity and Homogeneity: Language, Religion, and War

Expected versus actual pacifiers. "Few letters appear in the first compartments of (-/-/-)" (SDQ, p. 184). That is to say, few bonds of amity between belligerents, few actual pacifiers, were recorded by Richardson's historian sources. Richardson interpreted this to mean that historians have simply chosen to explain why there was war when wars occurred (SDQ, p. 184).

Among the eighteen situations "expected usually to make for amity," however, a number did make a significant appearance. By my count, in 780 belligerent pairs (1820-1952), magnitudes 3-7, these were a, c, d, g, i, and m, as listed in table 24.

A closer inquiry into restraints and delays on the outbreak of war could quite reasonably fix on these social relationships as pacifiers that may have been overlooked by historians chiefly concerned with explaining why war happened, not why it might conceivably not have happened. Similarly, inquiries into "peace periods" like that of Melko (1973) could reasonably treat these relationships as potential explanations of peace. There are several reasons:

1. Their expected valency in Richardson's classification;
2. The fact that when they are found in Richardson's list, it is never (with the partial exception of m, common government) as irritants;

TABLE 24

INCIDENCE OF a, c, d, g, i, m IN 780 PAIRS

		*In background**	*As irritant*
a	The two groups traded**	44 (5.6%)	0
c	Similar bodily characteristics	91 (11.7%)	0
d	Similar customs as to dress	53 (6.8%)	0
g	Similar religions or philosophies of life	172 (22.1%)	0
i	Common mother tongue	179 (22.9%)	0
m	Common government	237 (30.4%)	0***

*Or, very infrequently, as a pacifier: the count for the first and second compartments of $(-/-/-)$ is here combined but reflects the second compartment almost exclusively.

**Richardson defined this as "The tail-group sent goods to the tip-group as trade" but actually enters it without arrow modifiers so that in effect it indicates two-way trading.

***But 75 of the 237 pairs, i.e., 31.6% of them (but 9.6% of the whole 780), have rho (domination) as an irritant; to the degree that the common government and the domination were linked, the common government was possibly an irritant.

3.   The fact that where there was an "opposite" relation to these it customarily appeared more often in the war list, and sometimes as an irritant, as in table 25.

An additional reason has to do with Richardson's intriguing observation that the relations whose expected valency was pacific were mostly transitive and symmetrical: symmetrical in that if, for example, A is "of the same race" as B, then B is "of the same race" as A; transitive in that if in this instance B is "of the same race" as C, then A is also "of the same race" as C. In contrast the relations whose expected valency was ambivalent or irritant were either nontransitive ("of different race than") or not symmetrical ("richer than"). Richardson observed that the transitive-symmetrical relations convey the ideas of similarity, equality, and connectedness, while the others imply difference, inequality, and/or insulation. The notions of similarity, equality, and connectedness may be basic to a general theory of pacification; or they may require radical qualification and correction. Further investigation is needed. Richardson did it for similarity and difference of language and of religion.

Language and war.   Inclined initially to accept the belief of Ludwig Zamenhof, the inventor of Esperanto, "that a common language would do much to clear away misunderstandings and so to replace hatred by kindly feelings" (SDQ, pp. 211, 212), yet equally inclined to accept the insistence of Karl Pearson that "beliefs ought to be tested by statistics" (SDQ, p. ii),

TABLE 25
INCIDENCE OF C, D, G, I IN 780 PAIRS

		In background	*As irritant*
C	different bodily characteristics	114 (14.6%)	11 (1.4%)
D	different customary clothing	129 (16.5%)	8 (1.0%)
G	different religions or philosophies of life	223 (28.6%)	122 (15.6%)
I	languages different	451 (57.8%)	10 (1.3%)

Richardson undertook to examine the relationships that might be found to exist between languages and wars.This led him to count the number of pairs of opposed belligerents who used the same language; to devise a scheme for estimating expected colingual fighting if common language had no effect on fighting; and to compare expectation with actuality.

The symbols i (common language) and I (different languages) were applied to pairs of belligerents in accord with rough common sense made explicit. The presence of small minorities lacking the power to affect the decision to fight is disregarded; even large minorities are disregarded when a state "acted as a whole"; when portions of a state revolted, their language is *not* disregarded. The languages written in Chinese ideograms are treated as mutually intelligible. Bilingual populations are counted for the language that was politically most important. Serious ambiguities (auxiliaries with uncertain freedom of choice, coalitions with uncertain levels of integration) are noted and the counts made twice, once maximizing the number of pairs counted, once minimizing it. Pairs that are too puzzling are rejected into an unanalyzed class.

The symbols i and I almost always appear in the second or "background" compartment: historians seldom saw similarity or difference of language as obvious irritants or pacifiers; they were merely obvious.

Richardson's analysis was confined to pairs in wars of magnitudes 4–7, 1820–1929. When the count of pairs was minimized, Richardson found that 162 of 201 analyzed pairs (80.6%) had different languages, and 39/201 (19.4%) had the same language. When the count of pairs was maximized, 289/339 (85.3%) had different languages, 50/339 (14.7%) had the same language.

By my count, which simply tallies all i and I at magnitudes 3–7, 1820–1952, for 780 pairs, 461 of 780 total pairs (59.1%) had different languages; 179/780 (22.9%) had the same language. (In this count, 140 pairs are unanalyzed, i.e., assigned neither i nor I.) The ratio is by no means as marked, but still striking. The symbol I appears in my count more frequently than any other. (In second place is G, different religions, appearing in 345 pairs.)

These findings seem rather suggestive, all the more so as one may assume that there are far more opportunities for fighting between members of the same language-group, if only because such groups are more often geographically concentrated than dispersed.

Richardson was not satisfied with making this assumption. Instead he attempted a quantitative examination, utilizing three models to define in different ways the number of *conceivable* pairs of belligerents in the world. (The models vary the degree to which power is vested in a leading person, the range of action of any belligerent, and the compactness of the area in which a particular language is spoken.) From these models Richardson derived an underestimate and an overestimate of the theoretical probabilities "that a pair of opposed belligerents would happen to use the same language if sameness or difference of language had nothing to do with the causes of war" (SDQ, pp. 216–220). As these probabilities vary for different languages depending upon the proportion of the world's population who spoke those languages, the estimates must be made separately for each major language. For each language, Richardson then derived four actual numbers of pairs of belligerents colingual for that language, by using first the high count of pairs and then the low count, first for all wars magnitudes 4–7 and then for small wars of magnitude 4 only.

When the highest actual count of colingual pairs was lower than the *lowest* expected count produced by the models and the probability that such a difference could have arisen by chance in a sampling process is low enough to be discounted, Richardson concluded that the *particular* common language in question, or some correlate, restrained fighting between its speakers. If the lowest actual count was higher than the highest theoretical count and the deviation inexplicable by a chance of sampling, Richardson concluded that the particular language, or one of its associates, actually incited fighting (SDQ, pp. 221–223).

This stringent process of evaluation mostly demolishes the apparently promising discovery that twelve of the thirteen major languages examined have at least one actual figure below the high estimate and therefore might conceivably prevent fighting between their adherents. Had this preliminary finding been held up under scrutiny, Zamenhof's belief would have received strong support. But these findings, for all major languages but Chinese (and perhaps Bengali), failed to stand Richardson's severe test. He was left with the unexpected conclusion that there were fewer wars in which both sides used Chinese ideographs and more wars in which the opposed belligerents both spoke Spanish than could be explained by the populations using these languages (SDQ, pp. 223–227).

Why should this be so? Richardson resorted to historians' studies of the cultures allegedly shared by members of the Chinese and Spanish-language communities. Citing Latourette, Lin Yutang, and others, he concluded, "it seems probable that the comparative peaceableness of China, prior to A.D. 1911, was the result of instruction, and in particular of Confucian instruction" (SDQ, pp. 241–242).

Richardson rejected various theories that attributed the frequency of civil fighting in Spain and Spanish America to individuals, to the institutions or doctrines of church or army or monarchy or republic, and to the clash of property owners with the dispossessed. His reason was that, though satisfactory in individual cases, none of these theories covered the "wide field," encompassing the consistent and continuing frequency of fighting over many years, many countries, many caudillos, many doctrines, and many institutions. He took note of Salvador de Madariaga's assertion that there is a Spanish "national character"–individualistic, anticooperative, religious, dramatic, and pessimistic, yet given to bursts of optimistic idealism, of activity, energy, and force. Richardson drew no conclusions concerning the effects, causes, or even existence of these character traits; but he implied that if they existed they could easily induce frequent fighting over whatever objects of dispute were present; and the possibility that they exist, whether caused by biological inheritance of temperament or by socialization, or both, was one that he did not rule out (SDQ, pp. 228–229).

These speculations are not deep or detailed, nor are they conclusive. They are to the point. If there is any practical implication of Richardson's finding, it must lie somewhere in the field of national or group character and culture, and their manipulation by schemes of moral education and political indoctrination, by "cultural revolutions" or by "character-building." Precisely what schemes might be most appropriate for world pacification, and whether the deliberate pacification of a culture is truly feasible, remain to be considered by further research.

Richardson's investigation of languages and wars, intended to test Zamenhof's belief that a common world language would promote understanding and understanding concord in its turn, thus left that belief neither confirmed nor refuted. "There may be such an effect; but, if so, it is lost among the ambiguities" (SDQ, p. 230).

Could these ambiguities be resolved? The high and low theoretical estimates Richardson used to defend the null hypothesis are *very* far apart. If we sum, across all thirteen languages, Richardson's estimates of low and high percentages (colingual pairs as a percentage of all pairs) as predicted by his theoretical models, we find that the underestimate predicts 9.2 percent of all belligerent pairs will be colingual (for these thirteen languages), while the overestimate predicts 56.7 percent of pairs will be colingual. The actual fraction of pairs colingual in one of the thirteen languages varies, depending upon the definition of *actual*, between 10.2 percent and 23.7 percent: that is to say, it is below the midpoint and near the bottom of the theoretical range. If the underestimate is unrealistically low and needs to be raised, Zamenhof's belief may yet survive.

The underestimate (9.2%) seems intuitively to be very low, since the quantity being underestimated is the ratio (number of contacts within groups to number of contacts within and between groups), and since Richardson's later studies included estimates of the ratio of geographical opportunities for civil fighting to opportunities for civil plus foreign fighting that range not from 9.2 percent to 56.7 percent but from 28.6 percent to 97.3 percent (SDQ, p. 312). These later estimates seem intuitively plausible for colingual pairs as well—more plausible certainly than the range 9.2 percent to 56.7 percent! It will be noted that in the later figures the low estimate is higher than the high-actual datum.

The low estimate of 9.2 percent is derived by assuming all belligerents to have a worldwide range of action without any geographic restriction whatever, for example, via universal airpower (SDQ, pp. 216–217). Such a worldwide range of action does not exist today and certainly did not exist from 1820 to 1952. When introduced in later inquiries into the number of nations on each side of a war (SDQ, pp. 266–269) and into geographical opportunities for fighting (SDQ, pp. 292–294), the assumption of a worldwide range of action is found to create such gross distortions that it is promptly abandoned. On the whole, therefore, it seems that the low estimate of 9.2 percent for colingual pairs is so low as to be theoretically indefensible; that a reasonable underestimate would be much higher; and that there is a fair chance that a reasonable underestimate would rehabilitate Zamenhof's belief. It is good in itself to improve on theories of the way the world is, so I hope to see an attempt to correct the underestimate made.

But we had better be aware that the practical consequences of such a rehabilitation are doubtful. There are no signs that a single world language will soon, or ever, emerge. If undirected linguistic evolution means a persisting Babel, should we espouse political action to take control of that evolution? Coerced assimilation to national languages has incited wars of resistance. Violent resistance to a force-fed world language could be expected; the force-feeding apparatus, in effect a world state, would first have to be established, perhaps also by violence. Would more lives be saved by the success of the experiment (if Zamenhof's belief proved correct) than would be lost in setting it up and carrying it out? The era is one of conflicting nationalisms; the proposed remedy is dangerous and of uncertain value.

English is emerging as a worldwide second language for study and travel, science and business. That development can hardly fulfill Zamenhof's intent or test his belief. Its effects, if any, should however be mildly pacific; to encourage it seems at worst harmless, and thus in accord with the ancient medical principle that the physician's first duty is to do no injury.

Religions and wars. Richardson's statistical investigation of the connection between religions and wars paralleled his treatment of languages and wars. For this purpose he regarded "any firmly held belief about the world in general"–ideology, philosophy of life, or *Weltanschauung*, theist, atheist or otherwise–as a religion (SDQ, pp. 22, 24, 233). Each belligerent pair was classified g if just before the war began the belligerents felt their religions to be the same, G if they were felt to be in contrast. In the coding, Richardson counted as adherents all populations attached by conviction or by tradition, ardent or nominal in belief. All Christian pairs and all Muslim pairs were coded as of the same religion (g), except when there was evidence of strong contrary feeling, for example, persecution, declared holy war against heretics, and the like (SDQ, pp. 233-234).

The religious labels that Richardson recognized for the purpose of this analysis included the standard groups–Christians, Muslims, Hindus, Sikhs, Buddhists. They included also the labels C-T-B for the old Chinese mixture of Confucianism, Taoism, and Buddhism; and S-B for the Japanese mixture of Shinto and Buddhism. Marxist Communism is treated as a religion in Richardson's meaning. The Taiping religion is considered unique, neither Christian nor C-T-B. Primitive or animist tribal religions are classified within a single category, apparently on the grounds that as there is only one "primitive vs. primitive" pair it will not distort the count to treat this as a coreligious rather than an interreligious fight (SDQ, pp. 234–238).

Richardson counted pairs of opposed belligerent groups of different versus the same religion, in wars of magnitudes 4-7, 1820-1929. As with languages, he had high and low actual counts. The result is that the ratio of coreligious to all analyzed pairs must be calculated as at least 93/(93+37+97) = 93/227(41.0%) and as at its greatest 128/(128+35+76) = 128/239 (53.6%). Correspondingly, interreligious pairs may be as few as 46.4 percent or as many as 59.0 percent.

By my count, magnitudes 3-7, 1820-1952, of 780 pairs, 345 are coded G, 172 are coded g, and the remaining 263 are unanalyzed. Of the pairs analyzed, 345/517(66.7%) are interreligious and only 172/517(33.3%) are coreligious.

Richardson drew no conclusions from his overall data but proceeded to break them down by religion, as he earlier broke down his languages-and-wars data. This is entirely appropriate. Still it may be worth noting that Richardson seldom found difference of language cited as a direct cause of war by his sources and was therefore compelled to resort to indirect means (degree of association) to investigate causation. (In my count, difference of language is coded in the background of 451 of 461 interlingual pairs, and as an irritant in only 10.) However, difference of religion was frequently cited in the sources as a cause of fighting: in 35 to 37 of 111 to 134 interreligious pairs (hence 27.6 to 31.5% of such pairs) in Richardson's analysis (SDQ, p. 237); and in 122 of 345 interreligious pairs (thus 35.4% of such pairs) in my count. We are therefore already able to conclude that "different beliefs about the world in general" have been causes of fighting in a significant percentage (122/780, or 15.6%) of all belligerent pairs.

Richardson's tally of coreligious and interreligious pairs by religion, most of which he left in a half-analyzed table, holds several surprises. Of 93 to 128 coreligious pairs, 87 to 119 were Christian: taking the lowest count for the Christian pairs and the highest for the rest, no fewer than 87/96 (90.6%) of all coreligious pairs were Christian. By comparison, 4 to 8 were Muslim, 1 was C-T-B, 1 B-S, 0 to 2 Hindu, 1 "primitive," none Buddhist. Did Christianity incite Christians to fight one another? Did other religions block coreligious fighting? If not, some alternative explanation for these data is needed.

Of the 111 to 134 interreligious pairs, 96 to 105 had a Christian member. Minimizing the number of pairs with a Christian member and maximizing the rest, we find that, at minimum, 96/(96+134-105) = 96/125(76.8%) of all interreligious pairs had a Christian member. And of 65 to 80 interreligious pairs, no fewer than 65/(65+134-80) = 65/119(54.6%) of all interreligious pairs, had a Muslim member. Well below these two religions in interreligious participation were the C-T-B adherents, with a member in 20 interreligious pairs, or at maximum no more than 20/111(18.0%).

Again, of 111 to 134 interreligious pairs, 56 to 63 were Christian versus Muslim. Taking the lowest count for these, and the highest for the rest, no fewer than 56/127(44.1%) of all interreligious pairs were Christian-Muslim. Furthermore, there were only 7 to 12 interreligious pairs that had neither a Christian nor a Muslim member—at most, 12/(12+111-7) = 12/116(10.3%).

This evidence leads one to think that both Christianity and Islam, or some associates of theirs, strongly incited their members to fight those of other religions—or incited those of other religions to fight them, which is not the same thing; and that the two faiths, or their associates, especially incited their members to fight one another. Indeed, this may be taken as partly proved, if the historians Richardson used as sources were correct in their descriptions of the thirty-five to thirty-seven pairs for which religious differences were cited as a cause, since at least 30/36(83.3%) of these had a Christian member, at least 19/35(54.3%) had a Muslim member, at least 16/36(44.4%) were Christian-Muslim pairs, and no more than 2/35(5.7%) had neither a Christian nor a Muslim member. For this group of pairs, having G in the third compartment, the causal relationship needs no further statistical demonstration, but only careful comparative-historical analysis.

If one counts "participations" in the 204 to 262 pairs analyzed by Richardson, so that each religion is assigned a score of one for each interreligious pair and a score of two for each coreligious pair in which it participates, the tally is as follows:

Christians	270 to 343
Muslims	73 to 96
C–T–B	22
Hindus	5 to 16
Bolsheviks	11
B–S	10 to 11
Buddhists	4 to 5
All others	13 to 20
	408 to 491

Even minimizing the high participation of Christians and Muslims, at least $270/(270+524-343) = 270/451(59.9\%)$ of all participations were by Christian belligerents, and at least $73/(73+524-96) = 73/501(14.6\%)$ of all participations were by Muslim belligerents. Even maximizing the low C–T–B participation, no more than $22/408(5.4\%)$ of all participations were by C–T–B belligerents.

Still fewer belligerents were provided by other religious groups. The fact that communism was a widespread "belief" during only about 13 years of the 130-year span here analyzed by Richardson should probably be taken into account in interpreting the "Bolshevik" participations, all "interreligious," which during those 13 years were about as numerous as Muslim participations during the same years.

In order to assess the significance of these relationships, Richardson attempted, as he did in examining languages and wars, to construct models which would clearly represent overestimates and underestimates of the null hypothesis (that there is no association between religion and war).

For examination of coreligious pairs, Richardson found satisfactory population estimates only for Christians, Muslims, and C–T–B adherents. There is a suggestion that Christians fought one another more than their population and opportunities to fight would lead one to expect; but one out of four estimates of actual Christian pairs is less than the high estimate of the number of such pairs had sameness of religion been irrelevant (SDQ, p. 239). Richardson dropped the question of whether Christianity incited war between its adherents at this point in the analysis. It seems excessively conservative to do so. Better data on religious populations over time would allow a comparison of Christian participations/all participations and Christian coreligious pairs/all coreligious pairs to be corrected for the time-means of all populations. Until that has been done, I would strongly incline to accept the interim conclusion that Christianity *or a correlate* (wealth? armament? organization?) incited war among its adherents, or markedly failed to obstruct it.

Using the same method, Richardson overestimated and underestimated the frequency of C–T–B coreligious wars, found that the highest estimate of their actual frequency was far below the underestimate of their theoretically expected frequency, and concluded that "the C–T–B religion of China stands out conspicuously as being either itself a pacifier, or else associated with one" (SDQ, p. 239). (If acceptable population data were available, the same conclusion might well hold for Hinduism and Buddhism.)

There is a certain irony about this conclusion of Richardson's, as there is in his search for further explanation and his ultimate conclusion that "it seems probable that the comparative peaceableness of China, prior to A.D. 1911, was the result of instruction, and in particular of Confucian instruction [in pacifist ethics]. If China could thus be made peaceable, why not the whole world?" (SDQ, pp. 241–242). If Confucianism pacified China, it may also have made the Chinese less able to resist foreign attack or to repel attempts to reinstruct them by force. After 1949, Chinese Communists sought to uproot Confucian remnants, and ceased to espouse pacifist ethics. The durability of a pacific culture is, at least, uncertain. It might be interesting even so to consider prospects for resurrecting the old Chinese C–T–B ethos, deliberately revising it in the light of recent experience and social-scientific findings. Is it possible consciously to construct a pacific belief-system intended not only to compete successfully in a world of militant ideologies but also to overcome deliberate repression of the kind that the C–T–B ethos has apparently been able to endure but not to overcome? I cannot tell; but Richardson's work seems to me to suggest that the effort would be worth making, on the ground that if it were ever to take root such a belief system could prove both a durable and an effective means of restraining violence.

Richardson next turned to interreligious pairs. Employing a similar method to over- and underestimate the probability of a war between peoples professing different named religions on the null-hypothesis assumption that religion neither excites nor restrains the quarrel, Richardson concluded, not surprisingly, that "there were more wars between Christians and Muslims than would be expected from their populations, if religious differences had not tended to instigate quarrels between them" (SDQ, p. 245).

Richardson did not examine the question of whether adherents of these two religions took part in more external quarrels than their numbers would have led us to expect. For reasons already given, I am inclined to say that we ought to assume that they did, and seek an explanation.

Cultural militance and cultural disarmament.   One candidate explanation is a "just-war" hypothesis. The crusade, Armageddon, the jihad, more recently the revolutionary war, the war of liberation: these are moral entities in some

Christian or Muslim (or Marxist) historic or contemporary moral teachings. We may abstract from these various entities a more general just-war doctrine, as follows. "There are times when it is right to fight: it is right to resist and overthrow evil or unbelief or reaction; it is right to establish and defend the rule of right and the good society on earth." Is the presence of such a doctrine in the religious background of a culture, and even in the religious *past* of a secularized culture, associated with the tendency of public discussion to employ a rhetoric implicit in which is the assumption that by joining together and struggling against wrong we can establish or maintain the good society by force? Are there persistent, culturally embedded styles of discourse that predispose their users to believe that war can make sense, that some wars at any rate can be just, reasonable, and progressive? And could that predisposition work broadly to encourage or permit fighting in general, rather than narrowly and in particular instances? It seems possible. If so, we are confronted by the question of whether cultural disarmament is feasible. The fate of the Confucian ethos in China poses the question of whether a condition of cultural disarmament is durable under ordinary stresses of social change. But is general pacification conceivable without cultural disarmament?

Any inquiry into the connection between religions and wars is bound to touch on very sensitive issues of group pride, shame, and guilt. Nonetheless Richardson's conclusions and his data suggest that further probing of this sore topic is intellectually justifiable. More explicit criteria for coding, and intercoder reliability exploration, would be particularly worthwhile, since any findings on the subject that in any way deviate from a null hypothesis are bound to be harshly assailed on methodological grounds (among others). Extensive and deep comparative historical explorations of the relationship of just-war and general pacifist doctrines to public rhetoric and political decisions will be required if the explanatory hypotheses presented above are to be taken seriously enough to be tested. We may ponder whether cultural disarmament is necessary, whether it is possible, whether it is feasible and desirable, and whether it could last.

My inclination to search for economic causes leads me to speculate that an indirect approach may accomplish "cultural disarmament." Analysts of the Spanish national culture have been quick to attribute it to Spain's failure to undergo an industrial revolution, the poverty of the countryside, the availability of comfort only to a few. During the years of Richardson's study, Spanish and Spanish-American societies were among the most extreme in the distance that separated the impoverished many from the wealthy few. Conceivably, Spanish cultural militance actually belongs to a society never collectively prosperous, in which there is no faith that collective prosperity can exist, and in which self-concern, uncooperativeness, and pessimism all reflect objective economic conditions in which cooperation promises little gain while self-seeking offers a palpable chance to enter the privileged class.

Given such a set of facts and beliefs, militance needs no spiritual basis; it is rational.

The pacificity of the old Chinese culture, long remarked by Chinese and Westerners, Richardson attributed to Confucian instruction. But Confucius thought it proper to enrich the people before attempting to give them moral instruction (*Sayings* XIII.7). It is even more evident that the Confucianism successfully propagated by Mencius is not simply a moral teaching; it assumes that moral behavior has a material, environmental, economic basis. Mencius argued that collective prosperity was possible; that government drew its right to rule from the prosperity of the people (not their consent); and that the fundamental duty of the state, which it could and must fulfill, was to increase production, increase the community's wealth, and distribute that wealth so that all had a good and steady livelihood. To assist the state in doing its duty, Mencius tried to work out fundamental principles of economic planning. To encourage the state to do its duty, Mencius authorized the use of force to eliminate incompetent governments that prevented collective prosperity and to install competent and dutiful rulers. (*Mencius* IA, VIIA). The long history of peace and war in China seems to bear Mencius out: when Chinese governments have been notably capable and the people prosperous, Chinese history has been relatively tranquil; when governments have been inept, the people's livelihood has been insufficient, and internal violence has become intense (Wright 1965, p. 594, Reischauer and Fairbank 1958, pp. 117-118). Perhaps the peaceful periods of China's history combined economic conditions and economic doctrines which together made fighting seem irrational and become improbable.

Recollecting finally that the common theme of just-war doctrines is that it is right to fight, to overthrow the unholy by force, and by force to set up the rule of faith and the good society on earth, one must observe that, since Richardson wrote, the most vigorously advancing militant faith and culture seems to be that of Marxism-Leninism, whose "good society" has a notably materialistic ethos and structure, and whose gospel contends that collective prosperity cannot be achieved without a drastic, and probably violent, transformation of most existing political and economic institutions.

I would conjecture that the influence of militant cultures in the current international system would be minimized if people generally, and correctly, believed: (1) that collective prosperity (in this case worldwide) is possible, *and* (2) that the existing world order is actually creating it as quickly as is practicable.

A noticeable rapidly rising standard of living around the globe would be the only satisfactory evidence for both these propositions. Every stagnation, delay, and setback can be used to argue *either* that collective prosperity is impossible (so one must struggle to deprive another of his share, if one is to flourish), *or* that the established order is too inept or too selfish or too corrupt to deliver the goods, in which case, in Mao Tse-tung's eminently Confucian words, "It is right to rebel."

In our time, therefore, cultural disarmament seems extremely unlikely outside a social and political order that meets economic demands via economic growth; but not totally unlikely within one that does.

Heterogeneity and wars. Richardson's explorations of the connections between languages and wars, and between religions and wars, raise an issue which Richardson did not follow up: is there any pattern that relates group differences *in general* to warfare?

Richardson used many symbols that indicate ethnocultural contrasts or similarities between the members of a belligerent pair. The eight such symbols most frequently set were i (common language), I (different languages), g (common religion), G (different religions), c ("similar bodily characteristics," i.e., same "race"), C (different "races"), d (similar customs as to dress), and D (remarkably different customary clothing).

By my count, the symbols indicating a contrast occur more frequently than those indicating the corresponding similarity. For 780 pairs, magnitudes 3–7, 1820–1952:

> I appears in 461 (59.1%)
> i appears in 179 (22.9%)
> G appears in 345 (44.2%)
> g appears in 172 (22.1%)
> D appears in 137 (17.6%)
> d appears in 53 (6.8%)
> C appears in 125 (16.0%)
> c appears in 91 (11.7%)

The large proportion of pairs uncoded as between G and g, D and d, C and c, makes it impossible to draw any conclusions from this information, except that, where coding was possible, any symbol for heterogeneity appeared more often in the descriptions of belligerent pairs than did the matching symbol for homogeneity. Heterogeneity clearly predominated in I versus i, where 82.1 percent of all pairs were coded.

What is also lacking for D-d and C-c, and for heterogeneity overall, is the information needed to complete a two by two table relating heterogeneity/homogeneity to fighting/not fighting. We must have the numbers (i.e., the time-means) of pairs of heterogeneous versus homogeneous social groups who did *not* fight. Richardson did supply under- and overestimates of nonfighting pairs for I-i and G-g. Making such estimates for C-c should be possible with the assistance of ethnographic and ethnodemographic data; and Richardson's paper on "The Problem of Contiguity" (1961) might be helpful in the endeavor. It is possible, though less likely, that the same might be done for D-d, and for other specific cultural features as well.

Unsatisfactory as the data may be, there are patterns therein that are suggestive. 507/780 (65.0%) of pairs who fought had no coding for homogeneity (neither c nor d nor g nor i) while only 273/780 (35.0%) had some such coding. Only 23/780 (2.9%) of pairs who fought had all four c, d, g, i. The number of fighting pairs shrank as the number of homogeneity symbols grew: 507/780 (65.0%) with none of c, d, g, i; 139/780 (17.8%) with one; 69/780 (8.8%) with two; 42/780 (5.4%) with three; and 23/780 (2.9%) with four.

The data on heterogeneity are also suggestive, but less clearly so. 243/780, or only 31.2 percent of pairs who fought, had no coding for heterogeneity (neither C nor D nor G nor I), while 537/780 (68.8%) had one heterogeneity coding or more, and 94/780 (12.1%) had all four. The interpretation of the rest of the distribution for C, D, G, I is less patent.

Pairs with *none* of C, D, G, I:	243 (31.2%)
one	233 (29.9%)
two	171 (21.9%)
three	39 (5.0%)
all four of C, D, G, I	94 (12.1%)

To what degree is this distribution attributable to missing data? The columns of table 26 show the number of "homogeneity symbols" (c, d, g, and/or i) assigned to a given pair of belligerents. The rows show the number

TABLE 26

INCIDENCE OF c, d, g, i VERSUS INCIDENCE OF C,D,G,I IN 780 PAIRS

No. of heterogeneity symbols (C, D, G, I) \ No. of homogeneity symbols (c, d, g, i)	0	1	2	3	4	Total
0	88	43	60	29	23	243
1	129	83	8	13	0	233
2	159	11	1	0	0	171
3	37	2	0	0	0	39
4	94	0	0	0	0	94
Total	507	139	69	42	23	780

of "heterogeneity symbols" (C, D, G, and/or I) assigned to a given pair. The number in each cell is the count of the number of pairs with the column-number of homogeneity symbols and the row-number of heterogeneity symbols. Thus eighty-eight pairs were completely unanalyzed, receiving none of c, d, g, i, C, D, G, or I; eighty-three received one from c, d, g, i, and one from C, D, G, I; thirteen received three from c, d, g, i and one from C, D, G, I; and so on. As no pair can be assigned more than four of the eight symbols without contradiction, ten cells of the table are empty.

Arranging the data in this way permits us to make some use of those many pairs concerning which our information is incomplete, by counting pairs for which the amount of information is the same and comparing the counts. For instance, one item of homogeneity/heterogeneity information is known for 172 of the pairs: in 129/172 (75%) of those pairs that item is a coding for heterogeneity, in 43/172 (25%) of the pairs for homogeneity.

Two items of homogeneity/heterogeneity information are known for 302 of the pairs: in 159/302 (52.6%) both are codings for heterogeneity; in 83/302 (27.5%) one is a heterogeneity symbol and one a homogeneity symbol; in 60/302 (19.9%) both are homogeneity codings.

A similar relationship holds only partially for the three-item and four-item levels. At the extremes, more pairs (thirty-seven) have three heterogeneity symbols than have three homogeneity codings (twenty-nine), and more (ninety-four) have four heterogeneity codings than have four homogeneity codings (twenty-three); but more are all homogeneous than are partly homogeneous and partly heterogeneous. The last point is not evidently attributable to missing data, since it occurs at the four-item level for which information is complete, and I have no explanation to offer for it.

All features of the table except this last are consonant with the general hypothesis implied in Richardson's assignment of an expected valency of amity to c, d, g, i, and of hostility to C, D, G, I: ethnocultural contrast between two social groups is an irritant, and the more the contrast the greater the irritation; ethnocultural similarity is on the contrary a pacifier. The discrepancy might be explained if wholly homogeneous groups had so very many more contacts with one another (and therefore opportunities for fighting) than the partially heterogeneous groups that the higher number of fights between homogeneous pairs is attributable more to contact than to any irritation created by similarity.

The discrepancy either vanishes or is intensified depending upon how one treats the missing data. On the assumption least favorable to Richardson's implicit hypothesis, all missing symbols are assumed to be symbols of homogeneity, and the distribution of pairs from most heterogeneous to least heterogeneous is the puzzling distribution for C, D, G, I; 94–39–171–233–243. On the assumption most favorable to the hypothesis, all missing symbols are assumed to be symbols of heterogeneity, and the distribution of pairs from most heterogeneous to least heterogeneous is the less puzzling distribution of c, d, g, i, 507–139–69–42–23.

It is conceivable that a more thorough inquiry into ethnocultural similarities and differences between belligerents will support a fairly straightforward heterogeneity → irritation → fighting hypothesis; or a more complex heterogeneity-or-contiguity → irritation → fighting hypothesis; or neither of these, but an alternate hypothesis not now self-evident; or even the null hypothesis denying any connection between heterogeneity and fighting. The latter seems least likely, since the proportion of the total geographic opportunities to fight which any set of equally homogeneous groups possesses almost certainly will be found to vary directly and strongly with the homogeneity of the set. At the moment therefore we can probably feel safe in assuming that, other things being equal, the propensity of any pair of groups to fight varies directly with the degree of heterogeneity of the pair, that is, the number of ethnocultural contrasts between its member groups.

Homogeneity and peace. If ethnocultural heterogeneity does indeed irritate, and if deliberate global ethnocultural homogenization were a feasible policy, then that policy would also constitute a peace strategy. Richardson would doubtless concur: on anecdotal grounds he argued (1950b) that international intermarriage may have a pacifying effect for the intermarried groups, therefore deserved further research, and might prove to warrant political encouragement.

Homogenization has in the past often been a conqueror's policy, imposed by force or threat of force. The conqueror desecrates or reconsecrates sanctuaries, closes or opens schools, suppresses or subsidizes the dissemination of scriptures, liquidates or institutes priestly and teaching cadres, in order to change the religion, language, and culture of the conquered. The conquering soldiers, nobles, landlords, or owners mestisize the conquered, by marriage, rape, prostitution, and concubinage. Forced assimilation implies war as a precondition; whether in fact it pacifies more than it irritates remains to be researched. It seems no fit strategy for world peacemaking.

There do exist, however, significant voluntary and homogenizing tendencies. Interracial, international, and interreligious marriages do occur to a politically sensitive and significant degree when exogamy is not forbidden. Immigrant families often willingly change languages and cultures over three or four generations; many students, uncoerced, seek facility in some foreign language, usually a national, international, or world language. Print, radio, cinematic, audio-recorded and video-broadcast media increasingly diffuse cultural symbols and materials worldwide, with the consent, often enthusiastic, of their audiences.

Could voluntary homogenization be encouraged by any deliberate political means? I conjecture that a diplomatic strategy of promoting "human rights" would, if successful, have a net homogenizing effect, since state interference

with individual choice probably favors endogamy, segregation, and parochial-
ism more often than it coerces exogamy, integration, or cosmopolitan norms.

Another, more circuitous route to a unified world society may go by
way of modernization and development. These slogans are affirmed by and
indeed seem to guide some of the policies of most national governments
throughout the world. But successful modernization may have some unin-
tended consequences.

As a society develops or modernizes one expects to see it grow more
densely populated, more urban, more commercial and industrial, more
advanced and efficient technically, more productive and wealthier per capita
and absolutely, more literate and better read, less sectionalist, more ideologically perfused and enculturated, socially more complex and specialized,
more integrated, centralized, and bureaucratic. There will be an increase in
affective neutrality (impersonality, "objectivity," avoidance of emotion,
viewing at a distance, renouncing immediate self-gratification), collectivity-
orientation (taking into account the values and interests of a larger social
unit in making decisions), universalism (the tendency to judge in accordance
with generalized standards), performance orientation (judging others by what
they do rather than by who they are), functional specificity (explicit delimi-
tation and definition of the rights and obligations of others), and "rationality" (having and citing as reasons for doing a thing some empirical idea of
cause and effect relationships).[1]

Suppose this pattern were to dominate a modernized, developed world.
What then? That world need not be more homogeneous in language, religion,
or race; but it would be profoundly more homogeneous in cultural style.
The neutrality of that cultural style would distance individuals from identification with their ethnic groups; its collectivity-orientation would suggest
identification with the more inclusive collectivity (humanism) rather than
with national or communal egoism; its performance orientation would dis-
courage judging others by their ethnic attributes; its functional specificity
would impede the giving of total life-and-death allegiance to any communal
entity. Its universalism would tend to secularize competing religions by finding compatible (and discarding incompatible) norms and "facts" and in the
process converting theodicies to ethics and eschatologies to history; its
rationalism would tend to secularize by preserving empirical and displacing
miraculous theories of causation, and in the process converting mystery to
science.

Such a world may slowly be emerging. It is possible—I would agree with

---

[1] Most of these items are commonplaces among theorists of modernization. See
Banks and Textor (1963), Finished Characteristics 85–86, for a synchronic summary of
many of these relationships. For theoretical statements see Parsons and Shils (1951
Part 2), Modelski (1961), Levy (1966). The emphasis on social integration is Parsons'
(1966, p. 22–25).

those who assert it as a fact[2] —that the evolution of the world economy and world society is already creating and enlarging managerial, professional, technical, scientific, and clerical occupations, classes, and characters throughout the ecumene. Empirical, rational, worldly, humanistic, pragmatic, manipulative, utilitarian, contractual, epicurean, relativistic, scientistic, sensate norms are diffusing everywhere: Maoism, Khomeinism, and hip movements have represented reactions of protest which this tide meets and absorbs. As aristocrats, landowners and clergy are recruited to managerial, bureaucratic, and professional elites, and former peasants and proletarians become property-owning technicians and managers, there tends to be created an all-embracing, globally mobile, cosmopolitan world bourgeoisie that succeeds, engulfs, and abolishes all other classes. This holds for Marxist and Islamic countries that deny or resist it, as well as for those ex-Christian and ex-Confucian countries that especially hasten and affirm it.

It is possible that this class has a characteristic class culture more pacific than that of its predecessors and rivals, as Modelski (1961) suggested and Wright (1965, p. 1162) averred. If so, to accelerate and defend development and modernization would indeed be a strategy of ethnocultural as well as economic pacification. The meta-Faustian bargain involved has already been described: Modernization, before ever it pacifies, irritates and inflames discord.

Summary.   The data patterns invite the hypothesis that ethnocultural heterogeneity in general, and linguistic or religious heterogeneity in particular, is or is associated with an irritant. The character of the homogeneous culture is, however, of great importance. The Confucian-Taoist-Buddhist culture that seemed the most promising candidate for a world-pacifying religion fared poorly in the twentieth century. Extreme practical difficulties would stand in the way of deliberate social pacification by ethnocultural engineering; but economic growth, development, and modernization may help. In any case, the data and theory relating ethnocultural difference and character to war are far from complete and satisfactory. The subject is worth further study, on Richardsonian and comparative-historical lines.

[2] See for instance Kahn and Bruce-Briggs (1972).

10
Miscellaneous Factors

Militant ideology. Richardson coded G (religious or ideological contrast) as a background feature in 223/780 (28.6%) of pairs, but as an actual irritant in 122/780 (15.6%). In his analysis of G, Richardson grouped G-irritant with G-background pairs and examined only the degree to which an irritant effect could be statistically inferred from the frequency with which G occurred. Thus "no use whatever is made of [the historians'] assertions as to whether the religious difference was ... an active cause of quarrel" (SDQ, p. 245). Such a treatment fails to take advantage of some potentially useful information, not only in the count for G but also in the irritant count for L and S (differing beliefs concerning the degree of personal liberty to be allowed during peace, L; and civil power for the church, S). By my count, G and/or L and/or S appear as irritants in 158/780 (20.3%) of all pairs, magnitudes 3-7, 1820-1952.

The frequency with which these symbols occur suggests that some attempt at explanation is desirable. To interpret their meaning requires an inspection of the pairs by which the symbols are set. When I inspected those pairs, an obvious but nonquantitative and nonoperational hypothesis suggested itself, not only as a means of interpreting G, L, and S as irritants but also for the interpretation of other symbols—C, D, I, eta, and sometimes rho and T—when they are set as irritants.[1] It is as follows.

[1] They are set as irritants in the following fractions of all 780 pairs:
   C, different race—11/780;
   D, different dress—8/780;
   I, different language—10/780;
   eta, one sympathized with the subjects of the other—41/780;
   rho, resistance to actual or attempted domination—88/780;
   T, one desired territory occupied by the other—173/780.

Very frequently some abstract moral-political idea helped to bring on the fighting. Most often that element was nationalism or racism, in the form of a claim that a certain ethnocultural group (defined by language, race, and/or religion) had a right or a destiny

- to be independent of foreign rule
- to be united in a single state
- to take over and annex certain lands, or
- to rule over or massacre some other ethnic group.

I estimate that a nationalist or racist claim was active in about a quarter of the 315 cases. In approximately another quarter of the cases there was some other abstract idea or system of ideas that incited fighting: sometimes a direct claim for freedom, superiority, purity, or power for a particular world view or religion; sometimes a more limited claim to have a superior system for organizing the state and ordering political life. All told, some ideology, some scheme of ideas about how social matters should be run, by whom and for whom, incited or justified violence in about half the cases, and the ideologies that did so could therefore fairly be termed "militant."

Since this conclusion represents an opinion (mine) about an opinion (Richardson's) about opinions (the historians') about opinions (of the belligerents), methodological purists can safely relegate it to the realm of the yet-to-be-substantiated and the exceedingly-difficult-to-substantiate. Since the opinions in question reflect conventional wisdom, commonplace and established, traditionalists valuing a commonsense approach to history will assert that we may safely take them for granted and proceed to raise the truly interesting questions for policy: Can there be "ideological disarmament"? Under what circumstances? At what cost? By what means? With what likely effect? And how can an "ideologically disarmed" world stay disarmed?

As with the implicit militance of cultures, so with the explicit militance of ideologies am I minded to search for economic remedies. Historically militant ideologies are sometimes considered to have been sated by victory, inhibited by defeat, exhausted by protracted struggle, or diverted by material affluence. The fourth of these calmatives, which need not involve fighting, is especially attractive in an era when the strongest ideological appeal is this-worldly. The bitterest and most militant versions of contemporary nationalism and Marxism rest on accusations that poor classes and nations are poor because of exploitation by the rich; on demands for prosperity or economic betterment; and on the unstated assumption that what one gains the other must lose, so that coercive force or coercive threats will be required. But if economic growth can be sustained, economic concessions need not involve actual losses to the appeasers. High levels of affluence and high rates of economic growth are the social preconditions for continued diversion of national, class, and communal militance by continuing but essentially painless concessions. Therefore, even to assemble persuasive evidence that worldwide affluence, worldwide rapid growth, and economic redistribution without deprivation *could* exist, would be useful peace research and an important contribution to ideological disarmament.

Arms races. Many people believe that arms races commonly cause wars; Richardson's name has been associated with this theory. Indeed, a portion of the historical data collected in *Statistics of Deadly Quarrels* is cited in its companion volume, *Arms and Insecurity*, which contains mathematical models of arms races. The editors of *Arms and Insecurity*, N. Rashevsky and Ernesto Trucco, declare in their preface: "As Richardson correctly points out, most wars, at least recently, have been preceded by runaway arms races" (Richardson, 1960*a*, p. vi). A section of that volume is indeed titled "Have most wars been preceded by arms races?" Richardson's answer to that question reads, "Historians mention arms races only for 10 out of 84 wars that ended between 1820 and 1929" (1960*a*, p. 70. These 84 wars were presumably those at magnitudes 4-7 as tallied between 1948 and 1953, cf. SDQ, p. 31). My count of Richardson's 315 cases, magnitudes 3-7, ended 1820-1952, finds the arms-race symbol, omega (unusual preparations for war), set in 13/315 (4.1%) of cases; ten of the thirteen wars so marked began in the nineteenth century. One may therefore say that Richardson's data do *not* show that most wars have been preceded by "runaway arms races"; nor do they show that most recent wars have been preceded by arms races. Nor did Richardson make either assertion. On the contrary, he concluded that "the evidence, as far as it goes, is that only a minority of wars have been preceded by arms races" (1960*a*, p. 74).

Students of arms races may find the 26/780 pairs (3.3%) and 13/315 cases coded omega suitable for comparative study in depth. It may prove of some interest that twenty-two of the twenty-six pairs with omega were also coded I (different languages), while twelve were coded M (prior war between the two); or that eleven of the pairs with omega appear in the two world wars, but none in cases at the third magnitude.

Symbols infrequently set. Several other code symbols resemble omega in being assigned infrequently, yet often enough to make them useful for retrieving cases suited to comparative study of some interesting but apparently secondary aspect of the causation of war.

For instance, the symbol gamma (a third party wished the two to fight) appears in 47/780 (6.0%) of pairs and 38/315 (12.1%) of cases, always as an irritant. Most often gamma indicates the use of foreign mercenaries or auxiliaries; sometimes it denotes a firing up of the spirits or a filling up of the coffers of groups who have reason to fight on their own. The use of the symbol gamma will make it easier for those wishing to do a comparative case study of the use of mercenaries and auxiliaries or of what might be called provocation or proxy wars to retrieve appropriate cases.

The same observation holds for the 28/780 pairs (3.6%) and 23/315 cases (7.3%) in which N (personal resentment of a leader) appears as an irritant. (Here, however, I am bound to say that I believe Richardson may have substantially undercoded N, which, for instance, appears nowhere in the World War matrices nor in the matrix for the Mexican Revolution 1910–1920.) Similarly deserving of comparative study, as perhaps constituting special cases of some kind, would be the 44/780 pairs (5.6%) marked by the letter a as having traded before they fought, and the 51/780 pairs (6.5%) marked by the Greek letter mu as having intermingled on the same territory until the time the conflict began.

The analytical index prepared by John Askling (SDQ, p. 329-373) offers one convenient way for retrieving most of the chosen set of cases, since it contains all the coding symbols, their definitions and, as subheads to each definition, a list of cases in which the symbol is set. (Unfortunately the index listing of cases is not always quite complete.)

Political regimes. It is a vexing question whether certain types of political regime, or certain relations between such types, inhibit or provoke fighting. Richardson's data do not now help ask or answer that question: Richardson did not code for regime type. The lower-case symbol l, which indicates that two groups who fought enjoyed a similar degree of personal liberty, is Richardson's only indicator having to do with regime type; it is one of several symbols that Richardson defined but never used. (The cognate symbol L indicates differing ideologies rather than differing regimes.) In view of Terrell's finding (1977, p. 100) that for seventy-five countries, 1955-1960, there was some correlation ($r = 0.21$, $p < 0.05$) of a country's "war behavior" with the degree to which its regime differed from its neighbors' in "openness,"[2] and Jencks' assertion (1973, p. 12) that "no democratic Great Power has gone to war with another in this century," the topic is worth exploring.

Power parity and disparity. Though Richardson's data manifestly implicate great powers and war, they do not measure, and he did not deal with, the power relationship between belligerents as itself a potential irritant or pacifier. Claude (1962, pp. 56-62) presented an argument that "equilibrium is, on the whole, a situation favorable to the maintenance of peace." On the contrary, Organski (1958, pp. 293, 325) has asserted that a "preponderance of power on one side . . . increases the chances for peace . . . world peace has coincided with periods of unchallenged supremacy of power while the periods of approximate balance have been the periods of war." In thirty one-on-one interstate wars, 1816-1965, Garnham (1976*a*) has compared, for each war,

[2] Legitimacy, diffusion of power, and elite competition, all scored using data from Banks and Textor (1963); see Terrell (1977, pp. 95-96).

rank differences of the belligerent pair on various possible power indices (area, population, fuel consumption, steel production) with those of all pairs of states in the international system during the year of the war. His findings somewhat support a "parity → war, preponderance → peace" hypothesis. For sixteen "lethal conflicts," involving one death or more, between contiguous nation-states 1969–1973, Garnham (1976b) collected data on assorted power indices (area, population, gross national product, electrical power generation, military manpower, defense expenditures) for the twenty-four combatant states and their twenty-six noncombatant neighbors and compared the power parity on these indices of the sixteen lethal-violence dyads with the sixty-two nonlethal-violence dyads. He concluded that the data corroborate a "parity → war" hypothesis for contiguous states: If contiguous nation-states are of approximately equal power, lethal conflict is more probable between them than if they are of disparate power. Weede (1976) found that, among forty-one pairs of contiguous Asian nations during 1950–1969, war was much less frequent in the presence of overwhelming (ten-to-one) GNP or defense-expenditure preponderance then in the absence of overwhelming preponderance. (Minor insurgencies were less strongly inhibited than were interstate wars with battle deaths of 1,000 or more.)

Rosen (1972) examined forty international wars, 1815–1945, from the Singer-Small list. Of thirty-nine cases in which one party had more government revenue, it won in thirty-one (79%); of forty cases where one party suffered a lower population-loss rate, it won in thirty (75%); of thirty-one cases in which one party had both more government revenue and a lower loss-of-life rate, it won in twenty-six (84%). In eight cases where one party had more revenue but the other had the lower population-loss rate, the richer won in five (63%). Thus: "a party with either more revenue or a lower population-loss rate is favored to win by about 3 or 4 to 1. A party favored in both respects gets odds of almost 5 to 1" (1972, pp. 181–182).

Singer and Small themselves note (1972, p. 367) that initiators won thirty-four of forty-eight interstate wars. These findings would be consistent with a theory that belligerents occasionally go to war to prove, exploit, or enlarge a *slight* preponderance of strength. (If the preponderance were great, the stronger, and the initiator, should win more often.)

The question of the relationship of power parity and disparity to fighting is one that could be examined by an inquiry along Richardson's lines. Symbols for approximate parity and marked disparity would have to be defined and set. Richardson did not do so;[3] successors may be able to fill this lack.

Similarity, equality, connectedness, and cooperation. Certain symbols,

[3] The code symbol phi (one group *felt* itself stronger) could have measured perceived inequality and helped to test Blainey's assertion (1973, p. 246) that "wars usually begin when two nations disagree on their relative strength." But the symbol phi makes only eight appearances.

already in part analyzed above, often appear in the cases, but never as irritants. These symbols are a (the two groups traded, 44/780 of pairs), c (similar bodily characteristics, 91/780), d (similar customs as to dress, 53/780), g (similar religions or philosophies of life, 172/780), i (common mother tongue, 179/780), m (common government, 237/780), and lambda (ex-allies, 95/780). Most of these conditions seem, on evidence discussed elsewhere, to make for amity rather than enmity.

If we consider whether other social conditions, when cited, are mostly cited as present or as irritants, we may note that either mu (intermingling) or xi (interbreeding) appears in fifty-one pairs, only twice as an irritant; rho (domination) appears in ninety-four pairs, eighty-eight times as an irritant; E (inequality in wealth), sigma (a distinct entrepreneurial group), or theta (creditor-debtor) appear in seventy-five pairs, fifty-nine times as an irritant; F (contrasting marriage customs), O (incompatible legal systems), B (ban on intermarriage), H (ban on immigration), or K (mutual ignorance) appear in twenty-nine pairs, on twenty-two occasions as an irritant.

These various facts are collectively consistent with the general theory that *similarity, equality, and cooperation on the whole make for amity rather than enmity*. We must say "on the whole" because certain shared philosophies of life, cultures, and common governments seem not to have had this pacifying effect; and because complete nonintercourse and mutual isolation pacify even more effectively than cooperation.

H. G. Wells envisioned a sweeping transformation of the world system: a federal, constitutional, democratic world state; worldwide free trade, free migration, and economic development to universal prosperity; worldwide education in one cosmopolitan civic doctrine, libertarian-socialist, and humanistic rather than nationalistic; a world nation undivided in language, religion, or culture. This was Wells's vision of what was necessary and sufficient for world peace. He vacillated on how to accomplish this transformation (Wells 1930, pp. 15-31; 1939, pp. 40-43; 1940, pp. 11-12; 1942, pp. 188-192). Richardson's data seem consistent with Wells' belief that his utopian society, if constructed, would be unusually peaceable, but they provide no particular guidance on how to construct it. As elsewhere, I speculate that economic development is the key lever.

Summary. That "militant ideology" is a cause of war, and "ideological disarmament" accordingly a peace strategy, may reasonably be inferred from the frequent employment of certain code symbols. Many other symbols, such as those marking arms races, apply to so few cases that they are best used as search devices for comparative-historical analyses. Some topics, such as the relations between regime type or power balance and war, though not examined by Richardson, invite study using his approach. There is some basis for the general proposition that similarity, equality, connectedness, and cooperation on balance tend to pacify, and hence for a sweeping world-political reformism in the Wellsian manner.

11

A General Reappraisal

The "scientific" claims of Richardson's work. To what degree does Richardson's work meet the standards of scientific method or of scientistic ideology?

There are some shortcomings. The most important ones are virtually inescapable, and Richardson's study shares them with much political research animated by the scientistic spirit. In Richardson's scrutiny of the world's wars over a period of more than a century, there was no controlled or uncontrolled experimentation, no experimental intervention or manipulation whatever—nor could there be. There was no replication, no examination of a randomly chosen second "sample" from the same "population"—nor could there be. There was a minimum of direct observation by the researcher: Richardson "observed" World War I with an ambulance convoy and World War II as a retired citizen of one of the belligerents. He interviewed ten persons who had been at the scenes of several foreign quarrels, but his chief source was neither firsthand nor secondhand observation. He relied mainly on summaries written by historians, who had studied monographs written by other historians, who had searched and read and interpreted the reports and letters and memoirs of participants.

Whatever relationships are found in data that consist mostly of *very* indirect observations, without the possibility of controlled or uncontrolled experimentation, must always seem somewhat lame. No claim to inherent "scientific" superiority can properly be made on behalf even of the most striking and least ambiguous associations discovered in such data. Our belief in findings so insecurely based cannot be coerced or compelled. We are justified in weighing such findings against our intuitive or conventional or commonsense beliefs, and accepting—provisionally—only those findings that do not contravene our earlier beliefs but are consistent with them, *plus* those findings that *do* contravene our beliefs, but which are, however weak the case for them, better grounded than those beliefs themselves.

Richardson claimed no more. In *Arms and Insecurity* he disavowed "dogmatic certainty"; declared that he got his hypotheses by "intuition" and "luck" as well as by "laborious search"; conceded that it would be as reasonable to take the opinions of, say, psychoanalysts as of historians to be summarized, mathematized, and described or tested; admitted that the same data were likely to be consistent with different hypotheses or, at best, in rather better agreement with one than with another; and stated that his research objective was to compare hypotheses with observations and "to form an opinion" (1960*a*, pp. 145, 215, 231, 243). Even the sternest traditionalist ought to be willing to concede the merit of this modest claim.

Shortcomings that are inescapable simply have to be recognized and accepted. There are however some ways in which a study resting inevitably upon opinions can be enhanced, by attending to the number and quality of the opinions in question. The research represented by *Statistics of Deadly Quarrels* could be rendered more widely acceptable, and eventually no doubt more influential, by follow-up work intended to revise and improve most major features of the study. These features include: the list of prewar "social situations" and the coding scheme, the case list, the data sources, the codings of cases, the analysis of the data, and the interpretation of the analysis.

The "situation" list and code.   The fifty-nine defined "situations," a very large fraction of them never or hardly ever applied to a case, were selected and defined by Richardson alone from his inspection of the historical literature. It would be useful to have the code scheme revised in light of the substantial theoretical, prescriptive, and polemical literature on the topic of war, filled as that is with "beliefs" popular and unpopular that "ought to be tested by statistics" (SDQ, p. ii). As a preliminary to systematic overhaul, a number of particularly desirable revisions may be noted.

1. The ample literature on biography, personality, and the psychology of political leaders would argue for the inclusion of a code symbol intended to mark cases where personality was salient, cases in which one or a few political leaders had a notable influence on the decisions of one of the belligerent groups. The frequent, or the infrequent, appearance of such a symbol could prove informative to the designers of peace research and peace schemes.

2. Richardson's attention to economic factors would be sufficient if economic theories of war's origins were less important features of contemporary popular belief and political ideology. As such theories remain current, a reconsideration of the situation list in their light is in order. The type of economic regime and/or class basis

of each participant group would be appropriate new "situations"; likewise the condition of population and technological growth (Choucri and North, 1975) of the belligerents.

3. The now considerable literature of comparative politics could be drawn on to develop an appropriate political status typology for participants; from that of international politics, a power-status typology could be extracted.

4. The importance of contiguity and distance should be reflected in a few symbols designed to supplement mu (intermingling) by indicating, for example, a common boundary, a sea frontier, landlocked or coastal status, distance between capitals, and so on.

5. The presence or absence of a prewar acute crisis, and the length of time since that crisis, should be noted in a manner similar to that adopted for a prewar alliance.

6. Present symbols infrequently applied and of no particular theoretical significance should be dropped, or recycled for better use. Such would doubtless include: b, e, f, h, j, k, l, n, p, t, u, w; beta, chi, delta, pi, xi, zeta; B, F, H, K, Y.[1]

7. Some situations frequently met could be analyzed in more detail by the redefinition or reassignment of symbols, by application of more accents or suffixes, and so on. For instance: sources of desire for territory (symbol T), such as traditional claims and a drive for national union, should be specified; the vague symbol X (elated by pride) should be redefined to indicate that public opinion was favorable to fighting, and it should be matched by a small letter x to indicate antiwar sentiment.

8. Richardson used several symbols to indicate the various roles that third parties may play. Of these, beta, delta, and zeta go almost unused, while gamma, eta, and P are heavily used but rather too vaguely defined. No code symbol reflects the situation "had an ally."

9. The symbols E (difference in wealth), O (difference in legal systems), and Z (one fought for pay), should be reassigned to the ambivalent expected-valency group.

10. The set of ideological symbols G, L, S, should be augmented or particularized so as to take special note of desires for independence (or union) based on geography, race, language, or religion; and of desires for changes in government personnel, the constitution, and the social order.

11. A war involvement of those "religions" most often involved should receive a specific coding.

[1] For their definitions, see Appendix 4.

12.   Singer and Small found that in forty-eight interstate wars, the nation that made the first military attack on an opponent's army or territories was victorious in thirty-four (70.8%), and when a major power initiated war against a minor power, it was successful in 17/18 (94.4%) of the cases (1972, pp. 366–371). This suggests a need to examine instrumental rationality as a cause of war, by asking for each pair which, if either, was the initiator; which the victor; which expected victory; and for which the expectation of victory was a cause of its fighting.

Systematic reconsideration of the code scheme will doubtless reveal other needs. The above seem most pressing.

The war-criteria and the numerical variables. Singer and Small,[2] though agreeing with Wright that Richardson's list was the most complete for its period, found it and his casualty estimates inadequately refined and classified for their purposes (1972, p. 8–9). Their topic is "international war," and they chose to study this subject by "ignoring civil wars for the time being" (1972, pp. 4, 16–17). Should we follow their example or Richardson's? Since many wars are mixed (SDQ, p. 186), some difficulties arose when Singer and Small came to deal with "internationalized civil wars" (1972 pp. 31–35, 397–403). They themselves pointed out that "the clear division between civil and international wars" may be disappearing (1972, p. 35). Modelski (1972, p. 46) and Flora (1974, p. 152) have criticized the exclusion of civil war from the Correlates of War study. Richardson's device of marking civil *pairs* with m permits division of the wars into all-civil, all-international, and mixed categories for separate analysis and for comparisons as desired. On the whole, Richardson's device seems appropriate.

Singer and Small had, as they said, "more discriminating—as well as more complex—coding procedures" for listing wars and participants. The procedures were too complex to summarize here, but criteria in one way or another employed included the independence, population, diplomatic status, troop involvement, and battle deaths (total and per annum) of participants, as well as the total battle deaths in the war (1972, pp. 18–22, 30–32, 35–37, 381–382). Altogether, of Richardson's 315 cases, 147 were rejected by Singer and Small as having too few battle deaths, 62 as being civil wars, 19 as being between participants not in the interstate system (too small, lacking an independent foreign policy, or not recognized by Britain and France). Six cases were rejected on more than one ground: thus 315 – 222 = the 93 Singer and Small cases.

The point of having "membership in the interstate system" a criterion for exclusion rather than for special coding is somewhat obscure. Four-fifths of

[2] See Appendix 2.

the Richardsonian wars excluded on the battle-death criterion were coded by him as under magnitude 3.5 and could accordingly have been removed readily from any analysis if desired (1972, pp. 82–128); the other fifth included some cases where casualty data were poor and others where unarmed civilians were massacred, or where armed tribesmen or guerrillas were easily overwhelmed at low cost by professional Western armies. Again the argument for marking and including these, and then removing them as desired, seems rather stronger than the argument for excluding them entirely.

Singer and Small also collected measures of the battle-deaths among interstate-system participants' military personnel in the war; of the duration of the war in months; of the "nation months" of war experienced by all participants; and of the ratios of battle-deaths to nation months and to the prewar population and prewar armed forces' size of each participant (1972, pp. 44–54, 381–382). These indicators are more or less interesting, but the justification for excluding nonmilitary deaths stands or falls with the exclusion of civil wars (1972, p. 48). And the duration of the war in months is (and total casualties per war month would be) a measure more suitable for discussing wars as units of analysis than are those measures stated in nation months, suitable though the latter admittedly are for discussing the relative war-participation of individual nations.

Since the Singer and Small criterion and measures are more complex than those of Richardson, the labor cost of applying them is likely to be higher. It is not at all clear that the benefits of employing them are commensurately higher; in some respects they are likely to be lower. On the whole, future war collections would be most broadly useful if they were complete rather than selective; oriented toward casualties rather than battle deaths and durations rather than nation months; with markers for civil pairs, for massacres, and perhaps for tribesmen, guerrillas, and professional armies; and including more specialized indicators like nation months as the particular needs and predilections of the researchers who create them may dictate.

The case list. The case list is incomplete. We can be sure that it is incomplete, but not how incomplete. Richardson expected that it would prove nearly complete for wars of magnitudes 4 and above, 1820–1929, except for central African wars pre-1860 (SDQ, p. 31); and that though clearly incomplete at magnitude 3, it would there prove about half complete (SDQ, pp. 73, 151–153), though perhaps with many omissions for 1939–1945 (SDQ, p. 31, 108).

Wright called Richardson's estimate "optimistic," after comparing the 209 quarrels recorded at magnitude 3 with some 1,070 "military incidents . . . most of these probably above magnitude 2.5" in his own collection (SDQ, p. 73; Wright 1965, p. 636). The sources for Wright's statement are not easy to pin down but were surely the sixty-six manuscripts produced by the Causes of War project (Wright 1965, pp. 222, 410–413). Some of these I have been unable to trace. Most of the rest (Brumley 1928; Caine 1929; Garrick 1930; Melby 1936; Wallace 1930; White 1929) are organized in a nonstatistical narrative style, with "incidents" not clearly delineated. They will not suffice to resolve the question of the completeness of Richardson's list; but the best organized of the group (Brumley 1928) seems to support Richardson's opinion rather than Wright's.

Singer and Small (1972, pp. 78–79), who counted 289 wars on Richardson's list and 93 on a list of their own defined for different purposes, averred that 80.0 percent of their 93 (74.4?) are on Richardson's list (1972, p. 79), leaving, presumably, 18.6 that are not. Similarly they found that 32 of Wright's 133 and 35 of Sorokin's 97 cases (for comparable periods) are not in Richardson's list. The Singer and Small listing (1972, pp. 82–128) contains about 30 wars that, from what Wright, Sorokin, and/or Singer and Small had to say of them, appear to meet Richardson's criterion for inclusion, and their list of "wars that are excluded" (1972, pp. 395–398) contains perhaps three or four more that might do so. Given the differing purposes and criteria of these researchers, it is not to be taken for granted that all or any of these cases will be added to Richardson's list; but they may be.

Without knowing how incomplete the list is, we can reasonably anticipate certain sorts of lacunae. Taking into account Richardson's own reservations (SDQ, pp. 315–328), one may infer that he was more likely to have overlooked small wars than large, early wars than late, wars obscured by larger, simultaneous fighting than wars isolated in space and time, wars excluding Britain than wars with British participation. Similarly one worries about wars involving a nonliterate group, or only nonliterates; wars involving non-Westerners; wars far from the European core.

Further search at the fringes seems called for—search among histories of the early nineteenth century; histories of French colonies, Russia, Turkey, Central Asia, India, China, Latin America and especially Africa (SDQ, pp. 30–31); histories not written in English; histories published outside Europe; histories of small states and noncolonized areas; histories of guerrilla wars, frontier wars, colonial wars, massacres, raids, terrorism; and, of course, histories of Richardson's period published since 1949.

As for other emendations, it would be quite desirable and feasible to bring the case list up to date.[3] It might prove useful, though quite difficult, to push the listing back to some earlier date, say to the lull noted in Wright's list by Moyal (1949, pp. 447, 449; SDQ, p. 140) around A.D. 1740 or 1745. The main desideratum is, however, to find and fill the gaps in the extant list.

---

[3] Modelski (1972) provided a list, with duration and magnitude, of sixty-seven "armed conflicts" of magnitudes 3 and higher begun after January 1, 1945, with status as of December 13, 1970. See also Wright (1965, pp. 1544–1547). Singer and Small (1972), Starr and Most (1976), Garnham (1976b), SIPRI (1969), Denton (1968), Kende (1978).

The sources. Richardson's list contains references to some 135 sources, including multivolume histories, serials, books, articles, and consultations. Most frequently cited is the fourteenth edition (1929) of the *Encyclopaedia Britannica. Keesing's Contemporary Archives,* the *Cambridge Modern History,* and H. S. Williams' *Historian's History of the World* were also much used. Virtually all the sources, except for wars ended after 1939, date from the 1920s or 1930s.

Three citations per war is the median; the modal number of citations per war is one; the number of citations rises with the magnitude of the war.

Some belligerent pairs receive many code symbols—the one-pair Third Carlist war and Taiping Rebellion have thirteen—while others receive few or none. The mean number of symbols per pair is 3.6. 198/780 (25.4%) of pairs have no irritant noted; 56/780 (7.2%) have no symbols in the "pacifier" or the "background" compartments; and 21/780 (2.7%) have no symbols in any compartment.

From my own acquaintance with the wars examined I am inclined to judge that Richardson made very few, if any, type II coding errors (misstatements of a case, false affirmations, false positives) but may have made very many type I errors (omissions of true statements). He understated; he erred on the side of caution. As his findings are numerous and interesting nevertheless, his bias is in the right direction.

A complete re-researching of the wars would, it seems, be appropriate. It should take account of more than a generation of historical research and writing and should seek a substantial expansion in the number of sources researched, in the number of sources per war, and especially in the number of sources per pair with few symbols now set. A higher risk of type II errors might reasonably be run the second time around, if we assume that Richardson's data are likely to prove reliable but to underestimate rather than overestimate the frequency with which any symbol should be set.

The coding. The two race markers, C and c, may have been undercoded at high magnitudes (123/130 (94.6%) of pairs at magnitude 7 have neither C nor c); the two language-markers, I and i, at low magnitudes (101/312 (32.4%) of pairs at magnitude 3 have neither).

The former-alliance symbol, lambda, may have been underassigned at low magnitudes by comparison to the common-government symbol, m: 7/312 (2.2%) of pairs at magnitude 3 have lambda, as against 138/312 (44.2%) with m; yet if the commonly governed unit had ever fought as a unit before their civil war (and no earlier civil war had already broken the unity), lambda should have appeared alongside m.

If Wallace's reassertion of a direct link between arms levels or arms races and war is correct (1972, pp. 67, 69), the arms-race symbol, omega, may have been underassigned. Yet Richardson, as one particularly interested in arms races (1960*a*), is not likely to have missed any that his sources recorded. As

Wallace's data relate systemwide changes in military personnel to systemwide battle fatalities within five-year intervals, and the arms increases are not shown to be prewar or war-inciting, both Wallace and the historians may be right. Still it may prove worthwhile to go back of historians' assertions about arms races to actual military statistics for purposes of reconsidering the assignment of omega.

There would be some advantage to having the coding replicated by persons of markedly different biases. Richardson applied the symbol phi (the tail-group felt itself to be stronger than the tip-group) in 8/780 (1.0%) of pairs, and 6/315 (1.9%) of cases. Blainey, basing his book, as he said, on "a survey of all the international wars fought since 1700" or "almost one hundred wars" 1700–1971, and giving, among others, eighteen prominent instances in the 1820–1949 period, came to the general conclusion that "wars usually begin when two nations disagree on their relative strength" and that "when nations prepare to fight one another, they have contradictory expectations of the outcome of the war" (1972, pp. vii, ix-x, 44–50, 246). It is unlikely that both Richardson and Blainey were correct; it is likely that Blainey would have set phi (or some symbol designed to reflect his notion of "contradictory optimism") far more often than Richardson did; it would be desirable to get some sense of the degree of difference between and the amount of historical support for their views. To accomplish this aim, case-coding by persons of different ideological or theoretical backgrounds would be helpful.

One might assume that if Richardson, a Quaker and a pacifist presumably influenced by the political idealism of his time, were to have displayed any systematic bias in his coding, it would have been a bias toward overcounting and otherwise overemphasizing circumstantial (rather than deep-seated) causes of wars, particular (rather than general) causes, "environmental" (rather than "human-nature") causes, and generally those causes most subject to deliberate human manipulation and reform.

An inspection of Richardson's actual codings will not support this expectation. The irritant symbols most frequently set are T (desire for territory) and its variants, G (religious quarrels), M (desire for revenge for an old war), and rho (attempted domination and resistance). In general the coding does not seem such that it would persuade a political realist that only the problems readily solved are noticed: "realities of power politics" figure quite prominently; favorite idealist scapegoats like economic inequality, trade barriers, or arms races are present but in no way predominate. Since arms races were a major topic of Richardson's own work, his restraint in reading them into history was admirable and gives a contemporary reader greater confidence in the rest of his codings.

But I do have reservations about Richardson's employment of one code symbol. I suspect he may either have systematically tended to underuse the symbol N ("the leader of the tail-group felt a personal resentment against the leader of the tip-group") or may have defined it so narrowly that it fails to serve any useful purpose, even though it is the only symbol that reflects the impact of individual personality or character upon warfare. Richardson elsewhere admitted that his arms race description "cannot include anything so unpredictable" as "intelligent aggression planned by a leader"; he minimized the effectiveness of political leadership, emphasizing that the acts of leaders are "in part controlled by the great instinctive and traditional tendencies which are formulated in my description," and that "leaders lead peoples where they are willing to be led." He contended that his objective, "a theory which will indicate what might have happened [in the past] in such different circumstances as may arise in the future" cannot be derived from "the type of history which places all the emphasis on the personal characters of a few leading men ... because leaders retire and die." He admitted that the evidence "that Hitler and his associates planned the war" convinced him of the truth of a proposition that he was "loath to believe" (1960*a*, pp. 227, 231, 253). One feels that Richardson could easily have been inclined to minimize the role played by particular persons in the onset of war, partly out of sheer charity, but partly out of attachment to the hope of obtaining usable prescriptions for peace such as (he thought) a theory of the causes of war which rested on individual character could not provide. A political psychologist's coding of the cases is therefore to be desired.

The recoders should then include in their number a Blaineyite (if such there be), a political psychologist, and perhaps also an economist, in view of the small role that Richardson assigned to economic causes of war—though most economists would, I suspect, incline to agree with him. And a final recoder: an adversary. Richardson made many decisions that could have been reversed. This is most evident in his decisions about grouping pairs in a single "war," but also in his decisions on magnitude and duration, which are sometimes at variance with those of Singer and Small (1972, pp. 82–128). It is also undoubtedly true for his decision as whether to set a certain symbol in a certain case. Richardson declared that where decisions could reasonably be made in one of two ways, he alternated, attempting to give the average priority over the differences (SDQ, p. 125). Was he successful in that attempt? A new coding that set out deliberately to break up those wars Richardson decided to treat as one, accept higher casualty estimates where he accepted lower, and so on, would tell us.

We can take it for granted that it would be useful to have the coding done more explicitly, with coding rules more clearly laid down, sources more fully cited and readily checked, and intercoder agreement measured and evaluated. These methods are intended to *reduce* subjectivity; I would rather give priority to an attempt to *vary* it.

The analysis. Richardson's analysis of his own data was limited by the need to count his index cards by hand. Now-simple procedures, such as frequency counts, percentaging, and crosstabulations of symbols against magnitude, duration, and other symbols, were left to his successors; some are reported here. More complex procedures were also left to the future: Denton (1966) and Rummel (1967) factor analyzed Richardson's data; Weiss (1963), Horvath and Foster (1963), and Horvath (1968) used statistical models to produce functions and generate distributions to be fitted to the data. Many analyses no doubt remain to be performed—even conceived. In such conception, Richardson's own ingenious analytical methods will repay close scrutiny. Particularly worthy of examination with a view to further use are the method of "mapping by compact cells" in order to locate nonbelligerent pairs (SDQ, pp. 180, 215–227, 242–245, 308–309) and the chaos model for anticipating the number and complexity of wars (SDQ, pp. 247–287).

The interpretation. Richardson interpreted his own results, cautiously, in the light of his own opinions and experience. His interpretations, and those of other users of his data, have yet to be reconciled with and integrated into the diverse and disordered body of propositions on war contained in the works of writers on the subject over many generations. Such a reconciliation and integration will not be easy until the discipline of war/peace research produces a new collection and synthesis of extant knowledge and opinion—a successor to Wright's *A Study of War* (1965; but originally published in 1942, digesting research begun in 1926).

The need for such a contemporary synthesis within which to incorporate work on particular cases during a particular period is most striking when one considers a danger remarked by Richardson himself: "While diligently recording the special causes of each particular war, writers may perhaps have neglected to mention the general cause of all wars" (SDQ, p. 26). "Human nature," "international anarchy," Herz's "security dilemma" (1951, pp. 14–15), Han Fei Tzu's scarcity dilemma (1959, pp. 276–277): any of these, and not these alone, could be "the general cause of all wars." So many such causes could be asserted that any conclusion drawn from a systematic study of particular cases is endangered. Particular-cause collections and general-cause theories, collections and theories specific to the era of modern civilization and those specific to other times or social types (or to no particular time or type), even the human-species-specific theories of aggression and those specific to other species or generalized over many species—all must be compared and, as far as possible, reconciled. It is only in such a synthesis that the difficulty cited by Richardson, inescapable within the bounds of his research, might be resolved.

Priorities. I am led to conclude that first attention should be given to revising Richardson's coding scheme to satisfy the most obvious criticisms, applying the new scheme to a larger body of historical source material, and thereby producing a second Richardsonian data base different from but comparable to the first.

The Richardson data seem to justify further emphasis on certain lines of research: the causal background of the fluctuation in the frequency of war noted by Moyal (1949); the mechanism that generates the steady supply of new belligerents (SDQ, pp. 169–171); the distinct reasons for high-magnitude wars (or, better, for high-casualty pairs); the actual frequencies of incidence and of peaceful termination for prewar crises, which appear to be more numerous and less dangerous than is generally thought to be the case (SDQ, p. 129); life expectancy and actual sequels of the establishment of a common government, for example, years until civil war; discrimination of the pacifying effects of common government from those of ethnocultural similarities associated with it; and close comparative examination of historical transitions between conditions of high and low war-participation by a state.

The war/peace research field as a whole ought to give consideration to the organization of a project for collection and synthesis of the vast literature of the field in order to produce a logical and systematic digest to serve as a less legalistic and more contemporary successor to that of Quincy Wright. It is to be hoped that such a digest would render much easier the integration of Richardson's work, that of others using his or similar data, and ongoing war/peace research in general, into a body of organized, if not established, opinion.

It is, of course, always in order to call for more research. Are there any present and practical conclusions to be drawn from Richardson's research? In a broad sense there are. Practical attention should be directed, as it is, in fact, now largely directed, to the avoidance of inter-great-power wars and to the separate pacification of the major powers as the best hope for limiting frequency and magnitude of wars (cf. SDQ, pp. 153, 173). There is some justification for laborious efforts to postpone wars, even without getting at "deep-seated" motives for fighting (SDQ, pp. 190, 200). If there is any prospect for a long-term transformation of the world social system to a much more pacific condition, I believe that the levers will be found in economic growth, modernization, and prosperity, because of their apparent relationship to the economic, ethnocultural, and ideological incitements to fighting. Even while studying these processes and relations, it is imperative to do what can be done to accelerate worldwide economic growth.

12
Conclusion

Lewis Fry Richardson, one of the founders of the systematic study of the causes of war, published a series of papers during his lifetime. After his death two posthumous volumes, edited from his papers published and unpublished, were issued. The less known, but perhaps more important, of the two, *Statistics of Deadly Quarrels*, is a collection and analysis of data on wars and other killings.

Statistics of Deadly Quarrels is a work often referred to and generally well spoken of in the literature on war and peace. Its data, analytical techniques, and findings have been variously used and discussed in the considerable, though scattered, succeeding literature. It is now timely to reappraise this work to see whether it has been assimilated into political science as fully as it deserves, or whether there is still more to be learned by reading or analyzing, imitating or extending it.

RICHARDSON'S PURPOSE AND METHODS
Richardson approached war as a *pacifist*: he wanted to prevent it. He approached war as a *statistician*: he wanted to study it by counting cases of war and counting the occurrence of key causes and other features. He assumed that history shows continuity rather than periodic discontinuity or long-term progress, so he studied past wars to shed light on the present. Richardson held the metaphysical position that causation exists, that there is neither complete casual determinism nor complete freedom, and that as we become more aware of determinism we reduce its power. Richardson hoped to be a teacher of political engineers or political designers and saw his role as

revealing—and thereby challenging—the causes of violence by recording and counting them.

His approach was not merely statistical but comparative-historical as well. Since he accepted the category "causation" for himself, he also accepted historians' judgments about what causes each war had. Therefore his *Statistics* counts not just wars and their features, but wars and their alleged causes.

After grappling with numberous problems of terminology, data, and methods, Richardson collected (by my count) 315 wars that ended between 1820–1952, containing some 780 pairs of opposed belligerents. Each such pair was "coded" for 59 variables plus the duration of its fight. The war itself was assigned a duration and a "magnitude"—the logarithm of the number of those who died as a direct consequence of the war. The 59 variables are actually coding symbols that are set in a printed matrix. Each symbol may represent three to five statements by its definition, its typeface, its position in the matrix, and the suffix, accent, or arrows attached to it. The code is given in Appendix 4; the problems of converting such a dense, complex, technical, utterly *visual* information system to machine processing are discussed in Appendix 3.

TIME, MAGNITUDE, AND WAR

1. There is a pattern in the number of outbreaks of war in each year which suggests there are very many prewar crises every year, but that each has a low probability of actually leading to war.

2. The duration of wars can *almost* be accounted for on the assumption that, of all the wars ongoing in any year, 23.5 percent will end in that year. But this pattern does not hold true for very small wars, which have shorter durations.

3. A high death rate apparently tends to shorten wars and accelerate peacemaking.

4. Wars became shorter over Richardson's interval.

5. There was no clear trend in the frequency of war. Wars did not become more frequent; possibly they became slightly less frequent.

6. Smaller wars are very much more common than larger ones; frequency varies inversely with magnitude.

7. There is evidence that over Richardson's interval wars became larger, that is, there were more deaths per war; also that the total death toll from all wars in a given time span grew.

8. The death toll of wars is so much the product of the very few extremely large wars that the most pressing task in war prevention is to understand, predict, and impede these wars, the next of which would be World War III.

9.   There is evidence of a cycle with a 20–40 year period in war frequency and participation. There may also be a longer cycle, or two, with periods on the order of 100 or 200 years.

10.   Wars appear to arise independently, but to spread contagiously, through alliance structures, to neighbors, and otherwise.

COMMON GOVERNMENT, PRIOR ALLIANCE, AND PRIOR ENMITY

1.   An overarching common government (or some close associate) tends to inhibit fighting.

2.   The longer such common government endures, the greater its pacifying effect.

3.   The pacifying effect of common government between any two distinct groups is greater when rough equality prevails between them, but exists even when one group is dominated by the other.

4.   Having previously fought as allies may tend slightly to pacify; but more research is needed to clarify the complicating effects of power status, regime type, prior enmity, and contiguity upon this relationship.

5.   Having previously fought as enemies seems to be an incitement to fight again, though the effects of past wars diminish with time.

CONTIGUITY

The probability that any pair of groups will fight is increased by their being neighbors.

COMPLEX WARS

1.   Wars tend to be simple rather than complex: wars with more participants are less frequent than wars with fewer participants; wars with more belligerent pairs are less frequent than wars with fewer belligerent pairs; the least complex war (one versus one) is the most common type.

2.   There are nonetheless a few wars that involve many fighting pairs. Such wars also tend to be unusually long and unusually bloody. Ordinarily they are gang-ups (many against one, or many against a few).

3.   Richardson found that the occurrence, infrequency, and gang-up pattern of complex wars could all be explained by assuming that there exists a general propensity for states to fight anyone, modified by an overriding preference for fighting neighbors and a mild tendency for great powers to fight whomever they conveniently can; and that the propensity to fight one's neighbors

increases markedly when war breaks out or spreads among those neighbors.

4. Other studies suggest that complex wars are also propagated through alliance structures.

5. Reduction or elimination of long-range weapons systems (navies, air forces, missile forces), dissolution of peacetime alliances, and political unification of independent neighbor states would all probably tend to reduce the incidence of complex wars, which are particularly damaging.

PARTICIPATION

Although there was no chief aggressor nation, and although new belligerents continually appeared, nevertheless a group of eleven nations (former plus actual plus would-be great powers) did most of the fighting and suffered most of the casualties; and their participation, especially in opposition to one another, was associated with high casualties. It is therefore particularly important to pacify great powers and to harmonize their interrelations—or to abolish such powers.

ECONOMICS

Economic causes of war appear frequently, but not in all cases nor to the exclusion of other causes. There is no support for a single-factor theory that economics causes war, unless *economics* or *causes* are so broadly defined as to be uninteresting.

Furthermore, such economic causes are of many types, none of which preponderates, which makes it difficult to develop a consistent peace scheme even for dealing with economic causes alone. If such a scheme is possible, it must center on some plan for general prosperity and affluence; and it must understand that war today may be the price of the transition to prosperity and peace tomorrow.

ETHNOCULTURAL FACTORS

1. The propensity of any two groups to fight increases as the differences between them (in language, religion, race, and cultural style) increase. A homogeneous world would probably be a more peaceful one.

2. Some particular culture patterns themselves seem to be irritants or pacifiers or closely linked thereto: Christianity and the Spanish language on the one hand; Confucianism-Taoism-Buddhism and the Chinese language on the other. It is therefore meaningful to speak of "cultural disarmament," although a culture that simply discourages fighting may invite aggression.

3.   Economic growth, development, and modernization may well
        promote cultural homogenization and disarmament by universally
        establishing a cosmopolitan bourgeoisie, but only in the very long
        run, after many vicissitudes.

MISCELLANEOUS FACTORS

1.   It appears that "militant ideology" is a cause of war. "Ideological
        disarmament" is therefore more closely tied to peacemaking and
        detente than some choose to admit. Evidence for the belief that
        collective worldwide prosperity is possible within the current
        world order would tend to promote ideological disarmament.
2.   Several alleged causes of fighting—arms races, provocation of
        proxy wars, the psychology of leaders, regime types, power
        balances—merit further research, either on the assumption that
        Richardson may have overlooked or undercounted them or on
        the assumption that anything cited more than once as an actual
        cause is worthy of investigation.
3.   Similarity, equality, connectedness and cooperation tend toward
        pacificity. This provides some justification for H. G. Wells's radi-
        cal world-reform proposals, but no indication of how they might
        be realized.

A GENERAL APPRAISAL

Is Richardson's study scientific? It is as scientific as it claims to be; in
many respects it is as scientific as it could be; but in several key respects it
could be improved substantially.

1.   The fifty-nine code symbols need a thorough overhaul; some are
        of no use and should be discarded; others are overused and should
        be particularized; and there are nine or ten variables which should
        be represented by a symbol but are not.
2.   The war criteria used by Richardson are in respect of comprehen-
        sivity superior, not inferior, to those of his critics Singer and
        Small. Richardson's category of "war," however problematic, is
        less so than Singer and Small's category "international war." The
        Singer-Small critique of Richardson should be taken account of
        not by refusing to study civil wars, massacres, tribal wars, and
        one-sided routs, but by marking them and letting researchers who
        wish to exclude them do so.
3.   The list of 315 cases is certainly incomplete. Many small wars
        beyond the margin of Western (especially British) interests are
        likely to have been missed and should now be searched for.

4. We could probably use ten times as many historical sources as Richardson did before the diminishing information-returns of such an investment in time reach or approximate zero.

5. It would be worthwhile to bring Quincy Wright's massive digest of war theory up to date in order to be able to place Richardsonian findings more clearly in perspective.

6. Overall, Richardson's work is methodologically and theoretically fruitful and suggestive; it is far from obsolete. It can serve as a foundation for further research and speculation, but there is a pressing need for replicating in part and improving in part his collected list of wars and producing a second generation Richardsonian data collection.

These are among the many areas that need further research. As to practical conclusions, the key topics for contemporary peace strategy seem to be how to promote great-power detente, and how to accelerate world economic development.

Appendixes

APPENDIX 1
QUINCY WRIGHT'S WAR LIST

Quincy Wright (1965, pp. 636–651) listed 278 "wars of modern civilization," begun between 1482 (conquest of Granada) and 1940 (World War II). Information provided for each includes the date of beginning, date of ending, name of peace treaty, names of participants, number of participants, number of important battles, and type of war. Wright collected only wars of four types, which he coded with the letters B, C, D and I: wars between state members of the "modern family of nations" (B, balance-of-power); wars within such a state (C, civil); and wars between "modern civilization" and an "alien culture," either defending the former (D, defensive) or expanding it (I, imperial). A war may or may not be a "general war" (two years long or longer with a great power on each side). A "war" is an event (1) "recognized as war in the legal sense" or (2) "involving over 50,000 troops" or (3) leading to "important legal results such as the creation or extinction of states, territorial transfers, or changes of government" (1965, p. 636). Wars outside Europe involving no European state are not listed until one participant was recognized by European states as a member of the family of nations. Revolutionists, rebels, or insurgents are not listed as participants—unless they were successful (1965, p. 367). The ending date is by preference the effective date of a peace treaty, but in its absence the actual ending of active hostilities (1965, p. 638). These oddities and ambiguities stem from Wright's insistence on applying legalistic criteria wherever possible, and his retreat to practical criteria elsewhere. Richardson's criteria seem by comparison both more lucid and more consistent.

Among the more interesting of Wright's findings are these. The number of participants per war has increased from two or three in the sixteenth and seventeenth centuries to four in the nineteenth and 8.5 in the twentieth century (1965, pp. 638-639, 651). The number of important battles per war has risen dramatically, from one or two in the sixteenth century to 37.2 in the twentieth, and the number of battles per approximate half-century from 48 to 992 over the same interval (1965, pp. 639, 651). The average duration of war has declined from over five years to under four years since 1600. After the Napoleonic wars, the nineteenth century was "outstandingly peaceful," with shorter wars, fewer battles overall and per war, and fewer participants per war than the late eighteenth or early twentieth century—yet, strangely enough, wars were more frequent in this period than before or afterward (1965, pp. 638-639, 651). General wars have become briefer (from fourteen to four years' average duration) and less frequent (from six to twenty years' interval of general peace) since 1600 (1965, p. 650). Most great powers have taken part in most general wars, that is, when two great powers fought, most others, with very few exceptions, joined in (1965, p. 649). Certain states participated with notable frequency in the 278 wars:

England or Britain	78
France	71
Spain	64
Russia or USSR	61
Germanic Empire or Austria	52
Turkey	43
Poland	30
Sweden	26
Savoy or Italy	25
Netherlands	23
Prussia or Germany	23
Denmark	20
United States	13
China	11
Japan	9

Of these, Poland, Denmark, and China were not, to Wright, great powers at any time during this period. All the rest were; however, only England and France were great powers throughout (1965, pp. 649-650).

Wright's definitions are, relative to Richardson's, amorphous; his sources are far fewer; his collection cannot be divided by magnitude; information on background and causal factors is not collected. Wright's collection is superior to Richardson's only in the time span it covers.

APPENDIX 2
SINGER AND SMALL'S WAR LIST

J. David Singer and Melvin Small (1972, p. 38) listed ninety-three "international" wars, fifty of these "interstate" and forty-three "extra-systemic," begun after 1 January 1816 and ended before 31 December 1965. For each they collected information on participant actors, population, and armed forces; duration of the war; nation-months of fighting; and battle deaths, overall, per nation-month, per million participant population, and per thousand participant armed forces.

The war typology derived from Wright's, revised so as to be somewhat less legalistic and more replicable, though the result was even more ponderous. Rather elaborate criteria, involving population, recognition, control over foreign policy, and over armed force (1972, pp. 19–22), are used to discriminate a set of states, members of the "interstate" system (23 in 1816, 124 by 1965). Wars between such states are "interstate," their wars against nonmembers are "extra-systemic." Extra-systemic wars against independent entities are "imperial," against dependents "colonial," against insurgents within another member state "internationalized civil," against one's own insurgents "civil." Civil wars are on principle not listed; for various ad hoc reasons no internationalized civil wars are listed (1972, pp. 33–35); eighteen imperial and twenty-five colonial wars constitute the extra-systemic wars. Wars with fewer than one thousand battle fatalities among all participating system members are not listed; various casualty thresholds define "participants" (1972, pp. 30, 35–37).

Among the findings of Singer and Small are: 29 million battle deaths during their interval; only 24 of 150 years without a war; 4532.7 nation months of active combat, so that a nation was at war during an average of 5.2 percent of its existence. On average an interstate war began every three years, an extra-systemic war every three and a half years (1972, pp. 374–375). The years of greatest national participation were 1917 and 1944, with, respectively, 34.1 and 33.3 percent of all nations at war (1972, pp. 152–155). There were no significant trends noted in annual amounts of war begun or underway, nation months or battle deaths per war, or battle deaths per capita (1972, pp. 197–201); but there was some evidence of a twenty-year cycle in the amount of war underway (1972, pp. 208–212, 215). October is the preferred month for going to war (1972, p. 223). Major powers fought most of the wars, spent the most time at war, and suffered the most battle deaths (1972, pp. 282–287). England and France were persistent allies, often with the United States and Belgium; Anglo-Dutch, Anglo-Greek, Serbo-Greek alliances often recurred; Russia-Turkey, Austria-Italy, China-Japan and France-Germany were habitual enemies; otherwise hostility and alliance have been fluid, alignments irregular rather than consistent (1972, pp. 343–345).

There was no discernible battle-death threshold at which nations withdrew from interstate war; the vanquished generally, but not uniformly, suffered more (1972, pp. 349–357). The initiator of an interstate war usually won and suffered fewer battle deaths (1972, pp. 366–371).

Singer and Small did not, as Richardson did, publish coded background and causal data for each pair. By comparison with Richardson, Singer and Small appear to have used more sources, asked few questions of fewer cases, used more powerful tabulating devices but less theoretic imagination. Their study is, however, more widely accessible; their data, available in machine-readable form, are readily and frequently used by other researchers. Their decision to omit civil wars averted some problems, created others, and seems on balance regrettable.

APPENDIX 3
PROCESSING THE RICHARDSON DATA

To understand the problems of processing Richardson's data, it is necessary to know some of the twists of Richardson's coding procedure.

Richardson's data were designed to be handled by people not by machines—and especially designed to be handled easily by Richardson himself. They were entered on a card index that was to be sorted and counted by hand (SDQ, pp. 73, 287). His coding scheme required yes-or-no coding decisions[1] and was designed to provide visual emphasis for the positive decisions. The code was intended to be entered by an expert, with minimal physical effort, in a small space, and to be read and interpreted by a trained human eye. The printed case list contains some data (e.g., magnitudes), applicable to whole cases and other data (e.g., alleged causes of fighting), applicable to pairs of opposed belligerents.

The greatest technical problem is posed by the multidimensionality of Richardson's coding symbols. Such a symbol has a root meaning (definition); a meaning conveyed by its typeface (expected valency); a meaning conveyed by its location (actual valency); and sometimes a meaning conveyed by a suffix (duration), a footnote (third party involved), one or two following arrows (directionality), and a single, double, or triple accent (detailed specification of the relation).

For the purposes of this study, Richardson's cases were broken into pairs; the several dimensions of the coding system were reduced to two, with some attendant sacrifice of information; and the legibility of the coding was preserved in a machine-readable recoding, at some cost to the detail of analysis.

1. The case list (SDQ, pp. 32–111) was broken into pairs of opposed belligerents. All 315 cases, magnitudes 3–7, 1820–1952, were decomposed into a total of 780 pairs, including 7 of the 86 "minor" and "miscellaneous" pairs listed by Richardson as "omitted from the matrix of World War II" (SDQ, pp. 36–39). Each case received a number from 1 to 315, each pair a number from 1 to 780. Each pair also received its case number and, there being n pairs in a case, a number i from 1 to n indicating that it was the i-th pair in the case. To each pair was attached also the magnitude, starting date, and ending date of its *case*, the names of the "row actor" and "column actor"

---

[1] Richardson set a code symbol only when the characteristic in question was relevant to the pair being coded and meaningful for it, when information on the characteristic was available, and when the characteristic was unambiguously present. No symbol at all was set when the characteristic was absent or ambiguous or irrelevant or meaningless or undocumented (cf. Banks and Textor 1963, pp. 20–22, for an alternate procedure that goes very far toward the opposite extreme).

who together constituted the "pair of opposed belligerents," and a recoded version of Richardson's coding for the pair. The recoding was done on the system stated in the following paragraphs.

2. The most convenient available computing facility was the UCLA Center for Computer-Based Behavioral Studies PDP-10/PDP-15 timesharing system, which had available the BASIC conversational language, the PREP data preparation and analysis, and the SPSS data-analysis packages. For the recoded data file to be machine-readable when entered, visually meaningful when printed out, and similar to the original so as to reduce error and ease verification, the recode symbols were restricted to the twenty-six capital letters of the Roman alphabet. Expected valency was in consequence not coded. Suffixes, footnotes, and arrows were omitted from the recoding. Accents were mostly omitted; in a few instances they were reflected by a double recoding. The symbols set by Richardson in the pacifier compartment were so few that all were recoded into the background compartment.

The recoding scheme is given in detail in Appendix 4. In outline it is as follows:

Of Richardson's fifty-nine symbols defined and used, five were retained unchanged; sixteen were dropped; nine were replaced one-for-one by other symbols. C, D, G, I, N were used as in Richardson. Of the eighteen defined symbols with an expected valency of "amity," twelve seldom assigned by Richardson (b, e, f, h, j, k, l, n, p, t, u, w) were dropped from the analysis. The other six were recoded as Roman caps, a becoming Q; c, B; d, E; g, H; i, J; m, A. Of the sixteen symbols with an expected valency of "ambivalence," three seldom assigned (delta, pi, chi) were dropped; lambda became L; rho became R; and eta became S.

M incorporated M'; T incorporated T', T'', and T''', although each was also recoded elsewhere (see below); P incorporated P' and P''. As Y, infrequently set, indicated a desire for territory, it was recoded as T (and recoded a second time elsewhere). As beta, infrequently set, indicated a "contagion" relationship, it was recoded as P.

A new category (F) absorbed three symbols (omega, phi, psi), and an accented version of a fourth (T''') that had the common element of implying a "security dilemma." A new category (K) combined five minor symbols (B, F, H, K, O) that reflected various sorts of alienship or heterogeneity. A new category (O) combined three minor symbols (W, X, Z) that reflected odd features of the culture or of social psychology of a belligerent. A new category (V) combined two moderately important symbols (L and S) that represented differences of opinion on constitutional arrangements. A new category (X) combined two symbols (mu, xi) representing intermingling and "interbreeding." A new category (Y) combined one rather important symbol and one almost unused symbol (gamma, zeta) for the provocative influence of a third party. One new category (W) combined three symbols (theta, sigma,

E) of economic differences between belligerents; another new category (Z) combined several symbols (A, A', A'', Q, R, T', T'', U, V, Y) defined (or exclusively used) by Richardson to reflect an economic opposition or rivalry. The symbol U was set where Richardson had left a compartment blank.

3. The computer-entered data on a pair were reduced to those elements for which machine counting and sorting was essential: these proved to be the case number, the case-pair number, the background symbols, and the irritant symbols. The entry for "Serbs" and "Austro-Hungarians" in World War I, the first pair in the Richardson list, was thus reduced to l, l, I, SZ.

4. A 780-line BASIC file of pair data was created at the terminal and verified in BASIC. BASIC was used to create a 315-line file of case data from the pair data. Using BASIC, the case and pair files were each turned into three files, one containing background factors only, one containing irritant factors only, and one containing factors of both kinds. Pair numbers and case magnitudes were assigned to the appropriate files via the recode procedures of PREP. Frequencies, percentages, crosstabs, and statistics reported are those calculated via BASIC or PREP. SPSS was used only to retrieve case and pair numbers where these were needed to permit reexamination of Richardson's original coding, for example, for F and its component omega (arms races).

Other computations were done by hand count and pocket calculator.

APPENDIX 4
RICHARDSON'S CODE AND THE RECODING SCHEME

Original Symbol and Definition		*Recoded As*
a	The tail-group sent goods to the tip-group as trade	Q
b	Present intermarriage	omitted
c	Similar bodily characteristics	B
d	Similar customs as to dress	E
e	Common level of wealth or poverty	omitted
f	Similar marriage customs, e.g., monogamy or polygamy	omitted
g	Similar religions or philosophies of life (*Weltanschauungen*)	H
h	General philanthropy	omitted
i	Common mother tongue	J
j	Similar sciences and arts	omitted
k	The tail-group traveled in the tip-group's territory	omitted
l	Similar degree of personal liberty	omitted
m	Common government	A
n	The autocrats or ruling minorities of the two groups were personal friends	omitted
o	Unspecified	
p	Policy of nonintervention in other nations' quarrels	omitted
q	Unspecified	
r	Unspecified	
s	Unspecified	
t	Policy of not extending territory	omitted
u	Membership of the United Nations	omitted
v	Unspecified	
w	Objection to warfare in general	omitted
beta	The tail-group desired to join the winning side	P
gamma	This letter is used, like a repeated asterisk, to refer from the pair of belligerents to a third party which desired that they should quarrel	Y
delta	The tail-group issued propaganda to third parties . .	omitted
zeta	The tip-group was offered protection by a third party	Y
eta	The tail-group sympathized with those under the tip-group's control	S

APPENDIX 4 *(continued)*

theta	The tip-group owed money to the tail-group	W
lambda	The belligerents had previously fought as allies against a common enemy	L
mu	The belligerents had intermingled on the same territory up to the time when the conflict began	X
xi	The belligerent groups had been interbreeding with one another	X
pi	The tip-group issued propaganda to the tail-group . .	omitted
rho	The tail-group habitually ordered the tip-group to obey	R
sigma	The tail-group organized commercial enterprises on the tip-group's territory	W
phi	The tail-group felt itself to be stronger than the tip-group	F
chi	The tail-group competed successfully against the tip-group in intellectual occupations	omitted
psi	The government of the tail-group was insecure	F
omega	The tail-group had been making exceptional preparations for war	F
A	The tail-group put obstacles in the way of the movement of goods to (A') or from (A") the tip-group	Z
B	The tail-group banned intermarriage between its members and those of the tip-group	K
C	The two groups differed remarkably as to inborn bodily form, color, or odor	C
D	The customary clothing of the two groups was remarkably different	D
E	The individuals of the tail-group were on the average evidently richer than those of the tip-group	W
F	The marriage customs of the two groups were in marked contrast	K
G	The religions, or philosophies of life (*Weltanschauungen*), of the two groups were felt by the tail-group to be in contrast	G
H	The tail-group restricted immigration from the tip-group	K
I	Languages different, or more precisely, those persons whose only language was the dominant mother tongue of the one group could not	

	understand the dominant mother tongue of the other group	I
J	Unspecified	
K	The tail-group was generally ignorant of the tip-group	K
L	The tail-group believed in allowing a greater degree of personal liberty during peace than did the tip-group	V
M	The belligerents had fought one another previously. An accented M means chronic small fighting . . .	M
N	The leader of the tail-group felt a personal resentment against the leader of the tip-group	N
O	The legal systems of the two groups were annoyingly different	K
P	The tail-group was led into conflict with the tip-group because of the latter's action on a third group. On occasion the situation can be analyzed in more detail by accents, thus: P', the tip-group supported the tail-group's enemy or rival by favors, money, supplies, or fighting; P'', the tip-group injured or attacked the ally or friend of the tail-group	P
Q	The belligerents were rivals for concessions on the territory of third parties	Z
R	The belligerents were rivals in trading with third parties	Z
S	The tail-group was in favor of more civil power for the church than the tip-group would permit	V
T	The tail-group wished to acquire territory from the tip-group. On occasion the wish can be particularized, thus: T' for habitation, T'' for minerals or other portable goods, T''' for strategic strongholds	T*
U	The tail-group taxed the tip-group	Z
V	The tail-group wished to take loot	Z
W	The tail-group enjoyed fighting for its own sake . . .	O
X	The tail-group were elated by exceptionally strong pride	O
Y	The tail-group complained about the insufficiency of their land for their population	T*
Z	The tail-group fought for pay, regardless of the principles in dispute	O

*T' and T'' also recoded Z; T''' also recoded F; Y also recoded Z.

APPENDIX 5
RICHARDSON'S CASE LIST

Magnitude	Case Number	Name or Location	Intensity	Start	End	Number of Pairs	First Pair Number	Last Pair Number	Page Number In Richardson	Duration (In Years)
7	1	World War I	7.2	1914	1918	44	1	44	32-35	4
	2	World War II	7.3	1939	1945	86	45	130	35-39	6
6	3	Taiping Rebellion	6.3	1851	1864	1	131	131	40	13
	4	North American Civil War	5.8	1861	1865	1	132	132		4
	5	Great War in La Plata	6	1865	1870	6	133	138	40	5
	6	Sequel to the Bolshevik Revolution	5.7	1918	1920	9	139	147	41	2
	7	First Chinese-Communist War	6.1	1927	1936	1	148	148	41	9
	8	Spanish Civil War	6.3	1936	1939	16	149	164	42	3
	9	Communal Riots in the Indian Peninsula	5.9	1946	1948	8	165	172	43	2
5	10	Massacre of the Janissaries	4.6	1826	1826	1	173	173	44	0
	11	Russo-Turkish War	5	1828	1829	2	174	175		1
	12	Crimean War	5.4	1853	1856	4	176	179	44	3
	13	The European Revolutions	4.9	1848	1849	11	180	190	opp. 44	1
	14	Seven Weeks' War	4.6	1866	1866	5	191	195	45	0
	15	Franco-Prussian War	5.4	1870	1871	4	196	199		1
	16	Moslem Rebellions in West China	5.4	1861	1878	2	200	201		17
	17	Cuban Revolt	5.3	1868	1878	1	202	202	45	10
	18	Russo-Turkish War	5.4	1877	1878	6	203	208	46	1
	19	Armenian Massacres	4.6	1894	1897	2	209	210		3

No.	War	Magnitude	Year	Year					
20	Spanish-American War	5.3	1898	1898	2	211	212		0
21	Colombian Civil War	5.2	1899	1902	1	213	213	46	3
22	Russo-Japanese War	5.1	1904	1905	1	214	214	47	1
23	Maji-Maji Rebellion	5.4	1905	1907	1	215	215		2
24	War in Achin	5.4	1873	1908	3	216	218		35
25	Revolt in Southwest Africa	4.9	1903	1908	2	219	220	47	5
26	"First" Balkan War	4.8	1912	1913	4	221	224	48	1
27	The Mexican Revolution	5.4	1910	1920	23	225	247	49	10
28	War and Massacre in Anatolia	4.6	1919	1922	4	248	251		3
29	Moslem Rebellion in Kansu	5.3	1928	1928	1	252	252		0
30	Chinese Civil War	4.8	1930	1930	5	253	257	49	0
31	War in Libya	4.6	1920	1932	2	258	259	50	12
32	Japanese Invasion of China	4.8	1931	1933	1	260	260		2
33	Chaco War	5.3	1930	1935	1	261	261		5
34	Russo-Finnish War	4.83	1939	1940	1	262	262		1
35	Greek Civil War	4.65	1946	1949	1	263	263	50	3
36	Spanish-American War of Independence	4	1810	1824	9	264	272	51	14
37	"First" Burmese War	4.3	1823	1826	2	273	274	51	3
38	Siege of Bharatpur	3.7	1825	1826	3	275	277	52	1
39	War of Greek Independence	4	1821	1829	8	278	285		8
40	Revolt in Kashgaria	4.3	1822	1828	2	286	287	52	6
41	Rebellion in Central Java	4	1825	1830	3	288	290	53	6
42	Polish Rebellion	4.2	1830	1831	1	291	291		5
43	Revolt of Mehemet Ali	4	1831	1833	2	292	293	53	1
44	Miguelite War	4	1828	1834	6	294	299	54	2
45	Natal War	4.2	1838	1840	2	300	301		6
46	Caucasian Campaigns	4	1829	1840	1	302	302	54	2
47	First Carlist War	4	1833	1840	7	303	309	55	11
48	War in Syria	4	1839	1841	6	310	315		7
49	Dogra Invasion of Tibet	3.6	1841	1841	1	316	316	55	2
									0

4

APPENDIX 5 (continued)

Magnitude	Case Number	Name or Location	Intensity	Start	End	Number of Pairs	First Pair Number	Last Pair Number	Page Number In Richardson	Duration (In Years)
4	50	First Opium War	4	1839	1842	1	317	317	56	3
	51	First British-Afghan War	4.3	1838	1842	4	318	321		4
	52	Conquest of Sind	3.6	1843	1843	1	322	322		0
	53	First British-Sikh War	3.6	1845	1846	2	323	324	56	1
	54	Conquest of Algeria	3.6	1839	1847	4	325	328	57	8
	55	Mexico versus U.S.A.	4.2	1846	1848	1	329	329		2
	56	Second British-Sikh War	4	1848	1849	3	330	332	57	1
	57	War in La Plata	4.4	1836	1852	10	333	342	58	16
	58	Montenegrins versus Turks	3.8	1852	1853	1	343	343		1
	59	The Indian Mutiny	4	1857	1859	3	344	346	58	2
	60	War of Italian Union	4.34	1859	1859	5	347	351	59	0
	61	Second Opium War	4	1856	1860	2	352	353		4
	62	Spain versus Morocco	3.9	1859	1860	1	354	354	59	1
	63	Schleswig-Holstein War	3.6	1864	1864	2	355	356	60	0
	64	Mexican Expedition	4	1861	1867	3	357	359		8
	65	The Paris Commune	4.3	1871	1871	1	360	360		10
	66	Third Carlist War	4	1872	1876	1	361	361	60	4
	67	Egypt versus Abyssinia	3.8	1875	1876	3	362	364	61	2
	68	Satsuma Rebellion	4.0	1877	1877	1	365	365		0
	69	Bosnia and Herzegovina	3.8	1878	1878	1	366	366		0
	70	Zulu War	3.6	1879	1879	2	367	368	61	0
	71	Second British-Afghan War	3.6	1878	1880	2	369	370	62	2
	72	Sieges of Geok Tepe	4.3	1878	1881	1	371	371		3
	73	War of the Pacific	4.1	1879	1883	2	372	373		4
	74	Revolt of the Mahdi	4.44	1881	1885	2	374	375	62	4

75	Tongking War	4	1882	1885	3	376	378	63	3
76	Chilean Revolution	4.0	1891	1891	1	379	379		0
77	Invasion of Bornu	3.6	1893	1893	1	380	380		0
78	Eastern Congo War	4.3	1892	1894	4	381	384	63	2
79	Sudanese Independence	4	1885	1895	7	385	391	64	10
80	Sino-Japanese War	4	1894	1895	1	392	392		1
81	Italo-Abyssinian War	4.2	1894	1896	1	393	393		2
82	Sudan Campaigns	4.2	1896	1900	3	394	396	64	4
83	Chinese Boxer Rising	4.2	1899	1900	9	397	405	65	1
84	Conquest of Madagascar	3.8	1894	1901	2	406	407		7
85	Philippine Revolt	4	1899	1902	2	408	409		3
86	South African War	4.4	1899	1902	2	410	411	65	3
87	Zulu Revolt	3.7	1906	1906	1	412	412	66	0
88	Armenian Massacres	3.8	1909	1909	1	413	413		0
89	White Wolf War	4	1913	1914	1	414	414		1
90	Spanish-Moroccan War	4	1909	1910	1	415	415		1
91	Second Balkan War	4	1913	1913	4	416	419	66	0
92	Old versus New Systems in China	4	1913	1913	1	420	420	67	0
93	Russian Turkestan	3.95	1916	1916	1	421	421		0
94	War in Libya	4.2	1911	1917	5	422	426		6
95	War in Finland	4.3	1918	1918	3	427	429	67	0
96	Syria	3.7	1920	1920	1	430	430	68	0
97	Russo-Polish War	4	1918	1920	2	431	432		2
98	Fighting in Szechuan	3.6	1920	1920	1	433	433		0
99	Moplah Rebellion	4	1921	1922	2	434	435		1
100	Massacre of Koreans in Japan	4	1923	1923	1	436	436	68	0
101	War in Northern Morocco	4.4	1920	1927	3	437	439	69	7
102	Chinese Civil War	4	1926	1928	5	440	444	69	2
103	Rebellion in Chinese Turkestan	4.3	1931	1934	8	445	452	70	3
104	Ethiopian War	4	1935	1937	1	453	453	71	2
105	Greek Civil War	4	1944	1945	3	454	456	71	1

APPENDIX 5 (continued)

Magnitude	Case Number	Name or Location	Intensity	Start	End	Number of Pairs	First Pair Number	Last Pair Number	Page Number In Richardson	Duration (In Years)
4	106	Palestine	3.55	1940	1949	12	457	468	72	9
3	107	Argentina	3	1819	1820	1	469	469	73	1
	108	Aleppo	3	1820	1820	1	470	470	73	0
	109	Malay Peninsula	3	1821	1821	1	471	471	74	0
	110	Sumatra	3	1819	1821	1	472	472		2
	111	Naples and Sicily	3	1820	1821	1	473	473		1
	112	Piedmont	3	1821	1821	1	474	474		0
	113	Nubia	3	1820	1822	2	475	476		2
	114	Balkans	3	1820	1822	1	477	477	74	2
	115	Persia-Turkey	3	1821	1822	1	478	478	75	1
	116	Spain	3	1823	1823	2	479	480		0
	117	Southern Celebes	3	1825	1825	2	481	482		0
	118	Gold Coast	3.4	1821	1826	2	483	484		5
	119	La Plata	3.3	1825	1828	1	485	485		3
	120	Persia	3.5	1825	1828	2	486	487	75	3
	121	Central America	3	1827	1829	1	488	488	76	2
	122	Mexico	3	1829	1829	1	489	489		0
	123	Tasmania	3.3	1825	1830	1	490	490		5
	124	Algiers	3	1827	1830	1	491	491		3
	125	Chile	2.6	1829	1830	1	492	492		1
	126	Paris	3.3	1830	1830	1	493	493		0
	127	Kokand	3	1830	1830	1	494	494	76	0
	128	Argentina	2.6	1828	1831	1	495	495	77	3
	129	Bosnia	3	1830	1831	2	496	497		1
	130	Belgium	3.3	1830	1833	1	498	498		3

131	Buenos Aires	3	1833	1834	1	499	499		1
132	Palestine	3	1834	1834	1	500	500	77	0
133	South Africa	2.7	1834	1835	3	501	503	78	1
134	Zambezi-Delagoa	3	1833	1836	2	504	505		3
135	Texas	3	1836	1836	1	506	506		0
136	Central Sumatra	3	1807	1837	2	507	508		30
137	Zanzibar	3	1829	1837	1	509	509		8
138	Bosnia	3	1836	1837	1	510	510	78	1
139	South Africa	3	1836	1837	1	511	511	79	1
140	Ma-Kalanga War	3	1837	1837	1	512	512		0
141	Afghanistan	3	1837	1838	1	513	513		1
142	Annam	3.4	1833	1839	2	514	515		6
143	Chile	3	1836	1839	6	516	521	79	3
144	Khiva	3	1839	1839	1	522	522	80	0
145	Khelat	2.6	1839	1839	2	523	524		0
146	South Africa	3	1840	1840	1	525	525		0
147	Bosnia	3	1841	1841	1	526	526		0
148	Colombia	3	1839	1842	1	527	527		3
149	Gwalior	3.2	1843	1843	2	528	529		0
150	Brazil	3	1835	1845	1	530	530	80	10
151	Civil War in Syria	3	1845	1845	3	531	533	81	0
152	Bornean Piracy	3	1845	1845	1	534	534		0
153	Galicia	3	1846	1846	3	535	537		0
154	Kashgaria	3	1847	1848	1	538	538		1
155	Bali	3.3	1846	1849	2	539	540		3
156	Schleswig-Holstein	3	1848	1850	1	541	541	81	2
157	French Coup	2.7	1851	1851	1	542	542	82	0
158	Chile	3.3	1851	1851	1	543	543		0
159	South-East Africa	3.2	1850	1852	4	544	547		2
160	Burma	3	1852	1853	1	548	548		1
161	Gilgit	3.3	1852	1852	1	549	549		0
162	South Africa	3.45	1854	1854	1	550	550	82	0

APPENDIX 5 (continued)

Magnitude	Case Number	Name or Location	Intensity	Start	End	Number of Pairs	First Pair Number	Last Pair Number	Page Number In Richardson	Duration (In Years)
3	163	Colombia	3	1854	1854	1	551	551	83	0
	164	Bengal	3	1855	1855	1	552	552		0
	165	Nicaragua	3.3	1855	1857	2	553	554		2
	166	Anglo-Persian War	3	1856	1857	2	555	556		1
	167	Senegal	3	1857	1857	1	557	557		0
	168	Kashgaria	3.4	1857	1857	1	558	558	83	0
	169	Montenegro	3.4	1858	1858	1	559	559	84	0
	170	South Celebes	3	1859	1860	2	560	561		1
	171	Italy	3.3	1860	1860	1	562	562		0
	172	Lebanon-Damascus	3.4	1860	1860	2	563	564		0
	173	Mexico	3	1858	1861	1	565	565	84	3
	174	La Plata	3	1859	1861	1	566	566	85	2
	175	Abyssinia	3.3	1861	1861	1	567	567		0
	176	Colombia	3	1859	1862	1	568	568		3
	177	Montenegro	3	1862	1862	2	569	570		0
	178	Belgrade	3	1862	1862	1	571	571		0
	179	South Borneo	3	1859	1863	1	572	572	85	4
	180	Ambela	2.95	1863	1863	4	573	576	86	0
	181	Ecuador	3	1863	1863	1	577	577		0
	182	Circassia	3	1859	1864	1	578	578		5
	183	Japan	3	1862	1864	3	579	581		2
	184	Argentina	3	1863	1864	1	582	582	86	1
	185	Poland	3	1863	1865	1	583	583	87	2
	186	Bhutan	3	1865	1865	1	584	584		0
	187	Spain-Peru-Chile	3	1864	1865	2	585	586		1

188	Jamaica	2.67	1865	1865	1	587	587	87	0
189	Third Maori War	2.6	1863	1866	1	588	588	88	3
190	Minnesota and Dakota	3	1862	1867	1	589	589		5
191	South Africa	2.6	1865	1867	1	590	590		2
192	Rome	2.6	1867	1867	2	591	592		0
193	Abyssinia	3.5	1867	1867	1	593	593		0
194	Japan	3	1866	1868	1	594	594		2
195	British-Abyssinian War	3.0	1867	1868	2	595	596	88	1
196	Bokhara	3	1865	1868	1	597	597	89	3
197	Near Tabora	3	1860	1869	1	598	598		9
198	Bahr-el-Ghazal	3	1869	1869	1	599	599		0
199	Algeria	3	1871	1872	1	600	600		1
200	Ashanti	3	1873	1874	2	601	602	89	1
201	Tongking	3	1873	1874	2	603	604	90	1
202	Darfur	3	1873	1875	1	605	605		2
203	Argentina	3	1874	1875	1	606	606		1
204	Dakota	3	1876	1877	1	607	607		1
205	Colombia	3	1876	1877	1	608	608		1
206	South Africa	3	1877	1878	1	609	609	90	1
207	Bahr-el-Ghazal	3	1878	1879	1	610	610	91	1
208	Patagonia	3	1879	1879	1	611	611		0
209	Argentina	3	1880	1880	1	612	612		0
210	Uganda	3.3	1880	1880	1	613	613		0
211	Basutoland	3	1879	1881	1	614	614		2
212	Dalmatia	3	1881	1881	1	615	615		0
213	Tunisia	3	1881	1881	1	616	616	91	0
214	Egypt	3.2	1882	1882	1	617	617	92	0
215	Patagonia	3	1878	1883	1	618	618		5
216	Near 9° S. 27° E.	3	1883	1883	1	619	619		0
217	Arabia	3	1883	1884	1	620	620		1
218	Madagascar	3	1883	1885	2	621	622		2

APPENDIX 5 *(continued)*

Magnitude	Case Number	Name or Location	Intensity	Start	End	Number of Pairs	First Pair Number	Last Pair Number	Page Number In Richardson	Duration (In Years)
3	219	Colombia	3	1884	1885	1	623	623	92	1
	220	Pandjeh Incident	2.8	1885	1885	1	624	624	92	0
	221	Rumelia	3.4	1885	1885	1	625	625	93	0
	222	Eritrea	2.4	1887	1887	1	626	626		0
	223	Burma	3.8	1885	1886	2	627	628		1
	224	Uganda	3	1885	1890	6	629	634	93	5
	225	Near Zanzibar	3	1888	1890	1	635	635	94	2
	226	Dakota	2.6	1890	1891	1	636	636		1
	227	Upper Senegal	3	1890	1891	2	637	638		1
	228	Syria	3	1896	1896	1	639	639		0
	229	Uganda	3	1892	1892	1	640	640		0
	230	Uganda	3	1893	1893	1	641	641	94	0
	231	Malay Archipelago	3	1891	1894	2	642	643	95	3
	232	Dahomey	3	1892	1894	2	644	645		2
	233	Brazil	3	1892	1894	2	646	647		2
	234	Peru	3	1894	1895	1	648	648		1
	235	Nyasaland	3	1885	1896	4	649	652	95	11
	236	Kenya	3	1895	1896	1	653	653	96	1
	237	Bahia	3.2	1896	1897	1	654	654		1
	238	Southern Nigeria	3	1897	1897	1	655	655		0
	239	Greco-Turkish War	3.3	1897	1897	3	656	658		0
	240	Upper Niger	3	1890	1898	2	659	660	96	8
	241	German East Africa	3	1894	1898	1	661	661	97	4
	242	Northwest Frontier	3	1897	1898	2	662	663		1
	243	Sierra Leone	3.4	1898	1898	2	664	665		0
	244	Rhodesia	3	1896	1899	2	666	667		3

245	Ashanti	3	1900	1900	2	668	669	97	0
246	Uganda	3	1897	1901	5	670	674	98	4
247	Bornu	3	1899	1901	1	675	675		2
248	Northern Nigeria	3	1903	1903	1	676	676		0
249	Timbuctoo	3	1893	1904	2	677	678	98	11
250	British Somaliland	3.2	1899	1904	4	679	682	99	5
251	Tibet	3	1904	1904	2	683	684		0
252	St. Petersburg	3	1905	1905	1	685	685		0
253	Russian Pogroms	3.48	1905	1905		686	686		0
254	Near Victoria Nyanza	3	1905	1905	1	687	687		0
255	Tibet	3	1905	1906	1	688	688	99	1
256	Rumania	3	1907	1907	2	689	690	100	0
257	Morocco	3	1907	1908	2	691	692		1
258	Venezuela	3	1908	1908	1	693	693		0
259	Wadai	3	1904	1911	1	694	694		7
260	Morocco	3	1910	1911	2	695	696	100	1
261	Chinese Revolution	3	1911	1912	1	697	697	101	1
262	Fez	3.2	1912	1912	4	698	701		0
263	South Morocco	2.7	1912	1913	3	702	704		1
264	Tibet	3	1912	1913	1	705	705		1
265	In the Middle Atlas	3	1914	1917	2	706	707		3
266	Morocco	3.2	1916	1917	2	708	709	101	1
267	Near Agadès	3	1916	1917	1	710	710	102	1
268	Yunnan	2.6	1917	1918	1	711	711		1
269	Petrograd	2.6	1917	1917	1	712	712		0
270	Bolshevik Revolution	3	1917	1918	1	713	713		1
271	Kueichow	3.4	1917	1918	1	714	714	102	1
272	Tibet	3	1918	1918	1	715	715	103	0
273	Punjab	2.6	1919	1919	1	716	716		0
274	East Galicia	3	1919	1919	1	717	717		0
275	Afghan War	3	1919	1919	2	718	719		0
276	British Somaliland	3	1913	1920	1	720	720		7

APPENDIX 5 (continued)

Magnitude	Case Number	Name or Location	Intensity	Start	End	Number of Pairs	First Pair Number	Last Pair Number	Page Number In Richardson	Duration (In Years)
3	277	Haiti	3.35	1919	1920	1	721	721	103	1
	278	Hungary	3	1919	1920	2	722	723	104	1
	279	Vilna	3	1920	1920	1	724	724		0
	280	Iraq	3.3	1920	1921	2	725	726		1
	281	Ireland	3	1919	1922	1	727	727		3
	282	Waziristan	3	1919	1922	2	728	729		3
	283	Morocco	3	1923	1923	1	730	730	104	0
	284	Arabia	3	1924	1925	1	731	731	105	1
	285	Afghanistan	3	1924	1925	1	732	732		1
	286	Syria	3.4	1925	1926	6	733	738		1
	287	Dutch East Indies	3	1926	1927	1	739	739		1
	288	Afghanistan	3	1928	1929	2	740	741	105	1
	289	China	3	1929	1929	1	742	742	106	0
	290	China	3	1929	1929	1	743	743		0
	291	China	3	1929	1930	1	744	744		1
	292	China	3	1930	1930	1	745	745		0
	293	Indochina	3	1930	1931	1	746	746	106	1
	294	Brazil	3	1932	1932	1	747	747	107	0
	295	Quito	2.9	1932	1932	1	748	748		0
	296	Morocco	3.4	1929	1933	2	749	750		4
	297	Mosul	3	1933	1933	2	751	752		0
	298	Austria	3.2	1934	1934	2	753	754		0
	299	Germany	3	1934	1934	1	755	755		0
	300	Spain	2.7	1934	1934	1	756	756	107	0
	301	Suiyuan	3	1936	1937	1	757	757	108	1

302	Waziristan	3	1936	1938	2	758	759		2
303	Algeria	3	1945	1945	1	760	760		0
304	Syria-Lebanon	2.8	1945	1945	2	761	762	108	0
305	Bolivia	3	1946	1946	1	763	763	109	0
306	Formosa	3.2	1947	1947	1	764	764		0
307	Madagascar	3	1947	1947	2	765	766		0
308	Paraguay	2.7	1947	1947	1	767	767		0
309	Hyderabad	3.3	1948	1948	1	768	768	109	0
310	Colombia	2.7	1948	1948	1	769	769	110	0
311	South Korea	3	1948	1948	1	770	770		0
312	Java	3.2	1945	1949	4	771	774		4
313	Kashmir	3	1947	1949	4	775	778	110	2
314	Colombia	3.3	1949	1949	1	779	779	111	0
315	Bolivia	2.65	1952	1952	1	780	780	111	0

APPENDIX 6
RICHARDSON'S PAIR DATA

Pair Number	Case Number	Case-Pair Number	Background	Irritants	Row Actor	Column Actor
1	1	1	I	SZ	Serbs	Austro-Hungarians
2	1	2		P	Serbs	Germans
3	1	3	IL	M	Serbs	Bulgarians
4	1	4	IHL	F	Russians	Austro-Hungarians
5	1	5	QIHL	F	Russians	Germans
6	1	6	IGM		Russians	Turks
7	1	7	IL		Russians	Bulgarians
8	1	8	IHML	F	French	Austro-Hungarians
9	1	9	QIHL	PMTF	French	Germans
10	1	10	IGL		French	Turks
11	1	11	I		French	Bulgarians
12	1	12	IG		French Colonial Troops	Austro-Hungarians
13	1	13	IG		French Colonial Troops	Germans
14	1	14	IH		Belgians	Germans
15	1	15	IH	F	British	Austro-Hungarians
16	1	16	QIH	PZF	British	Germans
17	1	17	IGL		British	Turks
18	1	18	I		British	Bulgarians
19	1	19	IG		Indian Troops	Austro-Hungarians
20	1	20	IG		Indian Troops	Germans
21	1	21	I		Indian Troops	Turks
22	1	22	IGL	TP	Japanese	Austro-Hungarians
23	1	23	IGL		Japanese	Germans
24	1	24	IG		Japanese	Turks

1	25	IG	ZRGM	Japanese	Bulgarians
1	26	IAX	T	Armenians	Turks
1	27	IHML		Italians	Austro-Hungarians
1	28	IGL		Italians	Germans
1	29	IGM		Italians	Turks
1	30	I		Italians	Bulgarians
1	31	IH	P	Portugese	Austro-Hungarians
1	32	IH	P	Portugese	Germans
1	33	IG		Arabs of Hejaz	Austro-Hungarians
1	34	IG		Arabs of Hejaz	Germans
1	35	IHA	R	Arabs of Hejaz	Turks
1	36	IH	T	Rumanians	Austro-Hungarians
1	37	IH		Rumanians	Germans
1	38	ILM		Rumanians	Bulgarians
1	39	IH		Greeks	Germans
1	40	IGL	M	Greeks	Turks
1	41	I	MTP	Greeks	Bulgarians
1	42	IHA	R	Czechoslovaks	Austro-Hungarians
1	43	IHL		Americans	Austro-Hungarians
1	44	QIHL		Americans	Germans
2	1	IG	MZT	Chinese	Japanese
2	2	I	P	Chinese	Siamese
2	3	JAX	COG	Jews	Germans
2	4	JAX	CGP	Jews	Vichy French
2	5	JAX	CG	Jews	Fascist Rumanians
2	6	JX	MCG	Jews	Anti-Communist Hungarians
2	7	IA	TR	Czechoslovaks	Germans
2	8	I	T	Czechoslovaks	Anti-Communist Hungarians
2	9	I	T	Poles	Germans

APPENDIX 6 *(continued)*

Pair Number	Case Number	Case-Pair Number	Background	Irritants	Row Actor	Column Actor
54	2	10	IH	P	Poles	Fascist Italians
55	2	11	IG	TZ	French-Free French	Japanese
56	2	12	IVM	FPT	French-Free French	Germans
57	2	13	IL	PT	French-Free French	Fascist Italians
58	2	14	JXLA	P	French-Free French	Vichy French
59	2	15	IGL	PZT	British	Japanese
60	2	16	IVM	FPT	British	Germans
61	2	17	IL	PZ	British	Fascist Italians
62	2	18	ILM	P	British	Vichy French
63	2	19	IL	PZ	British	Fascist Rumanians
64	2	20	I	P	British	Anti-Communist Hungarians
65	2	21	IM	P	British	Fascist Bulgarians
66	2	22	IGC	P	British	Siamese
67	2	23	IGL	KTZ	Australians	Japanese
68	2	24	IVM	PT	Australians	Germans
69	2	25	IL	P	Australians	Fascist Italians
70	2	26	IL	P	Australians	Vichy French
71	2	27	IGC	P	Australians	Siamese
72	2	28	IGL		New Zealanders	Japanese
73	2	29	IVM	P	New Zealanders	Germans
74	2	30	IL	P	New Zealanders	Fascist Italians
75	2	31	IGL		Pro-British Indians	Japanese
76	2	32	IGM	P	Pro-British Indians	Germans
77	2	33	IGL	P	Pro-British Indians	Fascist Italians
78	2	34	IGL	P	Pro-British Indians	Vichy French
79	2	35	IG	P	Pro-British Indians	Siamese
80	2	36	IM	T	South Africans	Germans

81	2	IL	P	South Africans	Fascist Italians
82	2	IGL	PKTZ	Canadians	Japanese
83	2	IVM	P	Canadians	Germans
84	2	IL	P	Canadians	Fascist Italians
85	2	IVM	T	Danish Saboteurs	Germans
86	2	IV	TF	Norwegians	Germans
87	2	I	P	Norwegians	Vichy French
88	2	IVM	TF	Belgians	Germans
89	2	IL	P	Belgians	Fascist Italians
90	2	IG	TZ	Dutch	Japanese
91	2	IV	TF	Dutch	Germans
92	2	I	P	Dutch	Fascist Italians
93	2	IHA	TMR	Ethiopians	Fascist Italians
94	2	IM	TF	Greeks	Germans
95	2	IHM	PO	Greeks	Fascist Italians
96	2	I	TM	Greeks	Fascist Bulgarians
97	2	IGM	P	Communist Yugoslavs	Germans
98	2	IL	P	Communist Yugoslavs	Fascist Italians
99	2	I	TP	Communist Yugoslavs	Anti-Communist Hungarians
100	2	I	TM	Communist Yugoslavs	Fascist Bulgarians
101	2	IGM	PTZ	Russians	Japanese
102	2	IGM	TF	Russians	Germans
103	2	IGL	M	Russians	Fascist Italians
104	2	IG	MP	Russians	Finns
105	2	IGL	PT	Russians	Fascist Rumanians
106	2	I	PG	Russians	Anti-Communist Hungarians
107	2	BIG	P	Russians	Fascist Bulgarians
108	2	IGL	FKTZ	Americans	Japanese
109	2	IVM	FPS	Americans	Germans
110	2	IL	P	Americans	Fascist Italians
111	2	I	P	Americans	Vichy French

APPENDIX 6 (continued)

Pair Number	Case Number	Case-Pair Number	Background	Irritants	Row Actor	Column Actor
112	2	68	IL	ZP	Americans	Fascist Rumanians
113	2	69	I	P	Americans	Anti-Communist Hungarians
114	2	70	I	P	Americans	Fascist Bulgarians
115	2	71	IM	Z	Brazilians	Germans
116	2	72	I	Z	Brazilians	Fascist Italians
117	2	73	IGL	P	Democratic Italians	Germans
118	2	74	JHXLA	MVR	Democratic Italians	Fascist Italians
119	2	75	IGL	P	Communist Rumanians	Germans
120	2	76	XJA	G	Communist Rumanians	Fascist Rumanians
121	2	77	IL	P	Democratic Bulgarians	Germans
122	2	78	XJAM	P	Democratic Bulgarians	Fascist Bulgarians
123	2	79	IL	P	Democratic Hungarians	Germans
124	2	80	IG	TP	Vichy French	Siamese
125	2	81	IG	P	Iraq	British
126	2	82	I	G	Spanish Falangists	Russia
127	2	83	J		Bosnian Ustashis	Serbs
128	2	84	IGA	R	Burmese	British
129	2	85	JA	WG	Greeks of E.L.A.S.	Greeks of E.D.E.S.
130	2	86	J	GM	Yugoslav Chetniks	Yugoslav Partisans
131	3	1	BEJXAL	GWRZ	Taiping Rebels	Chinese Government
132	4	1	BEHJAL	SV	American South	American North
133	5	1	HJ	M	Uruguayan Colorados	Urguayan Blancos
134	5	2	HJ	FT	Uruguayan Colorados	Paraguayans
135	5	3	HIM	S	Brazilians	Uruguayan Blancos
136	5	4	HI	F	Brazilians	Paraguayans
137	5	5	HJM		Argentines	Uruguayan Blancos
138	5	6	HJ	FT	Argentines	Paraguayans

No.						
139	6	1	BJXLAM	GWPZV	Russian Nobles and Bourgeois	Bolsheviks
140	6	2	IG	Z	Russian Nobles and Bourgeois	Jews
141	6	3	BIL	TR	Ukrainians	Bolsheviks
142	6	4	IXG	Z	Ukrainians	Jews
143	6	5	BIL	P	Czechslovakians	Bolsheviks
144	6	6	BILM	PSGW	British	Bolsheviks
145	6	7	BILM	PSGW	French	Bolsheviks
146	6	8	CIGLM	PS	Japanese	Bolsheviks
147	6	9	BIL	PSGW	Americans	Bolsheviks
148	7	1	BEJLXA	WRG	Kuomintang	Communists
149	8	1	BEJX	WVGM	Spanish Republicans	Spanish Falangists
150	8	2	I	OVG	Spanish Republicans	Italian Contingent
151	8	3	I	OVG	Spanish Republicans	German Contingent
152	8	4	I	GV	Spanish Republicans	Eire Volunteers
153	8	5	I	G	Russian Contingent	Spanish Falangists
154	8	6	I	G	Russian Contingent	Italian Contingent
155	8	7	I	G	Russian Contingent	German Contingent
156	8	8	I	G	Russian Contingent	Eire Volunteers
157	8	9	I	V	French Volunteers	Spanish Falangists
158	8	10	I	V	French Volunteers	Italian Contingent
159	8	11	I	V	French Volunteers	German Contingent
160	8	12	I		French Volunteers	Eire Volunteers
161	8	13	I	V	British Volunteers	Spanish Falangists
162	8	14	I	V	British Volunteers	Italian Contingent
163	8	15	I	V	British Volunteers	German Contingent
164	8	16	J		British Volunteers	Eire Volunteers
165	9	1	A		British Government	Moslems
166	9	2	GA		Hindus	British Government
167	9	3	X	GTZ	Hindus	Moslems
168	9	4	G		Hindus	Pakistan Government
169	9	5	GA		Sikhs	British Government

APPENDIX 6 (continued)

Pair Number	Case Number	Case-Pair Number	Background	Irritants	Row Actor	Column Actor
170	9	6	X	GTZ	Sikhs	Moslems
171	9	7	G		Sikhs	Pakistan Government
172	9	8	G		Indian Government	Moslems
173	10	1	HAXKJMR		Janissaries	Turkish Regular Army
174	11	1	DI	GMS	Russians	Turks
175	11	2	IG		Bulgarians	Turks
176	12	1	DIML	GS	Turks	Russians
177	12	2	IHML	ZFN	French	Russians
178	12	3	IHL	Z	British	Russians
179	12	4	IH	P	Piedmontese	Russians
180	13	1	MA	RV	Autocrats of Italy	Liberals of Italy
181	13	2	I		Autocrats of France	Liberals of Italy
182	13	3	JXAM	WRV	Autocrats of France	Liberals of France
183	13	4	HJXAL	WRV	Autocrats of Germany	Liberals of Germany
184	13	5	IMA	RV	Autocrats of Austro-Hungary	Liberals of Italy
185	13	6	HJXA	WRV	Autocrats of Austro-Hungary	Liberals of Austria
186	13	7	HIAL	WRV	Autocrats of Austro-Hungary	Liberals of Hungary
187	13	8	HI	WV	Autocrats of Russia	Liberals of Hungary
188	13	9	HIL	W	Autocrats of Russia	Liberals of Wallachia
189	13	10	HJA	W	Autocrats of Wallachia	Liberals of Wallachia
190	13	11	GI		Autocrats of Turkey	Liberals of Wallachia
191	14	1	BJHML		Austrians	Prussians
192	14	2	HI	MVT	Austrians	Italians
193	14	3	BJH		Bavarians	Prussians
194	14	4	BJHM		Saxons	Prussians

195	5	BJH	NF	Hanoverians	Prussians
196	1	QMHI	F	North German Confederation	French
197	2	QIMH	F	Badeners	French
198	3	QIMH	F	Bavarians	French
199	4	QIMH	F	Wurtembergers	French
200	1	AJX	G	Moslems in Shensi and Kansu	Chinese
201	2	AIM	G	Moslems in Sinkiang	Chinese
202	1	HJA	YZRV	Cubans	Spaniards
203	1	IAM	GWZ	Christians in Herzegovina and Bosnia	Turks
204	2		GIR	Bulgarians	Turks
205	3	IM	G	Montenegrins	Turks
206	4	IM	G	Serbs	Turks
207	5	I	GMS	Russians	Turks
208	6	I	G	Rumanians	Turks
209	1	AI	GRZF	Turks	Armenians
210	2	XAI	GZ	Kurds	Armenians
211	1	HJA	MZRY	Cubans	Spaniards
212	2	HIL	TFSW	Americans	Spaniards
213	1	AJH	MV	Colombian Liberals	Colombian Conservatives
214	1	CDGIL	ZTF	Russians	Japanese
215	1	CDGIAW	R	Germans	Wangoni
216	1	QCDGI	MXTFO	Achinese	Dutch
217	2	BEHJ	O	Achinese	Teuku Uma's Legion
218	3	CDIG	O	Teuku Uma's Party	Dutch
219	1	CIHAML	RTZ	Germans	Hottentots
220	2	CDGIAM	RTZ	Germans	Hereros
221	1	GIM	TS	Montenegrins	Turks
222	2	IM	TS	Bulgarians	Turks
223	3	GIM	TS	Greeks	Turks
224	4	IM	TS	Serbs	Turks
225	1	JXA	WR	Diaz	Madero

APPENDIX 6 *(continued)*

Pair Number	Case Number	Case-Pair Number	Background	Irritants	Row Actor	Column Actor
226	27	2	J	WR	Diaz	Zapata
227	27	3	J		Diaz	Orozco
228	27	4	J	MWZ	Diaz	Villa
229	27	5	JXA	R	Diaz	Carranza
230	27	6	J	W	Zapata	Madero
231	27	7	J	W	Zapata	Huerta
232	27	8	J		Zapata	Carranza
233	27	9	J		Orozco	Madero
234	27	10	JL	Z	Orozco	Villa
235	27	11	J		Orozco	Huerta
236	27	12	JL	Z	Villa	Carranza
237	27	13	JL	W	Huerta	Madero
238	27	14	J	Z	Huerta	Villa
239	27	15	J		Huerta	Carranza
240	27	16	IW	Z	Americans	Villa
241	27	17	I		Americans	Huerta
242	27	18	I		Americans	Carranza
243	27	19			Obregon	Zapata
244	27	20			Obregon	Orozco
245	27	21			Obregon	Villa
246	27	22			Obregon	Huerta
247	27	23	L		Obregon	Carranza
248	28	1	IG	M	French	Turks
249	28	2	BJHA	V	Turkish Caliphate Army	Turks
250	28	3	GI	MT	Greeks	Turks
251	28	4	GI	MZ	Armenians	Turks

252	1	JA	GZM	Feng Yü-Hsiang	Chinese Moslems
253	1	BEHJ	N	Yen Hsi-Shan	Chiang Kai-Shek
254	2	HJ		Yen Hsi-Shan	Chang Hsueh-Liang
255	3	BEGJ	N	Feng Yü-Hsiang	Chiang Kai-Shek
256	4	HJ		Feng Yü-Hsiang	Chang Hsueh-Liang
257	5	BEHJ	NM	Chang Fa-Kuei	Chiang Kai-Shek
258	1	DWIK	MGT	Italians	Sanusi Bedouin
259	2	BJ	YO	Natives	Sanusi Bedouin
260	1	IG	MZOTW	Chinese	Japanese
261	1	BJH	TZF	Paraguayans	Bolivians
262	1	MZGI	TF	Finns	Russians
263	1	I	MGW	Greek Government	Communists
264	1	HJQA	ZR	Bolivians	Spaniards
265	2	HJQA	ZR	Ecuadorians	Spaniards
266	3	HJQA	ZR	Venezuelans	Spaniards
267	4	HJQA	ZR	Colombians	Spaniards
268	5	HJQAL	ZR	Argentines	Spaniards
269	6	HJQA	ZR	Uruguayans	Spaniards
270	7	HJQA	ZR	Chileans	Spaniards
271	8	HJQA	ZR	Peruvians	Spaniards
272	9	HJQAL	ZRW	Mexicans	Spaniards
273	1	CDGI	SKTOF	British	Burmese
274	2	CDGI	Y	Indians	Burmese
275	1	CDGI	MF	British	Jat Hindus
276	2		Y	Sepoys	Jat Hindus
277	3	I	Y	Gurkhas	Jat Hindus
278	1	QAI	GYZR	Greeks	Turks
279	2	IG	T	Greeks	Egyptians
280	3	IGM	STF	Russians	Turks
281	4	IG		Russians	Egyptians
282	5	IGM	S	French	Turks

APPENDIX 6 (continued)

Pair Number	Case Number	Case-Pair Number	Background	Irritants	Row Actor	Column Actor
283	39	6	IG		French	Egyptians
284	39	7	IGML	S	British	Turks
285	39	8	IG		British	Egyptians
286	40	1	QIA	MGZR	Jehangir's Party	Chinese
287	40	2	IG		Kokandians	Chinese
288	41	1	BEJA	NG	Court of Jogjakarta	Dipa Negara
289	41	2	QCIAM	RWKZG	Dutch	Dipa Negara
290	41	3		O	Auxiliaries	Dipa Negara
291	42	1	QRAIH	M	Russians	Poles
292	43	1	A	NPW	Syrians	Egyptians
293	43	2	HIRAL	ZTN	Turks	Egyptians
294	44	1	JXAM	NV	Portuguese Liberals	Dom Miguel
295	44	2	IH		Portuguese Liberals	British Government
296	44	3	I		Mercenaries	Dom Miguel
297	44	4	IHM	S	French Government	Dom Miguel
298	44	5	IHM		Spanish Government	Dom Miguel
299	44	6	IHL		British Government	Dom Miguel
300	45	1	CDGI	T	White Emigrants	Zulus
301	45	2	BEHJ	N	Zulu Exiles	Zulus
302	46	1	GI	TFO	Circassians	Russians
303	47	1	HJXA	N	Spanish Moderates	Spanish Conservatives
304	47	2	HI		Spanish Moderates	Basques
305	47	3	JXM	VGN	Spanish Liberals	Spanish Conservatives
306	47	4	I		Spanish Liberals	Basques
307	47	5	JLA		Spanish Liberals	Spanish Moderates
308	47	6	I	V	British Government	Spanish Conservatives

309	47	7	I		British Government	Basques
310	48	1	HARI	MTF	Turks	Egyptians
311	48	2	GIA	ZR	Maronites	Egyptians
312	48	3	GI		Maronites	Turkish Fleet
313	48	4	GIM		British	Egyptians
314	48	5	GI		Austrians	Egyptians
315	48	6	GIMA	ZR	Druses	Egyptians
316	49	1	GI		Tibetans	Dogras
317	50	1	CDGI	KOZ	Chinese	British
318	51	1	DGI	P	British	Afghans
319	51	2	JH	MN	Afghan Exiles	Afghans
320	51	3	G	MT	Sikhs	Afghans
321	51	4			Indians	Afghans
322	52	1	CDGI	TM	British	Baluchis
323	53	1	CDGIL	FT	British	Sikhs
324	53	2		Y	Sepoys	Sikhs
325	54	1	CDI	GMT	Abd El Kader	French
326	54	2	BEHJ	Y	Abd El Kader	North African Mercenaries
327	54	3	BEHJ		Abd El Kader	Moroccan Government
328	54	4	CDGI		Moroccan Government	French
329	55	1	QIH	MT	Mexicans	Americans
330	56	1	CDGIA	MR	British	Sikhs
331	56	2	DGI	M	British	Afghans
332	56	3	I	YO	Pathans	Sikhs
333	57	1	JHB		Uruguayan Colorados	Uruguayan Blancos
334	57	2	JHB		Uruguayan Colorados	Argentine Federalists
335	57	3	JHB		Argentine Unitarios	Uruguayan Blancos
336	57	4	JHBM		Argentine Unitarios	Argentine Federalists
337	57	5	IH		French	Uruguayan Blancos
338	57	6	IH		French	Argentine Federalists
339	57	7	IHM		British	Uruguayan Blancos

APPENDIX 6 (continued)

Pair Number	Case Number	Case-Pair Number	Background	Irritants	Row Actor	Column Actor
340	57	8	IHM		British	Argentine Federalists
341	57	9	IHM		Brazilians	Uruguayan Blancos
342	57	10	IHM		Brazilians	Argentine Federalists
343	58	1	GIM	RP	Turks	Montenegrins
344	59	1	CDIXA	MKGZRF	British	Bengal Army
345	59	2	AM	Y	Indian Troops	Bengal Army
346	59	3			Nepalese State Troops	Bengal Army
347	60	1	BHI	MFV	Piedmontese	Austrians
348	60	2	BHIAM	VR	Italian Volunteers	Austrians
349	60	3	MHA	V	Italian Volunteers	Papal Government
350	60	4	M	OV	Garibaldians	Austrians
351	60	5	BHIML	FVT	French	Austrians
352	61	1	QCDGI	KMZO	British	Chinese
353	61	2	QCDI	KGZO	French	Chinese
354	62	1	QDKGI	MF	Moroccans	Spaniards
355	63	1	BEI	MT	Prussians	Danes
356	63	2	HI		Austrians	Danes
357	64	1	I	WSV	French	Mexican Constitutionalists
358	64	2	JM	WS	Spaniards	Mexican Constitutionalists
359	64	3	I	WS	British	Mexican Constitutionalists
360	65	1	XHJAL	MW	French Government	National Guards
361	66	1	ABEHX	VRM	Spanish Government	Carlists
362	67	1	IG	TS	Northern Abyssinians	Egyptians
363	67	2	L		Northern Abyssinians	Bogos
364	67	3		M	Bogos	Egyptians

365	1	68	BEHJA	O	Japanese Government	Clan Satsuma
366	1	69	I	G	Austrians	Moslems
367	1	70	CDWKGI	TS	British	Zulus
368	2	70	B	Y	Native Troops	Zulus
369	1	71	DGI	MPY	British	Afghans
370	2	71		Y	Indians	Afghans
371	1	72	GI	FTP	Russians	Tekke Turkomans
372	1	73	JHM	TZW	Bolivians	Chileans
373	2	73	JHML	TZW	Peruvians	Chileans
374	1	74	AJ	GMZRS	Egyptians	Sudanese
375	2	74	CDI	GSV	British	Sudanese
376	1	75	QCDGI	MTZ	Annamese	French
377	2	75	CDGI	MZ	Black Flag Bandits	French
378	3	75	QCDGIM	P	Chinese	French
379	1	76	JHAXL	V	Chilean Congress	President Balmaceda
380	1	77	BH	TZ	Bornu Army	Rabeh
381	1	78	CDGIA	MZRFTV	Belgians	Arabs
382	2	78	CDGI		Belgians	Negroes
383	3	78	CDGI		Negroes	Arabs
384	4	78	BE		Negroes	Negroes
385	1	79	J	GMT	Egyptians	Sudanese
386	2	79	CDGI	MT	British	Sudanese
387	3	79	IG		Abyssinians	Sudanese
388	4	79	CI		Tribes near Suakin	Sudanese
389	5	79		G	Darfurians	Sudanese
390	6	79	DGI		Shilluks	Sudanese
391	7	79	IG	T	Italians	Sudanese
392	1	80	IG	TZO	Japanese	Chinese
393	1	81	HCDI	TZMR	Abyssinians	Italians
394	1	82	CDGIW	SMTF	British	Sudanese
395	2	82	GJW	SMTF	Egyptians	Sudanese
396	3	82	B	Y	Sudanese	Sudanese

APPENDIX 6 (continued)

Pair Number	Case Number	Case-Pair Number	Background	Irritants	Row Actor	Column Actor
397	83	1	BEJAX	G	Chinese Christians	Boxers
398	83	2	QM	K	Japanese	Boxers
399	83	3	QW	GKCDI	Russians	Boxers
400	83	4	QWM	GKCDI	British	Boxers
401	83	5	QW	GKCDI	Americans	Boxers
402	83	6	QWM	GKCDI	French	Boxers
403	83	7	QW	GKCDI	Germans	Boxers
404	83	8	QW	GKCDI	Austrians	Boxers
405	83	9	QW	GKCDI	Italians	Boxers
406	84	1	CDI	MFPTG	French	Hovas
407	84	2	CDI	Y	Senegalese	Hovas
408	85	1	QHIL	TZ	Americans	Filipinos
409	85	2		Y	Makabebe Scouts	Filipinos
410	86	1	BEH	MITZSW	Transvaal Boers	British
411	86	2	BEHI		Orange Free State Boers	British
412	87	1	CDWKGIR	ZM	British	Zulu
413	88	1	AXIR	MG	Armenians	Turks
414	89	1	BEHJ	Z	Peking Government	White Wolf's Bandits
415	90	1	DGI	MTW	Riffs	Spaniards
416	91	1	HIL	T	Greeks	Bulgarians
417	91	2	ILM	T	Serbs	Bulgarians
418	91	3	HIL	T	Rumanians	Bulgarians
419	91	4	GI	TM	Turks	Bulgarians
420	92	1	BEHJA	V	Imperial Remnants	Kuomintang
421	93	1	XAMGI	TZR	Russians	Kirghiz
422	94	1	DGI	WT	Italians	Turks

423	2	IDG	YT	Italians	Sanusi
424	3	I	YO	Eritreans	Turks
425	4	I	YO	Eritreans	Sanusi
426	5	DGI	P	British	Sanusi
427	1	JAXG	WR	White Finns	Red Finns
428	2	IG	W	White Finns	Russians
429	3	IG		Germans	Russians
430	1	IG	TM	Arabs	French
431	1	BIG	MT	Poles	Russian Bolsheviks
432	2	BIG	WSM	French Officers	Russian Bolsheviks
433	1	BEHJ	M	Yunnanese	Szechuanese
434	1	A	G	Hindus	Moplahs
435	2	CDIA	G	British	Moplahs
436	1	IA	R	Koreans	Japanese
437	1	QDGI	TM	Spaniards	Riffs
438	2	QDGI	T	French	Riffs
439	3	QBEHJ	T	Moors	Riffs
440	1	BEJH	FN	Wu Pei-Fu	Kuomintang
441	2	BEJ	G	Wu Pei-Fu	Communists
442	3	BEHJ	FN	Sun Chuan-Fang	Kuomintang
443	4	BEJ	G	Sun Chuan-Fang	Communists
444	5	GIM	W	Japanese	Kuomintang
445	1	GIA	ZM	Chinese Provincial Govt.	Hodja Nias Hadji
446	2	GIA	ZM	Chinese Provincial Govt.	Yollbars Khan
447	3	GJA	M	Chinese Provincial Govt.	Tungans
448	4	GIA		Russian Emigres	Yollbars Khan
449	5	GIA		Russian Emigres	Tungans
450	6	GI		Soviet Russians	Yollbars Khan
451	7	GI		Soviet Russians	Tungans
452	8	AHIL		Hodja Nias Hadji	Tungans
453	1	QHDCI	MT	Abyssinians	Italians
454	1	JBAXL	WGM	Right-Wing Greeks	Left-Wing Greeks

APPENDIX 6 (continued)

Pair Number	Case Number	Case-Pair Number	Background	Irritants	Row Actor	Column Actor
455	105	2	IBL		British	Left-Wing Greeks
456	105	3	IC		Gurkhas	Left-Wing Greeks
457	106	1	IAM	T	British	Irgun
458	106	2	IA	T	British	Stern Gang
459	106	3	A	T	British	Jews
460	106	4	IA		Palestinians	British
461	106	5	IA	T	Palestinians	Irgun
462	106	6	IA	T	Palestinians	Stern Gang
463	106	7	A	GT	Palestinians	Jews
464	106	8	I	GT	Egyptians	Jews
465	106	9	I	GT	Iraqis	Jews
466	106	10	I	GT	Transjordanians	Jews
467	106	11	I	GT	Syrians	Jews
468	106	12	I	GT	Lebanese	Jews
469	107	1	AHJ		Buenos Aires	Argentine Interior
470	108	1	A		Turks	Churchid Pasha
471	109	1			Kedah	Siamese
472	110	1	CDGIQM	R	Dutch	Palembang
473	111	1	HA	R	Naples Carbonarists	Austrians and King Ferdinand
474	112	1	HA	R	Piedmont Carbonarists	Austrians and King Charles Felix
475	113	1		T	Nubians	Mehemet Ali
476	113	2			Mamelukes	Mehemet Ali
477	114	1	A		Turkish Government	Ali Pasha
478	115	1	H		Turks	Persians
479	116	1	HJA	V	Spanish Royalists	Spanish Republicans
480	116	2	I		French	Spanish Republicans

ID	No.	n	Code1	Code2	Group 1	Group 2
481	117	1	CDGI	R	Bonians	Dutch
482	117	2			Bonians	Auxiliaries
483	118	1	CDIG	Z	British	Ashantis
484	118	2	BE	YZ	Africans	Ashantis
485	119	1	HI	T	Brazilians	Argentines and Uruguayans
486	120	1	I	TMG	Persians	Russians
487	120	2	I	GM	Persians	Armenians
488	121	1	BEJA	GWN	Central American Liberals	Central American Conservatives
489	122	1	HJ		Mexicans	Spaniards
490	123	1	CDWKGXA		Tasmanians	British
491	124	1	GI		Algerians	French
492	125	1	JA		Chilean Liberals	Chilean Conservatives
493	126	1	JA		French Government	French Liberals
494	127	1	IG		Chinese	Kokanese
495	128	1	JHA	Z	Bustos	Argentine Unitarios
496	129	1	KIA	N	Turks	Bosnians
497	129	2	A	M	Herzegovinians	Bosnians
498	130	1	A	GIR	Dutch	Belgians
499	131	1	C		Indians	Buenos Aires
500	132	1	A		Egyptians	Fellahin
501	133	1	CDI	ZT	British	Kaffirs
502	133	2	CDI	ZT	Boers	Kaffirs
503	133	3		Y	Hottentots	Kaffirs
504	134	1	CDGI	T	Portuguese	Matshangana
505	134	2			Negroes	Matshangana
506	135	1	A	T	Texans	Mexicans
507	136	1	BDJ	G	Malays	Padris
508	136	2	CDI	G	Dutch	Padris
509	137	1		T	Towns near Zanzibar	Sayyid Said
510	138	1	AH	M	Turks	Bosnians
511	139	1	CDGI	T	Matabele	Boers
512	140	1	C	T	Ma-Kalanga	Matabele

APPENDIX 6 (continued)

Pair Number	Case Number	Case-Pair Number	Background	Irritants	Row Actor	Column Actor
513	141	1		MT	Afghans	Persians
514	142	1	JA	G	Annamese	Annamese Christians
515	142	2	CI	G	Annamese	French
516	143	1	JH	N	Chileans	Bolivians
517	143	2	JH		Chileans	Peruvians
518	143	3	HJA		Chileans	Chilean Exiles
519	143	4	HJ		Peruvian Exiles	Bolivians
520	143	5	HJA		Peruvian Exiles	Peruvians
521	143	6	HJ		Peruvian Exiles	Chilean Exiles
522	144	1	GI	T	Khivans	Russians
523	145	1	IG		Khan of Khelat	British
524	145	2			Khan of Khelat	Sepoys
525	146	1			Mashonas	Matabele
526	147	1	IHA	RM	Turks	Turks of Bosnia
527	148	1	JA	G	Marquez	Obando
528	149	1	CDIG	R	British	Sindhiales
529	149	2		Y	Indians	Sindhiales
530	150	1	HJA	R	Brazilian Governments	Farrapos
531	151	1	JA	G	Maronites	Druses
532	151	2	IGA		Maronites	Turks
533	151	3	IGA		Turks	Druses
534	152	1	CDIG		British Navy	Borneo Pirates
535	153	1	HIA	R	Austrians	Polish Nobles
536	153	2	HIA	R	Polish Peasants	Austrians
537	153	3	XHJA	W	Polish Peasants	Polish Nobles
538	154	1	A	M	Chinese	Kashgarians

539	155	1	CDGI	Dutch	Balinese
540	155	2		Auxiliaries	Balinese
541	156	1	IH	Danes	Prussians
542	157	1	BJHA	T	French Republicans	Louis Napoleon
543	158	1	JHA	M	Chilean Conservatives	Chilean Liberals
544	159	1	CDI	MZT	Kaffirs	British
545	159	2		Y	Kaffirs	Hottentots
546	159	3	CDIL	Z	Hottentots	British
547	159	4	CDI	ZM	Basuto	British
548	160	1	CDGIM	Z	British	Burmese
549	161	1	E		Dogras	Dards
550	162	1	CDGI		Bantu	Boers
551	163	1	BEHJA	K	Colombian Constitutionalists	Melo
552	164	1	CDGIA		British	Santals
553	165	1		O	Nicaraguan Conservatives	Filibusters
554	165	2	JA		Nicaraguan Conservatives	Nicaraguan Liberals
555	166	1	GI	P	Persians	British
556	166	2		Y	Persians	Indians
557	167	1	CDGI	T	French	Fulani
558	168	1	IG	M	Chinese	Kokanese
559	169	1	GI	MR	Turks	Montenegrins
560	170	1	CDGIM	T	Dutch	Boninese
561	170	2	BEHJ	MN	Aru Palaka	Boninese
562	171	1	XJHA	V	Italian Autocrats	Italian Liberals
563	172	1	JA	GW	Syrian Christians	Druses
564	172	2	JA	G	Syrian Christians	Syrian Moslems
565	173	1	JA	V	Mexican Constitutionalists	Mexican Conservatives
566	174	1	BJHAM	Z	Argentine Confederation	Buenos Aires
567	175	1	A		Abyssinian Rebels	King Theodore
568	176	1	JA	V	Colombian Conservatives	Colombian Liberals
569	177	1	GI	M	Turks	Montenegrins
570	177	2	GIA		Turks	Herzegovinans

APPENDIX 6 (continued)

Pair Number	Case Number	Case-Pair Number	Background	Irritants	Row Actor	Column Actor
571	178	1	AIG		Serbs	Turks
572	179	1	QCDI	TZG	Dutch	Banjermasinese
573	180	1	IM	GZ	Bengal Moslems	British
574	180	2		OY	Bengal Moslems	Auxiliaries
575	180	3	I	GP	Hill Moslems	British
576	180	4		OY	Hill Moslems	Auxiliaries
577	181	1	J	V	Ecuadorian Clericals	Colombian Democrats
578	182	1	IGM		Circassians	Russians
579	183	1	CDGI		British	Japanese of Satsuma and Choshu Clans
580	183	2	CDGI		French	Japanese of Satsuma and Choshu Clans
581	183	3	CDGI		Dutch	Japanese of Satsuma and Choshu Clans
582	184	1	HJA		Argentines	Peñaloza's Guerrillas
583	185	1	GIA	MR	Russians	Poles
584	186	1	CDGI	MZ	British	Bhutanese
585	187	1	IG	M	Peruvians	Spaniards
586	187	2	JH		Chileans	Spaniards
587	188	1	CJXA	ZTK	British	Jamaican Blacks
588	189	1	CDGI	TM	British	Maoris
589	190	1	C	T	Americans	Sioux
590	191	1	CDGI	TZ	Basuto	Boers
591	192	1	JH	T	Papal Government	Italians
592	192	2	IH		French	Italians
593	193	1	A		Abyssinian Rebels	King Theodore

594	194	1	BEHJA		Japanese Government	Feudal Clans
595	195	1	CDI	S	Abyssinians	British
596	195	2		Y	Abyssinians	Indians
597	196	1	GI	T	Bokharians	Russians
598	197	1	CI	Z	Negroes	Arabs
599	198	1	A		Egyptians	Negroes
600	199	1	CDGIA		French	Algerians
601	200	1	CDGI	MST	British	Ashanti
602	200	2	B	O	Negroes	Ashanti
603	201	1	CDGI	TZ	Tonkinese	French
604	201	2	CDGI		Black Flag Bandits	French
605	202	1			Egyptians	Darfurians
606	203	1	BHJAM		Avellaneda	Porteños
607	204	1	CDAM	T	United States Army	Sioux
608	205	1	JA	G	Colombian Conservatives	Colombian Liberals
609	206	1	CDGI	MZ	Kaffirs	British
610	207	1	AM	S	Egyptians	Bahr-El-Ghazal
611	208	1	IM		Argentines	Patagonians
612	209	1	BJHAM	Z	Buenos Aires	Argentine Government
613	210	1	A		Victims	Metesa
614	211	1	CDGIA	R	British	Basutos
615	212	1	IA	R	Austrians	Dalmatians
616	213	1	GI	T	Tunisians	French
617	214	1	CDGI		Egyptians	British
618	215	1	C		Argentines	Patagonians
619	216	1	BE	ON	Black Tribes	Msidi
620	217	1	BJ		Indabayin	Oman Sultan
621	218	1	CDGI	T	French	Hovas
622	218	2	J		Sakalavas	Hovas
623	219	1	BEAJ		Colombian Conservatives	Colombian Radicals
624	220	1	DGI	T	Afghans	Russians

APPENDIX 6 *(continued)*

Pair Number	Case Number	Case-Pair Number	Background	Irritants	Row Actor	Column Actor
625	221	1	I	T	Serbs	Bulgarians
626	222	1	DI	T	Abyssinians	Italians
627	223	1	CDGIM	ZST	British	Burmese
628	223	2		O	Indians	Burmese
629	224	1	A	G	Heathen	Ba-ingleza
630	224	2	A	G	Heathen	Ba-fransa
631	224	3	A	G	Heathen	Ba-islamu
632	224	4	A	G	Ba-ingleza	Ba-fransa
633	224	5	A	G	Ba-ingleza	Ba-islamu
634	224	6	A	G	Ba-fransa	Ba-islamu
635	225	1	CDGI	R	Coast Arabs	Germans
636	226	1	CDM		Sioux	Americans
637	227	1	CDGIA	T	King Ahmadu	French
638	227	2	A	Y	King Ahmadu	Senegalese
639	228	1	AG	ZR	Turks	Druses
640	229	1	A	GM	Ba-ingleza	Ba-fransa
641	230	1			Bunyoro	Baganda
642	231	1	A	GMR	Sasaks	Balinese
643	231	2	GL	XK	Dutch	Balinese
644	232	1	CDGI	MTRS	Dahomeyans	French
645	232	2		YO	Dahomeyans	Senegalese
646	233	1	A		Peixoto	Rio-grandenses
647	233	2	A		Peixoto	Brazilian Fleet
648	234	1	HJA	N	Peruvian Countrymen	Peruvian Cities
649	235	1	CDGI	ST	British	Arabs
650	235	2	CDGI	ST	British	Yaos

651	235	3	CDGI	Y	Sikhs	Arabs
652	235	4	CDGI	Y	Sikhs	Yaos
653	236	1	CDGI	R	British	Arabs
654	237	1	JA	GR	Brazilian Government	Jaguncoes
655	238	1	CDGI	S	British	Beni
656	239	1	IAM	G	Turks	Cretan Christians
657	239	2	I	GT	Turks	Greeks
658	239	3	IAX	G	Cretan Moslems	Cretan Christians
659	240	1	QCDGIA	TRZ	French	Samory
660	240	2	A	Y	Senegalese	Samory
661	241	1	CDGIA	MP	Germans	Waheme
662	242	1	CDIA	GFW	British	Moslems
663	242	2	A	W	Indians	Moslems
664	243	1	CDGIA	RZST	British	Inland Tribes
665	243	2	BA		Coast Negroes	Inland Tribes
666	244	1	CDIA	MG	British	Matabele
667	244	2	A	Y	Cape Blacks	Matabele
668	245	1	CDIG	MT	British	Kumasi
669	245	2		Y	Auxiliaries	Kumasi
670	246	1	CDGIAW		Buganda	British
671	246	2	A	Y	Buganda	Sudanese
672	246	3	CDGIAL	RW	Sudanese	British
673	246	4	A	Y	Sudanese	Auxiliaries
674	246	5	CDGI		Bunyoro	British
675	247	1	CDGI	T	French	Rabeh
676	248	1	CDGI	T	Kano	British
677	249	1	DGI	T	French	Tuareg
678	249	2		Z	Natives	Tuareg
679	250	1	A	G	British	Mullah
680	250	2		Y	Auxiliaries	Mullah
681	250	3		G	Abyssinians	Mullah

APPENDIX 6 *(continued)*

Pair Number	Case Number	Case-Pair Number	Background	Irritants	Row Actor	Column Actor
682	250	4		G	Italians	Mullah
683	251	1	DGI	KZ	British	Tibetans
684	251	2			Nepalese	Tibetans
685	252	1	BHJA	W	Russian Workers	Czar's Guards
686	253	1	A		Jews	Russians
687	254	1	CDGI	Z	British	Nandi
688	255	1	AID	PRGT	Tibetans	Chinese
689	256	1	A	WT	Jews	Rumanian Peasants
690	256	2	BJHA	WT	Rumanian Government	Rumanian Peasants
691	257	1	DI	GT	Chaouians	French
692	257	2	BEJHA	N	Moulai Hafid	Abd el Aziz
693	258	1	I	O	Dutch	Venezuelans
694	259	1	I	MTG	Senussi	French
695	260	1	BEHJA		Moroccan Sultan	Fez
696	260	2	CDGI	T	French	Fez
697	261	1	BEJXA		Chinese Revolutionaries	Manchus
698	262	1	DGI	T	Makhzen	French
699	262	2	EHJA	R	Makhzen	Moroccan Sultan
700	262	3	DGI	MT	Fez	French
701	262	4	EHJA		Fez	Moroccan Sultan
702	263	1	DGI	T	French	El Hiba
703	263	2	EHJA		Moroccan Sultan	El Hiba
704	263	3	EHJA		Caids	El Hiba
705	264	1	DIA	MRT	Tibetans	Chinese
706	265	1	DI	T	French	Zaians
707	265	2	EJHA		Moroccans	Zaians

708	266	1	DI	M	French	El Hiba
709	266	2	EHJ	M	Caids	El Hiba
710	267	1			French	Kaossen
711	268	1	BEJHAL	WRY	Yunnanese	Szechuanese
712	269	1	BJXAL	W	Petrograd Workers	Russian Government
713	270	1	BJX	W	Bolsheviks	Russian Government
714	271	1	BEHJAL	R	Kueichow	Szechuanese
715	272	1	ID	MT	Chinese	Tibetans
716	273	1	A	R	British	Punjab Crowds
717	274	1	I	T	Poles	Ukrainians
718	275	1	CDIM	GF	British	Afghans
719	275	2	IG		Nepalese	Afghans
720	276	1	CDGI	M	British	Mullah
721	277	1			Cacos	Americans
722	278	1	BJAX	WR	Hungarian Bourgeoisie	Hungarian Communists
723	278	2	I	T	Rumanians	Hungarian Communists
724	279	1	HI	T	Poles	Lithuanians
725	280	1	DI	G	British	Arabs
726	280	2	I	Y	Indians	Arabs
727	281	1	BEJXA	MGR	British	Irish
728	282	1	IGM	ZO	British	Wazirs
729	282	2		Y	Indians	Wazirs
730	283	1		T	French	Tache de Taza
731	284	1	JM	T	Hejaz	Wahabi
732	285	1	A		Afghan Government	Khosts
733	286	1	IGA	R	Druses of Jebel Druse	French
734	286	2	IG	Y	Druses of Jebel Druse	Auxiliaries
735	286	3	IGA	MR	Arabs of Damascus	French
736	286	4	I	Y	Arabs of Damascus	Auxiliaries
737	286	5	IGA	RP	Druses of Lebanon	French
738	286	6	IG	Y	Druses of Lebanon	Auxiliaries

APPENDIX 6 (continued)

Pair Number	Case Number	Case-Pair Number	Background	Irritants	Row Actor	Column Actor
739	287	1	CDIA	G	Dutch	Communists
740	288	1	LBHJA	DK	Amanullah	Habibullah
741	288	2	A		Nadir Khan	Habibullah
742	289	1	BEJ	N	Chiang Kai-Shek	Kwangsi
743	290	1	BEJ	N	Chiang Kai-Shek	Feng Yü-Hsiang
744	291	1	BEJ	N	Chiang Kai-Shek	Chang Fa-Kuei
745	292	1	BEJ	N	Kuomintang	Tang Sheng-Chi
746	293	1	CDGIA		French	Indo-China Nationalists
747	294	1	BEJHAM	R	Brazilian Government	Paulistas
748	295	1	A		Ecuadorian Army	Ecuadorian Army
749	296	1	DGI	T	French	Great Atlas Tribes
750	296	2	BEHJA		Moors	Great Atlas Tribes
751	297	1	A	MG	Kurds	Assyrian Christians
752	297	2	A		Iraqis	Assyrian Christians
753	298	1	BJAG	W	Austrian Government	Austrian Socialists
754	298	2	BJAG	W	Austrian Fascists	Austrian Socialists
755	299	1	JA	N	Nazis for Socialism	Nazis for Hitler
756	300	1	BJAX	W	Spanish Government	Spanish Leftists
757	301	1	I		Kuomintang	Mongols
758	302	1	I	GMZ	British	Moslems
759	302	2		G	Hindus	Moslems
760	303	1	GIA		French	Algerians
761	304	1	I	M	French	Syrians and Lebanese
762	304	2		Y	Senegalese	Syrians and Lebanese
763	305	1	JXA	W	Bolivian Government	Bolivian Revolutionaries
764	306	1	A	R	Chinese Government	Formosans

765	307	1	A	R	French	Madagascar Nationalists
766	307	2	A	Y	Senegalese	Madagascar Nationalists
767	308	1	JHA	MN	Paraguayan Febreristas	Paraguayan Government
768	309	1		G	Hyderabad	Indian Government
769	310	1	JHA		Colombian Conservatives	Colombian Liberals
770	311	1	A	G	South Korean Government	Korean Army Mutineers
771	312	1	CI		British	Indonesians
772	312	2		Y	Indians	Indonesians
773	312	3			Chinese	Indonesians
774	312	4		T	Dutch	Indonesians
775	313	1			Kashmiri Army	Moslems
776	313	2			Kashmiri Army	Pakistanis
777	313	3		G	Indians	Moslems
778	313	4	X	GT	Indians	Pakistanis
779	314	1	JHA		Colombian Conservatives	Colombian Liberals
780	315	1	A	M	Bolivian Government	Movimiento Nacionalista Revolucionario

APPENDIX 7

RIDATA: FILE OF RECODED RICHARDSON DATA

This 780-line BASIC file has on each line the case number, pair-in-case
number, background factors, and irritant factors for one of the 780 pairs.
(Variations in spacing from line to line have no significance.)

00001	1,1,I,SZ	00038	1,38,ILM,U
00002	1,2,I,P	00039	1,39,IH,U
00003	1,3, IL,M	00040	1,40,IGL,M
00004	1,4,IHL,F	00041	1,41, I,MTP
00005	1,5,QIHL,F	00042	1,42,IHA,R
00006	1,6,IGM,U	00043	1,43,IHL,U
00007	1,7,IL,U	00044	1,44,QIHL,U
00008	1,8,IHML,F	00045	2,1,IG,MZT
00009	1,9,QIHL,PMTF	00046	2,2,I,P
00010	1,10,IGL,U	00047	2,3,JAX,COG
00011	1,11,I,U	00048	2,4,JAX,CGP
00012	1,12,IG,U	00049	2,5,JAX,CG
00013	1,13,IG,U	00050	2,6,JX,MCG
00014	1,14,IH,U	00051	2,7,IA,TR
00015	1,15,IH,F	00052	2,8,I,T
00016	1,16,QIH,PZF	00053	2,9,I,T
00017	1,17,IGL,U	00054	2,10,IH,P
00018	1,18,I,U	00055	2,11,IG,TZ
00019	1,19,IG,U	00056	2,12,IVM,FPT
00020	1,20,IG,U	00057	2,13,IL,PT
00021	1,21,I,U	00058	2,14,JXLA,P
00022	1,22,IGL,U	00059	2,15,IGL,PZT
00023	1,23,IGL,TP	00060	2,16,IVM,FPT
00024	1,24,IG,U	00061	2,17,IL,PZ
00025	1,25,IG,U	00062	2,18,ILM,P
00026	1,26,IAX,ZRGM	00063	2,19,IL,PZ
00027	1,27,IHML,T	00064	2,20,I,P
00028	1,28,IGL,U	00065	2,21,IM,P
00029	1,29,IGM,U	00066	2,22,IGC,P
00030	1,30,I,U	00067	2,23,IGL,KTZ
00031	1,31,IH,P	00068	2,24,IVM,PT
00032	1,32,IH,P	00069	2,25,IL,P
00033	1,33,IG,U	00070	2,26,IL,P
00034	1,34,IG,U	00071	2,27,IGC,P
00035	1,35,IHA,R	00072	2,28,IGL,U
00036	1,36,IH,T	00073	2,29,IVM,P
00037	1,37,IH,U	00074	2,30,IL,P

00075	2,31,IGL,U	00119	2,75,IGL,P
00076	2,32,IGM,P	00120	2,76,XJA,G
00077	2,33,IGL,P	00121	2,77,IL,P
00078	2,34,IGL,P	00122	2,78,XJAM,P
00079	2,35,IG,P	00123	2,79,IL,P
00080	2,36,IM,T	00124	2,80,IG,TP
00081	2,37,IL,P	00125	2,81,IG,P
00082	2,38,IGL,PKTZ	00126	2,82,I,G
00083	2,39, IVM,P	00127	2,83,J,U
00084	2,40,IL,P	00128	2,84,IGA,R
00085	2,41,IVM,T	00129	2,85,JA,WG
00086	2,42,IV,TF	00130	2,86,J,GM
00087	2,43, I,P	00131	3,1,BEJXAL,GWRZ
00088	2,44,IVM,TF	00132	4,1,BEHJAL,SV
00089	2,45,IL,P	00133	5,1,HJ,M
00090	2,46,IG,TZ	00134	5,2,HJ,FT
00091	2,47,IV,TF	00135	5,3,HIM,S
00092	2,48,I,P	00136	5,4,HI,F
00093	2,49,IHA,TMR	00137	5,5,HJM,U
00094	2,50,IM,TF	00138	5,6,HJ,FT
00095	2,51,IHM,PO	00139	6,1,BJXLAM,GWPZV
00096	2,52,I,TM	00140	6,2,IG,Z
00097	2,53,IGM,P	00141	6,3,BIL,TR
00098	2,54, IL,P	00142	6,4,IXG,Z
00099	2,55,I,TP	00143	6,5,BIL,P
00100	2,56,I,TM	00144	6,6,BILM,PSGW
00101	2,57,IGM,PTZ	00145	6,7,BILM,PSGW
00102	2,58,IGM,TF	00146	6,8,CIGLM,PS
00103	2,59,IGL,M	00147	6,9,BIL,PSGW
00104	2,60,IG,MP	00148	7,1,BEJLXA,WRG
00105	2,61,IGL,PT	00149	8,1,BEJX,WVGM
00106	2,62,I,PG	00150	8,2,I,OVG
00107	2,63,BIG,P	00151	8,3,I,OVG
00108	2,64, IGL,FKTZ	00152	8,4,I,GV
00109	2,65,IVM,FPS	00153	8,5,I,G
00110	2,66,IL,P	00154	8,6,I,G
00111	2,67,I,P	00155	8,7,I,G
00112	2,68,IL,ZP	00156	8,8,I,G
00113	2,69,I,P	00157	8,9,I,V
00114	2,70,I,P	00158	8,10,I,V
00115	2,71,IM,Z	00159	8,11,I,V
00116	2,72, I,Z	00160	8,12,I,U
00117	2,73,IGL,P	00161	8,13,I,V
00118	2,74,JHXLA,MVR	00162	8,14,I,V

APPENDIX 7 (continued)

00163	8,15,I,V	00204	18,2,U,GIR
00164	8,16,J,U	00205	18,3,IM,G
00165	9,1,A,U	00206	18,4,IM,G
00166	9,2,GA,U	00207	18,5,I,GMS
00167	9,3,X,GTZ	00208	18,6,I,G
00168	9,4,G,U	00209	19,1, AI,GRZF
00169	9,5,GA,U	00210	19,2,XAI,GZ
00170	9,6,X,GTZ	00211	20,1,HJA,MZRY
00171	9,7,G,U	00212	20,2,HIL,TFSW
00172	9,8,G,U	00213	21,1,AJH,MV
00173	10,1,HAXKJMR,U	00214	22,1,CDGIL,ZTF
00174	1,1,DI,GMS	00215	23,1,CDGIAW,R
00175	11,2,IG,U	00216	24,1,QCDGI,MXTFO
00176	12,1,DIML,GS	00217	24,2,BEHJ,O
00177	12,2,IHML,ZFN	00218	24,3,CDIG,O
00178	12,3,IHL,Z	00219	25,1,CIHAML,RTZ
00179	12,4,IH,P	00220	25,2,CDGIAM,RTZ
00180	13,1,MA,RV	00221	26,1,GIM,TS
00181	13,2,I,U	00222	26,2,IM,TS
00182	13,3,JXAM,WRV	00223	26,3,GIM,TS
00183	13,4,HJXAL,WRV	00224	26,4,IM,TS
00184	13,5,IMA,RV	00225	27,1,JXA,WR
00185	13,6,HJXA,WRV	00226	27,2,J,WR
00186	13,7,HIAL,WRV	00227	27,3,J,U
00187	13,8,HI,WV	00228	27,4,J,MWZ
00188	13,9,HIL,W	00229	27,5,JXA,R
00189	13,10,HJA,W	00230	27,6,J,W
00190	13,11,GI,U	00231	27,7,J,W
00191	14,1,BJHML,U	00232	27,8,J,U
00192	14,2,HI,MVT	00233	27,9,J,U
00193	14,3,BJH,U	00234	27,10,JL,Z
00194	14,4,BJHM,U	00235	27,11,J,U
00195	14,5,BJH,U	00236	27,12,JL,Z
00196	15,1,QMHI,NF	00237	27,13,JL,W
00197	15,2,QIMH,F	00238	27,14,J,Z
00198	15,3,QIMH,F	00239	27,15,J,U
00199	15,4,QIMH,F	00240	27,16,IW,Z
00200	16,1,AJX,G	00241	27,17,I,U
00201	16,2,AIM,G	00242	27,18,I,U
00202	17,1,HJA,YZRV	00243	27,19,U,U
00203	18,1,IAM,GWZ	00244	27,20,U,U

00245	27,21,U,U	00288	41,1,BEJA,NG
00246	27,22,U,U	00289	41,2,QCIAM,RWKZG
00247	27,23,L,U	00290	41,3,U,O
00248	28,1,IG,M	00291	42,1,QRAIH,M
00249	28,2,BJHA,V	00292	43,1,A,NPW
00250	28,3,GI,MT	00293	43,2,HIRAL,ZTN
00251	28,4,GI,MZ	00294	44,1,JXAM,NV
00252	29,1,JA,GZM	00295	44,2,IH,U
00253	30,1,BEHJ,N	00296	44,3,I,U
00254	30,2,HJ,U	00297	44,4,IHM,S
00255	30,3,BEGJ,N	00298	44,5,IHM,U
00256	30,4,HJ,U	00299	44,6,IHL,U
00257	30,5,BEHJ,NM	00300	45,1,CDGI,T
00258	31,1,DWIK,MGT	00301	45,2,BEHJ,N
00259	31,2,BJ,YO	00302	46,1,GI,TFO
00260	32,1,IG,MZOTW	00303	47,1,HJXA,N
00261	33,1,BJH,TZF	00304	47,2,HI,U
00262	34,1,MZGI,TF	00305	47,3,JXM,VGN
00263	35,1,I,MGW	00306	47,4,I,U
00264	36,1,HJQA,ZR	00307	47,5,JLA,U
00265	36,2,HJQA,ZR	00308	47,6,I,V
00266	36,3,HJQA,ZR	00309	47,7,I,U
00267	36,4,HJQA,ZR	00310	48,1,HARI,MTF
00268	36,5,HJQAL,ZR	00311	48,2,GIA,ZR
00269	36,6,HJQA,ZR	00312	48,3,GI,U
00270	36,7,HJQA,ZR	00313	48,4,GIM,U
00271	36,8,HJQA,ZR	00314	48,5,GI,U
00272	36,9,HJQAL,ZRW	00315	48,6,GIMA,ZR
00273	37,1,CDGI,SKTOF	00316	49,1,GI,U
00274	37, 2,CDGI,Y	00317	50,1,CDGI,KOZ
00275	38,1,CDGI,MF	00318	51,1,DGI,P
00276	38,2,U,Y	00319	51,2,JH,MN
00277	38,3,I,Y	00320	51,3,G,MT
00278	39,1,QAI,GYZR	00321	51,4,U,U
00279	39,2,IG,T	00322	52,1,CDGI,TM
00280	39,3,IGM,STF	00323	53,1,CDGIL,FT
00281	39,4,IG,U	00324	53,2,U,Y
00282	39,5,IGM,S	00325	54,1,CDI,GMT
00283	39,6,IG,U	00326	54,2,BEHJ,Y
00284	39,7,IGML,S	00327	54,3,BEHJ,U
00285	39,8,IG,U	00328	54,4,CDGI,U
00286	40,1,QIA,MGZR	00329	55,1,QIH,MT
00287	40,2,IG,U	00330	56,1,CDGIA,MR

APPENDIX 7 (continued)

00331	56,2,DGI,M	00372	73,1,JHM,TZW
00332	56,3,I,YO	00373	73,2,JHML,TZW
00333	57,1,JHB,U	00374	74,1,AJ,GMZRS
00334	57,2,JHB,U	00375	74,2,CDI,GSV
00335	57,3,JHB,U	00376	75,1,QCDGI,MTZ
00336	57,4,JHBM,U	00377	75,2,CDGI,MZ
00337	57,5,IH,U	00378	75,3,QCDGIM,P
00338	57,6,IH,U	00379	76,1,JHAXL,V
00339	57,7,IHM,U	00380	77,1,BH,TZ
00340	57,8,IHM,U	00381	78,1,CDGIA,MZRFTV
00341	57,9,IHM,U	00382	78,2,CDGI,U
00342	57,10,IHM,U	00383	78,3,CDGI,U
00343	58,1,GIM,RP	00384	78,4,BE,U
00344	59,1,CDIXA,MKGZRF	00385	79,1,J,GMT
00345	59,2,AM,Y	00386	79,2,CDGI,MT
00346	59,3,U,U	00387	79,3,IG,U
00347	60,1,BHI,MFV	00388	79,4,CI,U
00348	60,2,BHIAM,VR	00389	79,5,U,G
00349	60,3,MHA,V	00390	79,6,DGI,U
00350	60,4,M,OV	00391	79,7,IG,T
00351	60,5,BHIML,FVT	00392	80,1,IG,TZO
00352	61,1,QCDGI,KMZO	00393	81,1,HCDI,TZMR
00353	61,2,QCDI,KGZO	00394	82,1,CDGIW,SMTF
00354	62,1,QDKGI,MF	00395	82,2,GJW,SMTF
00355	63,1,BEI,MT	00396	82,3,B,Y
00356	63,2,HI,U	00397	83,1,BEJAX,G
00357	64,1,I,WSV	00398	83,2,QM,K
00358	64,2,JM,WS	00399	83,3,QW,GKCDI
00359	64,3,I,WS	00400	83,4,QWM,GKCDI
00360	65,1,XHJAL,MW	00401	83,5,QW,GKCDI
00361	66,1,ABEHX,VRM	00402	83,6,QWM,GKCDI
00362	67,1,IG,TS	00403	83,7,QW,GKCDI
00363	67,2,L,U	00404	83,8,QW,GKCDI
00364	67,3,U,M	00405	83,9,QW,GKCDI
00365	68,1,BEHJA,O	00406	84,1,CDI,MFPTG
00366	69,1,I,G	00407	84,2,CDI,Y
00367	70,1,CDWKGI,TS	00408	85,1,QHIL,TZ
00368	70,2,B,Y	00409	85,2,U,Y
00369	71,1,DGI,MPY	00410	86,1,BEH,MITZSW
00370	71,2,U,Y	00411	86,2,BEHI,U
00371	72,1,GI,FTP	00412	87,1,CDWKGIR,ZM

00413	88,1,AXIR,MG	00456	105,3,IC,U
00414	89,1,BEHJ,Z	00457	106,1,IAM,T
00415	90,1,DGI,MTW	00458	106,2,IA,T
00416	91,1,HIL,T	00459	106,3,A,T
00417	91,2,ILM,T	00460	106,4,IA,U
00418	91,3,HIL,T	00461	106,5,IA,T
00419	91,4,GI,TM	00462	106,6,IA,T
00420	92,1,BEHJA,V	00463	106,7,A,GT
00421	93,1,XAMGI,TZR	00464	106,8,I,GT
00422	94,1,DGI,WT	00465	106,9,I,GT
00423	94,2,IDG,YT	00466	106,10,I,GT
00424	94,3,I,YO	00467	106,11,I,GT
00425	94,4,U,YO	00468	106,12,I,GT
00426	94,5,DGI,P	00469	107,1,AHJ,U
00427	95,1,JAXG,WR	00470	108,1,A,U
00428	95,2,IG,W	00471	109,1,U,U
00429	95,3,IG,U	00472	110,1,CDGIQM,R
00430	96,1,IG,TM	00473	111,1,HA,R
00431	97,1,BIG,MT	00474	112,1,HA,R
00432	97,2,BIG,WSM	00475	113,1,U,T
00433	98,1,BEHJ,M	00476	113,2,U,U
00434	99,1,A,G	00477	114,1,A,U
00435	99,2,CDIA,G	00478	115,1,H,U
00436	100,1,IA,R	00479	116,1,HJA,V
00437	101,1,QDGI,TM	00480	116,2,I,U
00438	101,2,QDGI,T	00481	117,1,CDGI,R
00439	101,3,QBEHJ,T	00482	117,2,U,U
00440	102,1,BEJH,FN	00483	118,1,CDIG,Z
00441	102,2,BEJ,G	00484	118,2,BE,YZ
00442	102,3,BEHJ,FN	00485	119,1,HI,T
00443	102,4,BEJ,G	00486	120,1,I,TMG
00444	102,5,GIM,W	00487	120,2,I,GM
00445	103,1,GIA,ZM	00488	121,1,BEJA,GWN
00446	103,2,GIA,ZM	00489	122,1,HJ,U
00447	103,3,GJA,M	00490	13,1,CDWKGXA,U
00448	103,4,GIA,U	00491	124,1,GI,U
00449	103,5,GIA,U	00492	125,1,JA,U
00450	103,6,GI,U	00493	126,1,JA,U
00451	103,7,GI,U	00494	127,1,IG,Z
00452	103,8,AHIL,U	00495	128,1,JHA,N
00453	104,1,QHDCI,MT	00496	129,1,KIA,M
00454	105,1,JBAXL,WGM	00497	129,2,A,U
00455	105,2,IBL,U	00498	130,1,A,GIR

APPENDIX 7 *(continued)*

00499	131,1,C,U	00540	155,2,U,U
00500	132,1,A,U	00541	156,1,IH,T
00501	133,1,CDI,ZT	00542	157,1,BJHA,U
00502	133,2,CDI,ZT	00543	158,1,JHA,M
00503	133,3,U,Y	00544	159,1,CDI,MZT
00504	134,1,CDGI,T	00545	159,2,U,Y
00505	134,2,U,U	00546	159,3,CDIL,Z
00506	135,1,A,T	00547	159,4,CDI,ZM
00507	136,1,BDJ,G	00548	160,1,CDGIM,Z
00508	136,2,CDI,G	00549	161,1,E,U
00509	137,1,U,T	00550	162,1,CDGI,U
00510	138,1,AH,M	00551	163,1,BEHJA,K
00511	139,1,CDGI,T	00552	164,1,CDGIA,U
00512	140,1,C,T	00553	165,1,U,O
00513	141,1,U,MT	00554	165,2,JA,U
00514	142,1,JA,G	00555	166,1,GI,P
00515	142,2,CI,G	00556	166,2,U,Y
00516	143,1,JH,N	00557	167,1,CDGI,T
00517	143,2,JH,U	00558	168,1,IG,M
00518	143,3,HJA,U	00559	169,1,GI,MR
00519	143,4,HJ,U	00560	170,1,CDGIM,T
00520	143,5,HJA,U	00561	170,2,BEHJ,MN
00521	143,6,HJ,U	00562	171,1,XJHA,V
00522	144,1,GI,T	00563	172,1,JA,GW
00523	145,1,IG,U	00564	172,2,JA,G
00524	145,2,U,U	00565	173,1,JA,V
00525	146,1,U,U	00566	174,1,BJHAM,Z
00526	147,1,IHA,RM	00567	175,1,A,U
00527	148,1,JA,G	00568	176,1,JA,V
00528	149,1,CDIG,R	00569	177,1,GI,M
00529	149,2,U,Y	00570	177,2,GIA,U
00530	150,1,HJA,R	00571	178,1,AIG,U
00531	151,1,JA,G	00572	179,1,QCDI,TZG
00532	151,2,IGA,U	00573	180,1,IM,GZ
00533	151,3,IGA,U	00574	180,2,U,OY
00534	152,1,CDIG,U	00575	180,3,I,GP
00535	153,1,HIA,R	00576	180,4,U,OY
00536	153,2,HIA,R	00577	181,1,J,V
00537	153,3,XHJA,W	00578	182,1,IGM,U
00538	154,1,A,M	00579	183,1,CDGI,U
00539	155,1,CDGI,U	00580	183,2,CDGI,U

00581	183,3,CDGI,U	00624	220,1,DGI,T
00582	184,1,HJA,U	00625	221,1,I,T
00583	185,1,GIA,MR	00626	222,1,DI,T
00584	186,1,CDGI,MZ	00627	223,1,CDGIM,ZST
00585	187,1,IG,M	00628	223,2,U,O
00586	187,2,JH,U	00629	224,1,A,G
00587	188,1,CJXA,ZTK	00630	224,2,A,G
00588	189,1,CDGI,TM	00631	224,3,A,G
00589	190,1,C,T	00632	224,4,A,G
00590	191,1,CDGI,TZ	00633	224,5,A,G
00591	192,1,JH,T	00634	224,6,A,G
00592	192,2,IH,U	00635	225,1,CDGI,R
00593	193,1,A,U	00636	226,1,CDM,U
00594	194,1,BEHJA,U	00637	227,1,CDGIA,T
00595	195,1,CDI,S	00638	227,2,A,Y
00596	195,2,U,Y	00639	228,1,AG,ZR
00597	196,1,GI,T	00640	229,1,A,GM
00598	197,1,CI,Z	00641	230,1,U,U
00599	198,1,A,U	00642	231,1,A,GMR
00600	199,1,CDGIA,U	00643	231,2,GL,XK
00601	200,1,CDGI,MST	00644	232,1,CDGI,MTRS
00602	200,2,B,O	00645	232,2,U,YO
00603	201,1,CDGI,TZ	00646	233,1,A,U
00604	201,2,CDGI,U	00647	233,2,A,U
00605	202,1,U,U	00648	234,1,HJA,N
00606	203,1,BHJAM,U	00649	235,1,CDGI,ST
00607	204,1,CDAM,T	00650	235,2,CDGI,ST
00608	205,1,JA,G	00651	235,3,CDGI,Y
00609	206,1,CDGI,MZ	00652	235,4,CDGI,Y
00610	207,1,AM,S	00653	236,1,CDGI,R
00611	208,1,IM,U	00654	237,1,JA,GR
00612	209,1,BJHAM,Z	00655	238,1,CDGI,S
00613	210,1,A,U	00656	239,1,IAM,G
00614	211,1,CDGIA,R	00657	239,2,I,GT
00615	212,1,IA,R	00658	239,3,IAX,G
00616	213,1,GI,T	00659	240,1,QCDGIA,TRZ
00617	214,1,CDGI,U	00660	240,2,A,Y
00618	215,1,C,U	00661	241,1,CDGIA,MP
00619	216,1,BE,ON	00662	242,1,CDIA,GFW
00620	217,1,BJ,U	00663	242,2,A,W
00621	218,1,CDGI,T	00664	243,1,CDGIA,RZST
00622	218,2,J,U	00665	243,2,BA,U
00623	219,1,BEAJ,U	00666	244,1,CDIA,MG

APPENDIX 7 *(continued)*

00667	244,2,A,Y	00708	266,1,DI,M
00668	245,1,CDIG,MT	00709	266,2,EHJ,M
00669	245,2,U,Y	00710	267,1,U,U
00670	246,1,CDGIAW,U	00711	268,1,BEJHAL,WRY
00671	246,2,A,Y	00712	269,1,BJXAL,W
00672	246,3,CDGIAL,RW	00713	270,1,BJX,W
00673	246,4,A,Y	00714	271,1,BEHJAL,R
00674	246,5,CDGI,U	00715	272,1,ID,MT
00675	247,1,CDGI,T	00716	273,1,A,R
00676	248,1,CDGI,T	00717	274,1,I,T
00677	249,1,DGI,T	00718	275,1,CDIM,GF
00678	249,2,U,Z	00719	275,2,IG,U
00679	250,1,A,G	00720	276,1,CDGI,M
00680	250,2,U,Y	00721	277,1,U,U
00681	250,3,U,G	00722	278,1,BJAX,WR
00682	250,4,U,G	00723	278,2,I,T
00683	251,1,DGI,KZ	00724	279,1,HI,T
00684	251,2,U,U	00725	280,1,DI,G
00685	252,1,BHJA,W	00726	280,2,I,Y
00686	253,1,A,U	00727	281,1,BEJXA,MGR
00687	254,1,CDGI,Z	00728	282,1,IGM,ZO
00688	255,1, AID,PRGT	00729	282,2,U,Y
00689	256,1 A,WT	00730	283,1,U,T
00690	256,2,BJHA,WT	00731	284,1,JM,T
00691	257,1,DI,GT	00732	285,1,A,U
00692	257,2,BEJHA,N	00733	286,1,IGA,R
00693	258,1,I,O	00734	286,2,IG,Y
00694	259,1,I,MTG	00735	286,3,IGA,MR
00695	260,1,BEHJA,U	00736	286,4,I,Y
00696	260,2,CDGI,T	00737	286,5,IGA,RP
00697	261,1,BEJXA,U	00738	286,6,IG,Y
00698	262,1,DGI,T	00739	287,1,CDIA,G
00699	262,2,EHJA,R	00740	288,1,LBHJA,DK
00700	262,3,DGI,MT	00741	288,2,A,U
00701	262,4,EHJA,U	00742	289,1,BEJ,N
00702	263,1,DGI,T	00743	290,1,BEJ,N
00703	263,2,EHJA,U	00744	291,1,BEJ,N
00704	263,3,EHJA,U	00745	292,1,BEJ,N
00705	264,1,DIA,MRT	00746	293,1,CDGIA,U
00706	265,1,DI,T	00747	294,1,BEJHAM,R
00707	265,2,EJHA,U	00748	295,1,A,U

00749	296,1,DGI,T	00765	307,1,A,R
00750	296,2,BEHJA,U	00766	307,2,A,Y
00751	297,1,A,MG	00767	308,1,JHA,MN
00752	297,2,A,U	00768	309,1,U,G
00753	298,1,BJAG,W	00769	310,1,JHA,U
00754	298,2,BJAG,W	00770	311,1,A,G
00755	299,1,JA,N	00771	312,1,CI,U
00756	300,1,BJAX,W	00772	312,2,U,Y
00757	301,1,I,U	00773	312,3,U,U
00758	302,1,I,GMZ	00774	312,4,U,T
00759	302,2,U,G	00775	313,1,U,U
00760	303,1,GIA,U	00776	313,2,U,U
00761	304,1,I,M	00777	313,3,U,G
00762	304,2,U,Y	00778	313,4,X,GT
00763	305,1,JXA,W	00779	314,1,JHA,M
00764	306,1,A,R	00780	315,1,A,U

APPENDIX 8
RICHEK: DATA VERIFICATION PROGRAM

This BASIC program checks two files, RIDATA and RIDAT2, to see if they are identical. Each of the two files contains the 780 lines of Richardson pair data (case number, pair-in-case number, background factor code letters, irritant factor code letters). Where the two files are not identical, an error is presumed to have been made in entering one of them, and the discrepancy is reported back to the researcher for correction.

```
00100   FILES RIDATA, RIDAT2          00240   FOR K=1 TO C(0)
00110   RESTORE #1, #2                00250   IF C(K)=G(K) THEN 270
00120   FOR I=1 TO 780                00260   GOSUB 500
00130   READ #1, A,B, C$, D$          00270   NEXT K
00140   DIM C(20), D(20)              00280   FOR K=1 TO D(0)
00145   DIM G(20), H(20)              00290   IF D(K)=H(K) THEN 305
00150   READ #2, E, F, G$, H$         00300   GOSUB 500
00160   IF A=E THEN 180               00305   NEXT K
00170   GOSUB 500                     00310   NEXT I
00180   IF B=F THEN 200               00320   STOP
00190   GOSUB 500                     00500   PRINT "ERROR IN LINE":
00200   CHANGE C$ TO C                00501   PRINT I; ",
00210   CHANGE D$ TO D                          CASE #"; A; PAIR #"; B
00220   CHANGE G$ TO G                00505   PRINT TAB 10;
00230   CHANGE H$ TO H                00510   PRINT A, B, C$, D$
00231   IF C(0)=G(0) THEN 233         00515   PRINT TAB 10;
00232   GOSUB 500                     00520   PRINT E, F, G$, H$
00233   IF D(0)=H(0) THEN 240         00530   RETURN
00234   GOSUB 500                     00540   END
```

APPENDIX 9
RICHARDSON DATA FREQUENCY COUNTS

Table A1

Pair Frequencies: 780 Pairs

		Background	*Irritants*	*Both*
A.	Com. Govt:	237	0	237
B.	Sim. Race:	91	0	91
C.	Dif. Race:	114	11	125
D.	Dif. Dress:	129	8	137
E.	Sim. Dress:	53	0	53
F.	Insecure:	0	48	48
G.	Dif. Ideol:	223	122	345
H.	Sim. Ideol:	172	0	172
I.	Dif. Lang:	451	10	461
J.	Com. Lang:	179	0	179
K.	Misc. Het:	7	22	29
L.	Exallies:	95	0	95
M.	Oldwar:	103	116	219
N.	Leader:	0	28	28
O.	Cult Psych:	0	30	30
P.	Contag:	0	80	80
Q.	Traded:	44	0	44
R.	Ruled:	6	88	94
S.	Symp. Subj:	0	41	41
T.	Terr.:	0	173	173
U.	Blank:	56	198	233*
V.	Pol. Conf:	10	43	53
W.	Ec. Dif:	16	59	75
X.	Mingled:	49	2	51
Y.	Provoc.:	0	47	47
Z.	Ec. Conf:	1	104	105

*Twenty-one pairs had blanks in all compartments.

APPENDIX 9 *(continued)*

Table A2

Pair Percentages

		Background	*Irritants*	*Both*
A.	Com. Govt:	30.3846	0	30.3846
B.	Sim. Race:	11.6667	0	11.6667
C.	Dif. Race:	14.6154	1.41026	16.0256
D.	Dif. Dress:	16.5385	1.02564	17.5641
E.	Sim. Dress:	6.79487	0	6.79487
F.	Insecure:	0	6.15385	6.15385
G.	Dif. Ideol:	28.5897	15.641	44.2308
H.	Sim. Ideol:	22.0513	0	22.0513
I.	Dif. Lang:	57.8205	1.28205	59.1026
J.	Com. Lang:	22.9487	0	22.9487
K.	Misc. Het:	0.897436	2.82051	3.71795
L.	Exallies:	12.1795	0	12.1795
M.	Oldwar:	13.2051	14.0718	28.0769
N.	Leader:	0	3.58974	3.58974
O.	Cult. Psych:	0	3.84615	3.84615
P.	Contag:	0	10.2564	10.2564
Q.	Traded:	5.64103	0	5.64103
R.	Ruled:	0.769231	11.2821	12.0513
S.	Symp. Subj:	0	5.25641	5.25641
T.	Terr.:	0	22.1795	22.1795
U.	Blank:	7.17949	25.3846	29.8718
V.	Pol. Conf:	1.28205	5.51282	6.79487
W.	Ec. Dif:	2.05128	7.5641	9.61538
X.	Mingled:	6.28205	0.25641	6.53846
Y.	Provoc.:	0	6.02564	6.02564
Z.	Ec. Conf:	0.128205	13.3333	13.4615

Table A3

Case Frequencies: 315 Cases

		Background	*Irritants*	*Both*
A.	Com. Govt:	155	0	155
B.	Sim. Race:	68	0	68
C.	Dif. Race:	91	2	92*
D.	Dif. Dress:	102	2	104
E.	Sim. Dress:	44	0	44
F.	Insecure:	0	27	27
G.	Dif. Ideol:	123	63	172*
H.	Sim. Ideol:	91	0	91
I.	Dif. Lang:	192	4	194*
J.	Com. Lang;	114	0	114
K.	Misc. Het:	7	12	19
L.	Exallies:	35	0	35
M.	Oldwar:	49	91	129*
N.	Leader:	0	23	23
O.	Cult. Psych:	0	23	23
P.	Contag:	0	17	17
Q.	Traded:	19	0	19
R.	Ruled:	6	63	68*
S.	Symp. Subj:	0	28	28
T.	Terr.:	0	111	111
U.	Blank:	45	107	132**
V.	Pol. Dif:	1	23	23*
W.	Ec. Dif:	9	38	45*
X.	Mingled:	36	2	38
Y.	Provoc.:	0	38	38
Z.	Ec. Conf:	1	63	64

*One case or more had this symbol set in the background for one pair, and as an irritant for another.

**Twenty cases had all cells blank.

APPENDIX 9 *(continued)*

Table A4

Case Percentages

		Background	*Irritants*	*Both*
A.	Com. Govt.	49.2063	0	49.2063
B.	Sim. Race:	21.5873	0	21.5873
C.	Dif. Race:	28.8889	0.634921	29.2063
D.	Dif. Dress:	32.381	0.634921	33.0159
E.	Sim. Dress:	13.9683	0	13.9683
F.	Insecure:	0	8.57143	8.57143
G.	Dif. Ideol:	39.0476	20	54.6032
H.	Sim. Ideol:	28.8889	0	28.8889
I.	Dif. Lang:	60.9524	1.26984	61.5873
J.	Com. Lang:	36.1905	0	36.1905
K.	Misc. Het:	2.22222	3.80952	6.03175
L.	Exallies:	11.1111	0	11.1111
M.	Oldwar:	15.5556	28.8889	40.9524
N.	Leader:	0	7.30159	7.30159
O.	Cult. Psych:	0	7.30159	7.30159
P.	Contag:	0	5.39683	5.39683
Q.	Traded:	6.03175	0	6.03175
R.	Ruled:	1.90476	20	21.5873
S.	Symp. Subj:	0	8.88889	8.88889
T.	Terr.:	0	35.2381	35.2381
U.	Blank:	14.2857	33.9683	41.9048
V.	Pol. Conf:	0.31746	7.30159	7.30159
W.	Ec. Dif:	2.85714	12.0635	14.2857
X.	Mingled:	11.4286	0.634921	12.0635
Y.	Provoc.:	0	12.0635	12.0635
Z.	Ec. Conf:	0.31746	20	20.3175

Bibliography

Banks, Arthur S., and Robert B. Textor
1963 *A Cross-Polity Survey*. Cambridge: M.I.T. Press
Bazard, Saint-Amand, et al.
1830 *The Doctrine of Saint-Simon*. Translated by George G. Iggers. Boston: Beacon Press, 1958.
Beer, Francis A.
1974 *How Much War in History: Definitions, Estimates, Extrapolations and Trends*. Sage Professional Papers in International Studies 3 (02-030). Beverly Hills: Sage.
Bellany, Ian
1973 "The Problems of Balancing Reductions in Conventional Forces." *Journal of Conflict Resolution* 17 (4): 657-672.
Binyon, Laurence
1918 *For Dauntless France*. London: Hodder and Stoughton.
Black, Cyril E.
1966 *The Dynamics of Modernization*. New York: Harper and Row.
Blainey, Geoffrey
1973 *The Causes of War*. New York: Free Press
Boulding, Elise
1972 "Peace Research: Dialectics and Development." *Journal of Conflict Resolution* 16 (4): 469-475.
Brumley, Mary Jane
1928 "Minor Wars and Interventions of the British Empire, 1900-1926." Master's thesis, University of Chicago.
Bueno de Mesquita, Bruce, and J. David Singer
1973 "Alliances, Capabilities, and War: A Review and Synthesis." *Political Science Annual*, edited by Cornelius Cotter, 4: 237-280.

Caine, Lula
  1929 "Conditions Underlying Minor Wars and Interventions of the Unit-
         ed States." Ph.D. dissertation, University of Chicago.
Choucri, Nazli, and Robert C. North
  1972 "Dynamics of International Conflict: Some Policy Implications of
         Population, Resources, and Technology." *World Politics* 24 supple-
         ment (Spring): 80–122.
  1975 *Nations in Conflict.* San Francisco: W. H. Freeman.
Claude, Inis L., Jr.
  1962 *Power and International Relations.* New York: Random House.
Comte, Auguste
  1875 *Social Statics. System of Positive Polity.* Vol. 2. Translated by
         Frederic Harrison. London: Longmans, Green.
  1877 *Theory of the Future of Man. System of Positive Polity.* Vol. 4.
         Translated by Richard Congreve and Henry Dix Hutton. London:
         Longmans, Green.
Davis, William W., George T. Duncan, and Randolph M. Siverson
  1976 "Stochastic Models of the Distribution of Dyadic Warfare in
         Time." Technical Report No. 120. Pittsburgh: Department of Sta-
         tistics, Carnegie-Mellon University.
  1978 "The Dynamics of Warfare: 1816–1965." *American Journal of
         Political Science* 22 (4): 772–792.
Denton, Frank Hardy
  1966 "Some Regularities in International Conflict, 1820–1949." *Back-
         ground* 9 (4): 283–296.
  1968 "Patterns in Political Violence and War, 1751–1960." Ph.D. disser-
         tation, University of Southern California.
  1969 *Factors in International System Violence–1750 to 1960.* P–4216
         (October). Santa Monica: The Rand Corporation.
Denton, Frank Hardy, and Warren Phillips
  1968 "Some Patterns in the History of Violence." *Journal of Conflict
         Resolution* 12 (2): 182–195.
Deutsch, Karl W., and J. David Singer
  1964 "Multipolar Power Systems and International Stability." *World
         Politics* 16 (3): 390–406.
Dowty, Alan
  1970 "Conflict in War Potential Politics: An Approach to Historical
         Macroanalysis." Peace Research Society (International) *Papers* 13:
         85–101.
Eckstein, Harry
  1962 "Internal War: The Problem of Anticipation." *Social Science Re-
         search and National Security.* 102–147. Washington, D.C.: Smith-
         sonian Institution Research Group in Psychology and the Social
         Sciences.
  1964 *Internal War.* New York: Free Press.

Finsterbusch, Kurt, and H. C. Greisman
1975 "The Unprofitability of Warfare in the Twentieth Century." *Social Problems* 22 (3): 450–463.

Fisher, R. A.
1936 *Statistical Methods for Research Workers*, 6th ed. Edinburgh: Oliver & Boyd.

Flora, Peter
1974 "A New Stage of Political Arithmetic." *Journal of Conflict Resolution* 18 (1): 143–165.

Garnham, David
1976a "Dyadic International War 1816–1965: The Role of Power Parity and Geographical Proximity." *Western Political Quarterly* 29 (2): 231–242.
1976b "Power Parity and Lethal International Violence, 1969–1973." *Journal of Conflict Resolution* 20 (3): 379–394.

Garrick, Ruby
1930 "Uses of Military Force in the Pacific Area." Master's thesis, University of Chicago.

Gold, E.
1954 "Lewis Fry Richardson." *Obituary Notices of Fellows of the Royal Society* 9: 217–235.

Gurr, Ted Robert
1974 "The Neo-Alexandrians: A Review Essay on Data Handbooks in Political Science." *American Political Science Review* 68 (1): 243–252.

Han Fei Tzu
1959 "Five Vermin." *The Complete Works of Han Fei Tzu* 2: 275–297. Translated by W. K. Liao. London: Arthur Probsthain.

Hayes, Richard E.
1973 "Identifying and Measuring Changes in the Frequency of Event Data." *International Studies Quarterly* 17 (4): 471–494.

Herz, John H.
1951 *Political Realism and Political Idealism*. Chicago: University of Chicago Press.

Horvath, William J.
1968 "A Statistical Model for the Duration of Wars and Strikes." *Behavioral Science* 13 (1): 18–28.

Horvath, William J., and Caxton C. Foster
1963 "Stochastic Models of War Alliances." *Journal of Conflict Resolution* 7 (2): 110–116.

Hsün Tzu
1928 *The Works of Hsüntze*. Translated by Homer H. Dubs. London: Arthur Probsthain.

Jeffreys, Harold
1939 *Theory of Probability*. Oxford: Clarendon.

Jencks, Harlan W.
  1973 "The Great Powers and War: 1902-1971." Paper prepared for the
        Peace Science Society (Western) Conference, San Francisco, Febru-
        ary 1973.
Kahn, Herman, and B. Bruce-Briggs
  1972 *Things to Come*. New York: Macmillan.
Kende, Istvan
  1978 "Wars of Ten Years (1967-1976)." *Journal of Peace Research* 15
        (3): 227-241.
Klingberg, Frank L.
  1966 "Predicting the Termination of War: Battle Casualties and Popula-
        tion Losses." *Journal of Conflict Resolution* 10 (2): 129-171.
Levy, Marion J., Jr.
  1966 *Modernization and the Structure of Societies*. Princeton: Princeton
        University Press.
Lijphart, Arend
  1974 "The Structure of the Theoretical Revolution in International
        Relations." *International Studies Quarterly* 18 (1): 41-74.
Melby, John Frémont
  1936 "Hostilities in Latin America." Master's thesis, University of Chi-
        cago.
Melko, Matthew
  1973 *52 Peaceful Societies*. Oakville, Ontario: CPRI Press.
Midlarsky, Manus I.
  1970 "Mathematical Models of Instability and a Theory of Diffusion."
        International Studies Quarterly 14 (1): 60-84.
  1974 "Power, Uncertainty, and the Onset of International Violence."
        Journal of Conflict Resolution 18 (3): 395-431.
  1975 *On War*. New York: Free Press.
Modelski, George
  1961 "Agraria and Industria." *The International System*, edited by Klaus
        Knorr and Sidney Verba, 118-143. Princeton: Princeton University
        Press.
  1972 "War and the Great Powers." Peace Research Society (Interna-
        tional) *Papers* 18: 45-59.
Moyal, J. E.
  1949 "The Distribution of Wars in Time." *Journal of the Royal Statisti-
        cal Society* 115, ser. A, pt. IV: 446-449.
Organski, A. F. K.
  1958 *World Politics*. New York: Knopf.
Parsons, Talcott
  1966 *Societies: Evolutionary and Comparative Perspectives*. Englewood
        Cliffs, N. J.: Prentice-Hall.
Parsons, Talcott, and Edward A. Shils
  1951 *Toward a General Theory of Action*. New York: Harper and Row.

Parvin, Manoucher
  1973 "Economic Determinants of Political Unrest." *Journal of Conflict Resolution* 17 (2): 271-296.
Pearson, Frederic S.
  1974 "Geographic Proximity and Foreign Military Intervention." *Journal of Conflict Resolution* 18 (3): 432-460.
Phillips, Warren R.
  1974 "Where Have All the Theories Gone?" *World Politics* 26 (2): 155-188.
Rapoport, Anatol
  1957 "Lewis F. Richardson's Mathematical Theory of War." *Journal of Conflict Resolution* 1 (3): 249-299.
Ray, James Lee
  1974 "Status Inconsistency and War Involvement in Europe, 1816-1970." Peace Research Society (International) *Papers* 23: 69-80.
Reischauer, Edwin O., and John K. Fairbank
  1958 *East Asia: The Great Tradition.* Boston: Houghton Mifflin.
Richardson, Lewis F.
  1944 "The Distribution of Wars in Time." *Journal of the Royal Statistical Society* 107 n.s., pts. 3 and 4: 242-250.
  1950a "Statistics of Deadly Quarrels." *Psychological Factors of Peace and War,* edited by T. H. Pear, 237-255. London: Hutchinson.
  1950b "War and Eugenics." *Eugenics Review* 42 (1): 25-36.
  1952 "Is It Possible To Prove Any General Statements about Historical Fact?" *British Journal of Sociology* 3 (1): 77-84.
  1960a *Arms and Insecurity.* Pittsburgh: Boxwood.
  1960b *Statistics of Deadly Quarrels.* Pittsburgh: Boxwood.
  1961 "The Problem of Contiguity: An Appendix to *Statistics of Deadly Quarrels." General Systems* 6: 139-187.
Richardson, Stephen A.
  1957 "Lewis Fry Richardson (1881-1953): A Personal Biography." *Journal of Conflict Resolution* 1 (3): 300-304.
Rosecrance, Richard N.
  1963 *Action and Reaction in World Politics.* Boston: Little Brown.
Rosen, Steven
  1972 "War Power and the Willingness to Suffer." *Peace, War, and Numbers,* edited by Bruce M. Russett, 167-183. Beverly Hills: SAGE.
Rummel, R. J.
  1967 "Dimensions of Dyadic War, 1820-1952." *Journal of Conflict Resolution* 11 (2): 176-183.
  1972 *The Dimensions of Nations.* Beverly Hills: SAGE.
Russett, Bruce M.
  1965 *Trends in World Politics.* New York: Macmillan.
Russett, Bruce M., et al.
  1964 *World Handbook of Political and Social Indicators.* New Haven: Yale University Press.

Saint-Simon, Henri, Comte de
  1825*a* "Nouveau Christianisme." *Oeuvres de Saint-Simon & d'Enfantin*
       23: 99–192. Aalen: Otto Zeller, 1964.
  1825*b* "De l'organisation sociale." *Oeuvres de Saint-Simon & d'Enfantin*
       39: 107–172. Aalen: Otto Zeller, 1964.
Singer, J. David
  1970 "From *A Study of War* to Peace Research: Some Criteria and
       Strategies." *Journal of Conflict Resolution* 14 (4): 527–542.
  1972 "The 'Correlates of War' Project: Interim Report and Rationale."
       World Politics 24 (2): 243–270.
  1973 "The Peace Researcher and Foreign Policy Prediction." Peace Re-
       search Society (International) *Papers* 21: 1–13.
Singer, J. David, Stuart Bremer, and John Stuckey
  1972 "Capability Distribution, Uncertainty, and Major Power War,
       1820–1965." *Peace, War, and Numbers*, edited by Bruce M.
       Russett, 19–48. Beverly Hills: SAGE.
Singer, J. David, and Melvin Small
  1966*a* "The Composition and Status Ordering of the International Sys-
       tem: 1815–1940." *World Politics* 18 (2): 236–282.
  1966*b* "Formal Alliances, 1815–1939: A Quantitative Description." *Jou-
       rnal of Peace Research* 3 (1): 1–32.
  1966*c* "National Alliance Commitments and War Involvement, 1815–
       1945." Peace Research Society (International) *Papers* 5:109–140.
  1968 "Alliance Aggregation and the Onset of War, 1815–1949." *Quanti-
       tative International Politics: Insights and Evidence*, edited by J.
       David Singer, 247–286. New York: Free Press.
  1972 *The Wages of War 1816–1965, A Statistical Handbook*. New York:
       John Wiley.
Singer, J. David, and Michael Wallace
  1970 "Intergovernmental Organization and the Preservation of Peace,
       1816–1964: Some Bivariate Relationships." *International Organi-
       zation* 24 (3): 520–547.
SIPRI
  1969 *Yearbook of World Armaments and Disarmament: 1968/1969.*
       Stockholm: Almqvist Wiksell.
Siverson, Randolph M., and George T. Duncan
  1975 "Stochastic Models of the Distribution of Dyadic Warfare in
       Time." Paper presented to the International Studies Association,
       February 1975.
Siverson, Randolph M., and Joel King
  1978*a* "Alliances and the Expansion of War, 1815–1965." Paper pre-
       sented to the Western Section, Peace Science Society (Interna-
       tional), February 1978.
  1978*b* "Alliance Attributes and War Participation, 1815–1965." Paper
       presented to the International Studies Association/West, March
       1978.

Small, Melvin, and J. David Singer
1969 "Formal Alliances, 1816–1965: An Extension of the Basic Data." *Journal of Peace Research* 6 (3): 257–282.
1970 "Patterns in International Warfare, 1816–1965." *Annals of the American Academy of Political and Social Science* 39: 145–155.
1973 "The Diplomatic Importance of States, 1816–1970: An Extension and Refinement of the Indicator." *World Politics* 25 (4): 577–599.
Sorokin, Pitirim A.
1937 *Fluctuation of Social Relationships, War and Revolution. Social and Cultural Dynamics* 3. New York: American Book.
Starr, Harvey
1972 *War Coalitions.* Lexington, Mass.: D. C. Heath.
1974 "The Quantitative International Relations Scholar as Surfer." *Journal of Conflict Resolution* 18 (2): 336–368.
1975 *Coalitions and Future War: A Dyadic Study of Cooperation and Conflict.* Sage Professional Papers in International Studies 3 (02–034). Beverly Hills: Sage.
Starr, Harvey, and Benjamin A. Most
1976 "The Substance and Study of Borders in International Relations Research." *International Studies Quarterly* 20 (4): 581–620.
Stefflre, Volney
1974 "Long-term Forecasting and the Problem of Large-scale Wars." *Futures* 6 (4): 302–308.
Taylor, Charles Lewis, and Michael C. Hudson
1972 *World Handbook of Political and Social Indicators*, 2d ed. New Haven: Yale University Press.
Terrell, Louis M.
1972 "Patterns of International Involvement and International Violence." *International Studies Quarterly* 16 (2): 167–186.
1977 "Attribute Differences Among Neighboring States and Their Levels of Foreign Conflict Behavior." *International Journal of Group Tensions* 7 (1–2): 89–108.
Wallace, Edna
1930 "French Military Operations in the Western Sahara." Master's thesis, University of Chicago.
Wallace, Michael D.
1972 "Status, Formal Organization, and Arms Levels as Factors Leading to the Onset of War, 1820–1964." *Peace, War, and Numbers*, edited by Bruce M. Russett, 49–70. Beverly Hills: Sage.
1975 "Clusters of Nations in the Global System, 1865–1964: Some Preliminary Evidence." *International Studies Quarterly* 19 (1): 67–110.
Wallace, Michael, and J. David Singer
1970 "Intergovernmental Organization in the Global System, 1815–1964: A Quantitative Description." *International Organization* 24 (2): 239–287.

1971 "The Use and Abuse of Imagination: A Reply to Samuel A. Bleicher." *International Organization* 25 (4): 953-957.

Waltz, Kenneth
1954 *Man, The State, and War.* New York: Columbia University Press.

Weede, Erich
1976 "Overwhelming Preponderance as a Pacifying Condition Among Continguous Asian Dyads, 1950-1969." *Journal of Conflict Resolution* 20 (3): 395-411.

Weiss, Herbert K.
1963 "Stochastic Models for the Duration and Magnitude of a 'Deadly Quarrel.' " *Operations Research* 11 (1): 101-121.

Wells, H. G.
1930 *The Way to World Peace.* London: Ernest Benn.
1939 *The Fate of Man.* New York: Longmans, Green.
1940 *The New World Order.* London: National Peace Council.
1942 *Phoenix.* London: Secker and Warburg.

Wesley, James Paul
1962 "Frequency of Wars and Geographical Opportunity." *Journal of Conflict Resolution* 6 (4): 387-389.

White, Wilbur W.
1929 "Wars in Arabia 1900-1926." Master's thesis, University of Chicago.

Wilkinson, David
1975 *Revolutionary Civil War.* Palo Alto: Page-Ficklin.

Wright, Quincy
1965 *A Study of War,* 2d ed. Chicago: University of Chicago Press.

Zinnes, Dina A.
1976 *Contemporary Research in International Relations.* New York: Free Press.

Index

www.ingramcontent.com/pod-product-compliance
Lightning Source LLC
Chambersburg PA
CBHW031132270326
41929CB00011B/1589